The
EVERYTHING®
Astrology Book

Dear Reader:

Welcome to the world of astrology! The concepts are not always easy to understand, but the benefits absolutely outweigh the hard work. In fact, the study of astrology is a little addictive. You're hooked before you know it! I became curious about astrology when I was fifteen. At that time, my best friend Alexandra started nurturing my curiosity by pushing loads of astrology information onto me—literally. Book after heavy book was set in my lap. "Here, here! Look! You see? I told you!" We grew breathless with excitement as every suspicion we set out to prove regarding friends and family was right there, on the money, evident as could be.

Alex showed me that nothing in this world happens by coincidence. With our incredible host of information, we were able to turn luck in our favor and succeed in jobs, friendships, and even relationships. Some say astrology is not a science, but nothing could be further from the truth. Just remember: Life is not like a fortune cookie. You can't just crack it open and find your destiny laid out before you. You have to work for it. So, why not start now? Turn the page!

Warmest Wishes for Your Future,

Jenni Kosarin

The EVERYTHING® Series

Editorial

Publishing Director	Gary M. Krebs
Associate Managing Editor	Laura M. Daly
Associate Copy Chief	Brett Palana-Shanahan
Acquisitions Editor	Gina Chaimanis
Development Editor	Katie McDonough
Associate Production Editor	Casey Ebert

Production

Director of Manufacturing	Susan Beale
Associate Director of Production	Michelle Roy Kelly
Cover Design	Paul Beatrice
	Erick DaCosta
	Matt LeBlanc
Design and Layout	Colleen Cunningham
	Holly Curtis
	Erin Dawson
	Sorae Lee
Series Cover Artist	Barry Littmann

Visit the entire Everything® Series at *www.everything.com*

THE
EVERYTHING®
ASTROLOGY
BOOK

2ND EDITION

Follow the stars to find love, success, and happiness!

Jenni Kosarin

Adams Media
Avon, Massachusetts

For my zany but wonderful friend, Alexandra G.,
who put the "spirit" back into "spiritual."

An Everything® Series Book.
Everything® and everything.com® are registered trademarks of F+W Publications, Inc.

Published by Adams Media, an F+W Publications Company
57 Littlefield Street, Avon, MA 02322 U.S.A.
www.adamsmedia.com

ISBN: 1-59337-373-2

Printed in the United States of America.
J I H G F E D C B

Library of Congress Cataloging-in-Publication Data
Kosarin, Jenni.
The everything astrology book : follow the stars to find love, success, and happiness!
/ Jenni Kosarin.-- 2nd ed.
p.   cm. -- (An Everything series book)
Rev. ed. of: The everything astrology book / Trish MacGregor. c1999.
ISBN 1-59337-373-2
1. Astrology. I. MacGregor, Trish, 1947- Everything astrology book. II. Title. III. Series: Everything series.

BF1708.1.M29 2005
133.5--dc22
2005026437

This publication is designed to provide accurate and authoritative information with regard to the subject matter covered. It is sold with the understanding that the publisher is not engaged in rendering legal, accounting, or other professional advice. If legal advice or other expert assistance is required, the services of a competent professional person should be sought.

—From a *Declaration of Principles* jointly adopted by a Committee of the American Bar Association and a Committee of Publishers and Associations

Many of the designations used by manufacturers and sellers to distinguish their products are claimed as trademarks. Where those designations appear in this book and Adams Media was aware of a trademark claim, the designations have been printed with initial capital letters.

This book is available at quantity discounts for bulk purchases.
For information, please call 1-800-289-0963.

Contents

Squares: 90 Degrees / 153

Sextiles and Trines: 60 and 120 Degrees / 169

Oppositions: 180 Degrees / 185

Love Compatibility: Fire / 201

Love Compatibility: Air / 211

Acknowledgments

A very heartfelt thank-you to Kate McBride, Laura Daly, Gina Chaimanis, and Katie McDonough for your wonderful support and guidance in shaping this book.

All my love to Paul and Donna Kosarin (the perfect astrological match, Sagittarius and Pisces). Thank you for everything you are and everything you've done.

Last, but not least, my deepest gratitude to Alexandra Guarnieri, without whom I couldn't have written this book. You gave me inspiration; you have been selfless with your time; and, most of all, you have led me toward a passion that will flourish for all time—like our friendship.

Thank you all!

Top Ten Things You'll Accomplish Through Reading This Book

1. **Learn how to gauge romance with the signs:** You'll find out the truth about all signs in love.

2. **Discover what your baby will be like, according to his or her sign:** You'll discover all you need to know about children and astrology.

3. **Learn how to analyze your chart and the charts of others:** You'll find out how to do your own chart and do it well!

4. **Learn all about your Sun sign:** You'll find all the details about what your Sun sign really means.

5. **Learn more about the planets:** You'll find out about placements and translations—for you—and how planets affect the entire world, too.

6. **Discover what "aspects" are:** Between conjunctions and oppositions, aspects can be tricky! Here, you'll get a clear understanding of it all.

7. **Learn what a "rising sign" is:** You'll get the scoop on your rising sign and how it affects your life and the way you act with the people around you.

8. **Discover how your Moon plays a part in everything:** You'll learn about your moon to make connections in your life.

9. **Become familiar with astrological symbols:** Getting to know these symbols will help you work with astrological charts.

10. **Learn how to construct your own birth chart:** You'll find out how astrologers have done this since the very beginning of the study of astrology.

Introduction

▶ If this book is your first encounter with astrology, you may be surprised to know that the science of astrology is not a recent phenomenon. On the contrary, the origins of astrology date back to around 2000 B.C. and can be traced to ancient Egypt, ancient Greece, and ancient China. From Greece, astrology came to Rome, where Augustus, the first emperor, used astrology as a science. He was an avid believer.

Modern astrology originated around A.D. 200 when Claudius Ptolemaeus (Ptolemy), the most important astronomer of the time, wrote *Tetrabiblos,* his four-volume book on the subject. Many of the astrological practices found today are based on Ptolemy's theories. Like many people today, Ptolemy regarded astrology and astronomy as adjuncts. The origins of astrology are so intimately entwined with those of astronomy that it is nearly impossible to separate the two. Throughout its evolution, astrology has been ridiculed and condemned by many religions. Christianity has always been the religion that has most strongly opposed the principles and practices of astrology. For example, Saint Augustine, a fourth-century bishop, asserted that belief in astrology meant denial of the power of God. This attitude prevailed with such force that the practice of astrology nearly vanished from the Christian world until the twelfth century, when scholars began translating Arabic texts on the subject. It was during this time that the Arabic intricacies of astrology started to surface. These discoveries included thirty-two points in a chart that were believed to be the most significant parts of horoscope interpretation.

By 1610, Galileo was speaking of new stars and four new planets he had discovered, which ancient astrologers, apparently, had not accounted for. (The planets were later found to be four of Jupiter's moons.) In 1660, Copernicus claimed that the Earth wasn't the center of the universe and that, instead, the Earth revolved around the Sun.

With each successive scientific pronouncement—such as those of famous scientists like Newton and Darwin—astrology was driven further underground into a state of public disrepute. This state could not be blamed on the masses. Scientific "fact" was always changing—no one knew just what to believe.

Today, some people have faith in astrology, and some don't. Fundamentalists and pious, puritanical religious societies have called astrology the work of the devil, while modern scientists—who believe less in spirituality and energy and more in simple, cold facts—generally consider astrology to be irrelevant.

However, astrology has survived through thousands of years of adversity. Those who are familiar with astrology believe that there are just too many "coincidences" for it to be fiction. A recent poll revealed that more than half of Americans believe in astrology. Whether you're already one of them or are looking to learn more before confirming your beliefs, this book will guide you. It will steer you through the awesome intricacies of astrology and teach you how influential this exciting phenomenon can be in your life.

Chapter 1

What Is Astrology?

Astrology is based on the belief that the movement of the stars and other celestial bodies affects our lives here on Earth. Not everyone acknowledges these effects, but those who study astrology have many reasons to believe that all things, both terrestrial and celestial, are strongly connected. In fact, scientists have absolutely determined that the moon has influence over certain phenomena on Earth such as ocean tides. This chapter will catch you up on the basics of astrology, from philosophy to signs and symbols.

A Few Basics

One common misinterpretation of astrology is that it determines our fate. The truth, however, is that astrology describes our potential; it is our choice to live up to that potential or to deny it. Astrology is organic rather than mechanistic; its meaning grows and deepens as we learn its symbols and begin to understand its language. Astrology can't really predict what happens to us in day-to-day life because it deals with trends—not minute-to-minute occurrences.

In other words, astrology examines patterns that prevail in our lives—opportunities or gateways that are made available to us. Astrology is a highly effective way of interpreting our individual realities. The study of astrology increases our awareness and knowledge of ourselves and of the people around us. It empowers us.

QUESTION?

Can astrology predict the future?
Yes and no. By studying your chart and its relation to the stars and planets, you'll get a glimpse of periods of time. For example, you'll get a sense of a good time to ask for a raise, a great time for new love, the right time to sign or not sign a contract, or the time to move or to stay put. However, *you* are the one who needs to take advantage of the good timing.

In natal astrology, the patterns in a chart are created by the date, time, and place of birth. These three elements individualize the chart and place the planets within particular signs and within the twelve houses of the horoscope. In addition to the Sun and the Moon, a chart includes the sign and placement of the other planets in relation to Earth: Mercury, Venus, Mars, Jupiter, Saturn, Uranus, Neptune, and Pluto.

Philosophy

To learn the language of astrology (so that you may draw up charts), you must also consider a philosophical side. For example, are the specifics of our birth—date, time, and place—as random as they appear to be? If so, are the tendencies of our birth charts merely coincidental? Are they simply the product of a physical act that produces a child nine months later? Not according to astrological philosophy.

Though some suspect our universe to be completely random, most people have an intuitive sense of pattern and connectedness. Shrugging our shoulders and deciding that all the coincidences we encounter are purely accidental is easy to do, but delving deeper often generates other philosophies.

Over the years, as people have explored the concepts of astrology and other facets of metaphysics, they have come to regard the birth chart as a blueprint of the soul's intent. If you view life as an opportunity to achieve those intentions, astrology begins to make more sense. Students of astrology discovered that certain aspects (geometrical angles formed between planets) in our birth charts coincide with certain tensions and stresses in our lives. Additionally, it was determined that some of these aspects also matched areas of ease and pleasure in our experiences.

From this point on, any time you do a birth chart, you need to interpret the chart as an organic whole—a living pattern of whom the individual is and what he or she could become. A birth chart should become a kind of hologram encoded with information that could be used for self-awareness. It doesn't matter whether you or anyone else is the product of a random sexual union; you need to recognize the practical value of astrology. The question of whom or what sets the whole thing in motion will matter less than the fact that you'll have found a tool for discovery that works for you.

A Hologram

Think of a horoscope as a hologram—a symbolic projection from a level of reality vastly different from our own. A hologram is composed of interconnected parts that we have to understand before we can grasp the meaning of the whole. In our attempt to understand, we interact with the hologram by bringing our own intuitive perceptions to the overall pattern.

Bear in mind the idea of a birth chart as a hologram as you read through the descriptions of planets in the houses in future chapters. To correctly interpret a chart, though, you must consider the other elements, as well as the aspects. Aspects can dramatically alter the meanings of planets in the houses. The concept of aspects will be discussed later in this chapter.

Intuition

Eventually, as you learn from this book and begin trusting your intuition, you'll come to realize that we really are masters of our own destiny. We choose it all; before birth our souls select the circumstances into which we are born. They pick the optimal astrological conditions that will allow us the opportunity to develop and evolve spiritually. These conditions are outward expressions of internal needs and help create the reality we experience. Within these patterns, our free will reigns supreme.

ALERT!

Don't discount free will! Nothing in this life is set in stone—you only have to reach out and make your destiny happen. Remember that astrology deals with patterns and gateways—opportunities we're given at birth that make it either easier or harder for us to achieve what we want. But no matter what the obstacles, we'll succeed if we go for it!

Free Will

The concept of astrology and free will working together seem deceptively easy to grasp at first. But as you work with both, peeling back the layers, you realize that everything that happens to you—from the grand to the mundane—is the result of a belief that you hold. And if it's simply your belief, you can change it. When you change a core belief, your experience also changes. This is what empowers you.

Signs and Symbols

Astrological signs and symbols were created for practical reasons. Consider them astrological shorthand. Once you learn about them, working with astrology and understanding astrological charts will be much easier. This understanding is important, as these charts are essential in your journey. The next three tables show the various symbols you'll become familiar with in this book.

TABLE 1-1 Signs and Symbols

There are twelve signs and each has a symbol:

Sign	Symbol	Sign	Symbol
Aries	♈	Libra	♎
Taurus	♉	Scorpio	♏
Gemini	♊	Sagittarius	♐
Cancer	♋	Capricorn	♑
Leo	♌	Aquarius	♒
Virgo	♍	Pisces	♓

TABLE 1-2 Planets and Symbols

Besides the Sun and the Moon, we'll be using eight planets, two nodes, and the Part of Fortune in birth charts:

Planet/Node	Symbol	Planet/Node	Symbol
Sun	☉	Saturn	♄
Moon	☽	Uranus	♅
Mercury	☿	Neptune	♆
Venus	♀	Pluto	♇
Mars	♂	North Node	☊
Jupiter	♃	South Node	☋

TABLE 1-3 Aspects and Symbols

Due to the placement of planets in the houses, geometric angles are created between the planets and also between the planets and the angles of the houses. These angles are called aspects. Each aspect has a particular symbol and meaning. In this book, the following aspects are used:

Aspect	Symbol	Meaning
Conjunction	☌	A separation of 0 degrees between two or more planets
Sextile	✶	A separation of 60 degrees between two or more planets
Square	□	A separation of 90 degrees between two or more planets
Trine	△	A separation of 120 degrees between two or more planets
Opposition	☍	A separation of 180 degrees between two or more planets

Other symbols used in a birth chart are:

- **Ascendant or Rising Sign (AS):** The sign and degree of the zodiac rising at the time of birth
- **Descendant (DS):** Opposite the Ascendant, cusp of the seventh house.
- **Midheaven or Medium Coeli (MC):** The highest point of the zodiac at the time of birth
- **Imum Coeli or Nadir (IC):** The zodiac point opposite the midheaven

Other symbols you'll see in the charts, but which won't be discussed in this book because they are much more complicated are:

- **Equatorial Ascendant (Eq):** The ascendant of the chart if you were born at the equator. Symbolizes who you think you are.
- **Vertex (Vtx):** A point of fate or destiny.

Birth Charts

A birth chart is circular, with 360 degrees. The ascendant, represented by a horizontal line through the middle of the chart (**FIGURE 1–1**), forms the horizon. The space above it is south of the horizon; the space below it is north. The ascendant (AS) is intersected by the meridian, the axis that connects the Midheaven (MC) and the Nadir or Imum Coeli (IC). The space to the left of the meridian is east; the space to the right is west.

These directions are the opposite of what they usually are because we live in the northern hemisphere, on the "top" of the planet. This means the Sun is due south when it reaches the peak of its daily arc at noon.

FIGURE 1-1

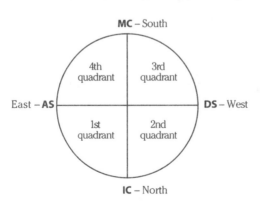

MC – South

4th quadrant

3rd quadrant

East – **AS**

DS – West

1st quadrant

2nd quadrant

IC – North

The birth chart (**FIGURE 1–2**) shows an ascendant in Pisces, a Sun in Virgo, and a Moon in Virgo. The numbers inside each of the pieces of the pie represent the houses. In the lower left-hand corner is a graph that depicts the various aspects of the chart.

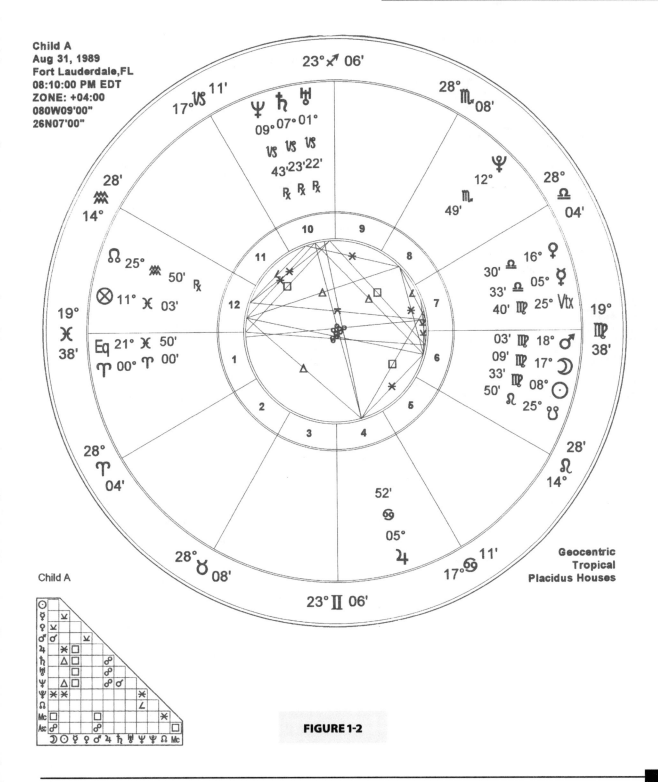

Child A
Aug 31, 1989
Fort Lauderdale, FL
08:10:00 PM EDT
ZONE: +04:00
080W09'00"
26N07'00"

Child A

FIGURE 1-2

Geocentric
Tropical
Placidus Houses

This is a child's chart (1989 birth year). This chart is quite straightforward and shows clearly defined areas of the soul's intent. We'll be referring back to it in later chapters as you begin to put together everything you're learning.

Twelve Houses

Think of the sky as a circle. Now divide it into twelve parts. Each "part" is a house. As the Sun travels over the course of a year, it makes a circle, passing from one house to the next. Your "Sun sign" is where the Sun was on the day you were born, in relation to where you were born, i.e., which part of the world. Your ascendant is determined by what hour and minute of the day you were born in relation to this.

Because there are no "lines" in the sky dividing up the universe into precise parts, there are some discrepancies that remain in terms of determining a person's Sun sign. Those who were born at the edge of a house—during the days when one Sun changes to another—are considered to have been born "on the cusp" and may show traits from the two signs they border.

To fully understand how it all works, it's necessary to talk briefly about the signs and their rulers. In the natural order of the zodiac, the signs begin with Aries and progress through the months to Pisces. Why couldn't the signs start with January? Why April and Aries? And why end up in March and Pisces instead of in December and Sagittarius?

Part of the reason for the order that starts with Aries in Western astrology is due to the nature of the signs themselves. In other words, in astrology, we believe that Aries is the pioneer who goes out into the world first. Pisces swims through the waters of the imagination, and his dreams eventually root in the physical world and become the reality of Aries.

House Cusps

The division between one house and another is called the cusp. The sign on the ascendant sets up the structure of the various house cusps. If, for instance, you have Taurus rising—on the cusp of the first house—then Gemini sits on the cusp of your second house, Cancer on the cusp of the third, and so on around the horoscope circle.

The exception to this structure is an "intercepted sign," which means a sign that doesn't appear on the cusp of a house but is completely contained within the house. The chart in **FIGURE 1-3** shows an interception in the sixth house and in the opposite twelfth house as well. In the first instance, the cusps leap from Virgo on the cusp of the sixth to Scorpio on the cusp of the seventh. Libra has been swallowed. Directly opposite, the cusp of the eleventh house leaps from Taurus on the ascendant to Pisces. Aries has been subsumed.

ALERT!

Some astrologers believe an interception portends trouble for the ruler of the intercepted sign. Others think the house that holds the interception is more powerful. Actually, the outcome depends on the overall chart. Sometimes, with an interception, you're attracted to people born under the subsumed sign. Or you manifest those attributes more strongly than you might otherwise.

In the birth chart in **FIGURE 1-3**, ruling planets affected by the interception are Neptune, which rules Pisces, and Mars, which rules Aries.

Each house cusp is ruled by the planet that governs the sign on the cusp. In **FIGURE 1-3**, Taurus is on the ascendant, so Venus rules the first house. Since the Sun is so close to the ascendant in this chart, the Sun could be said to co-rule. Gemini is on the cusp of the second house, so Mercury is the ruler of that house.

However, the natural order of the horoscope begins with Aries, then Taurus, then Gemini, and so on around the zodiac. This means that regardless of what sign is on the cusp, Mars is the natural ruler of the first house because Mars governs Aries. The attributes of the natural rulers must be taken into account when interpreting a chart.

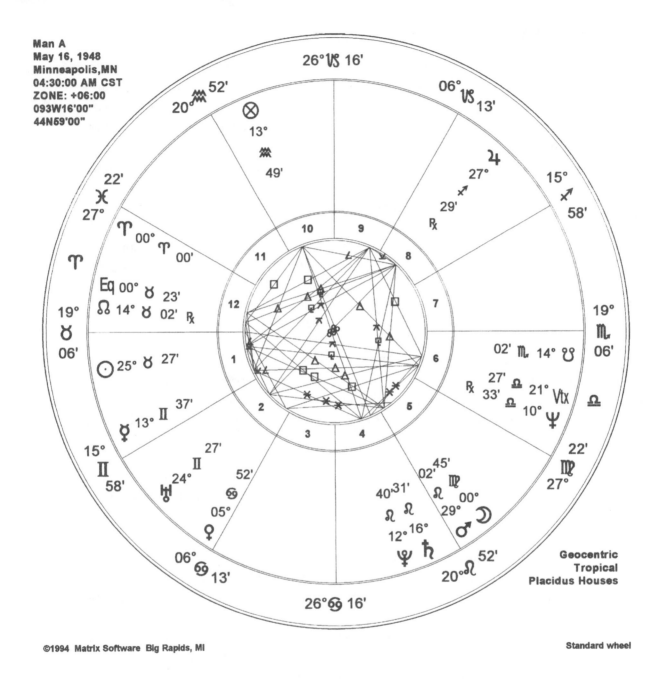

Man A
May 16, 1948
Minneapolis,MN
04:30:00 AM CST
ZONE: +06:00
093W16'00"
44N59'00"

Geocentric
Tropical
Placidus Houses

©1994 Matrix Software Big Rapids, MI

Standard wheel

FIGURE 1-3

Past-Life Astrology

Even if you don't believe you've lived previous lives, your astrologer proba-bly believes it and can pinpoint elements in your chart that seem to confirm it. In *Astrology and Your Past Lives*, famous astrologer Jeanne Avery empha-sizes the sign, house placement, and aspects to the planet Saturn as hints about lives you might have lived before. Mary Devlin, author of *Astrology & Past Lives*, contends "the incarnating entity chooses the time most astrologi-cally advantageous for its mission on Earth."

FACT

Edgar Cayce, the famed sleeping prophet of Virginia Beach, gave many readings that included astrological information on past lives. These read-ings were studied by the Association of Research and Enlightenment (ARE), the organization that Cayce's sons and grandsons perpetuated, and ARE now offers past-life astrology charts based on Cayce's reading.

Most astrologers eventually arrive at some aspect or configuration that tells them about the past lives of the people whose charts they erect. It might be Saturn or the Moon's nodes; but it might be something else. The prac-tice of astrology, particularly in relation to past lives, is a highly acclaimed pursuit.

Hypnotic Regression

Jeanne Avery backs up her research with Saturn through hypnot-ic regression. Astrologer Mary Devlin accumulated 400 horoscopes that included reincarnational histories derived through hypnotic regression as the basis for her book, *Astrology & Past Lives*.

She notes that past life birth charts are obtained through two methods, which are sometimes combined. In the first method, research has located the recorded birth date for a past personality. In the second method, an indi-vidual, while under regression in hypnosis, is asked to tune in psychically to his or her birth date in a particular past life.

According to Devlin, "The birth data is then run through a computer. The resulting natal-chart features are analyzed carefully to make sure they fit the life and personality (as revealed through regression) of the prior incarnation. About one half of our cases involve subjects with one past-life birth chart; the rest have at least two." By studying the patterns in the birth charts, Devlin was able to formulate the theories in her book.

The Nodes of the Moon

The lunar nodes are the degrees where the plane or the Moon's orbit intersects or crosses the ecliptic (Earth's orbit around the Sun). The nodes are important in the interpretation of a chart, but astrologers differ about what they mean. Astrologer Robert Hand believes that nodes "relate to connections with other people; that is, they are an axis of relationship. In this context, the North Node has a joining quality, while the South has a separating quality."

In Hindu astrology, both nodes are considered to be malefic ("bad"). In Western astrology, the North Node, called the Dragon's Head, is considered an easier aspect, the equivalent of Jupiter, and the South Node or Dragon's Tail is considered the equivalent of Saturn.

Another theory ties the nodes in with reincarnation. In this theory, the South Node represents our karma, deeply embedded patterns of behavior and thought we acquired in previous lives. We need to overcome these patterns through the North Node, which represents the area of our most profound growth in this life.

In *The Inner Sky*, astrologer Steven Forrest writes: "the South Node of the Moon symbolizes our karma . . . it shows a kind of behavior that is instinctive and automatic . . . it speaks of mindset and a pattern of motivations that arise spontaneously." "The North Node," according to Forrest, "represents the point that puts the most unrelenting tension on the past. As we allow ourselves to experience it, we open up to an utterly alien and exotic reality. We are stretched to the breaking point."

Sometimes, the nodes seem to work in a symbiotic relationship with Saturn. As we encounter restrictions in the area where Saturn sits in our chart, we are seemingly forced to rid ourselves of South Node prejudices by working through our North Node energies. The North Node also represents the types of people we gravitate toward, and the South Node represents the types of people we avoid.

ALERT!

Constant dependence on karma implies denial of free will. Instead, think of the South Node as an unconscious bias—either from previous incarnations or that which builds up during our lives. It's what we need to release in order to grow. The North Node sign and house placement indicate the area of our lives we need to expand so we can evolve toward our fulfillment as spiritual beings.

How Important Are Sun Signs?

Generalities in your chart—using just Sun signs without Moon, ascendant, etc.—aren't wrong, but they're hardly the full story. They don't take into account the vast diversity inherent in every human being. However, they are a convenient way to immediately get a handle on someone you've just met.

FACT

Another part of the astrological pattern that appears in a natal chart is formed by the distribution of the planets in the twelve houses of the horoscope. One famous astrologer, Marc Edmond Jones, identified seven such patterns or shapes. All horoscopes fall into one of them. These are called "Jones's Patterns."

Your Sun sign is the pattern of your overall personality and represents your ego. The sign in which your Sun falls influences the goals you choose and how you accomplish those goals. The twelve Sun signs are divided roughly by months, but because those divisions don't follow the months exactly, you may have been born on the cusp between two signs. If you were, then read the interpretations for both signs. For instance, if you were born on April 19, the cutoff date for Aries, also read the interpretation for Taurus, because some of those attributes probably apply to you.

Chapter 2

Sun Signs: Aries–Virgo

During the 1960s, when astrology enjoyed a boom unlike anything it had known since the late 1800s, it seemed that everyone knew everyone else's Sun sign—even if no one knew exactly what it meant. A Gemini was pegged as bright and fun, flighty and flirtatious, but basically two-faced and superficial. Virgos were known as being fussy about details. But what is the truth about Sun signs? You'll find out in this chapter and the following one. The descriptions of Sun signs are broken down into six sections: women, men, work, finances, physical traits, and spirituality.

Aries

THE RAM (MARCH 21–APRIL 19)

Element: Fire

Quality: Cardinal

Keyword: Leadership, the pioneer spirit

Planetary Ruler: Mars

Rules: Head and face; natural ruler of first house

Aries are bold, courageous, and resourceful. They always seem to know what they believe, what they want from life, and where they're going. Aries people are dynamic and aggressive (sometimes, to a fault) in pursuing their goals—whatever they might be. They're also survivors.

The challenge with this sign is lack of persistence: Aries people sometimes lose interest if they don't see rapid results. But this tendency is compensated for by their ambition and drive to succeed. They can be argumentative, lack tact, and have bad tempers. On the other hand, their anger rarely lasts long, and they can be warm and loving with those they care about.

Aries Woman

The bottom line with an Aries woman is that you shouldn't offend or anger her. If you do, she'll never forget it, and you won't see much of her after that. She'll turn her energy to someone or something else. If you're involved with an Aries woman, the relationship had better be one of equality, or she won't stick around. This isn't a woman who tolerates chauvinism.

FACT

In romance, the Aries woman's passions are fervent and sometimes all-consuming. She may even like sexual adventure, and the bedroom is the one place she'll allow—no, want—to be dominated. Suffice it to say that the Aries woman can get bored easily.

Professionally, she's driven. She sets goals and pursues them with all the relentless energy she possesses. She's great at initiating projects, launching ideas, and putting things into action. But she isn't particularly good at seeing a project or idea through to its completion unless she passionately believes in it. She can hold her own in most situations and certainly can compete with any man on the professional front. She exudes an aura of success and dresses to enhance that aura.

Aries Man

This man is as bold and brash as his female counterpart and just as impatient and driven. Thanks to his innate courage, he may recklessly take up daredevil sports. He wants to prove himself and takes unnecessary chances and risks.

He's an excellent executive—the kind of man who relies on his own judgment and intuition to make decisions. Like the female Aries, he projects a successful image even if he has failed at some endeavors in the past.

ESSENTIAL

Some women may find the Aries man too audacious for her tastes, but life with him is never boring. This is the guy who, on a whim, flies to the Caribbean for a long weekend simply to see what's there. If he's got the money, he will absolutely spend it all. And no one is as creative as the Aries man when it comes to wooing a woman.

Once an Aries man is smitten, watch out. He brings his considerable energy to the relationship and pursues the woman in a whirlwind of romance. But if the emotion isn't reciprocated quickly, he'll be gone in a flash. On the other hand, if it is—and he falls out of love—he'll be out the door before a woman could even try to convince him to stay. He's not easily talked into or out of something. Once he makes up his mind, it's usually a done deal.

Work

An Aries excels at anything in which leadership ability is paramount. These people like giving orders, and they're terrific at delegating responsibilities. They have numerous ideas and want to put them all into effect yesterday. As a fire sign, they pour energy into whatever they do.

They aren't particularly interested in having power over others. They simply want the power to do what they want without restriction.

Finances

No two ways about it: Aries people spend money as fast as it comes in. An Aries knows something should be tucked away, but retirement seems such a long way off. And besides, money always comes in when needed! The challenge for an Aries is to develop the habit of saving.

Physical Traits

These people often have ruddy complexions, arched brows, narrow chins, and in men, profuse body hair. An Aries requires adequate rest and good nutrition to replenish all the energy he burns. He shouldn't eat much red meat and will benefit from herbs that belong to this particular sign: mustard, eye-bright, and bay.

ALERT!

Since Aries rules the head and face, these areas are considered to be the weakest parts of the body for him. Common ailments are tension headaches, dizziness, and skin eruptions. In fact, many Aries suffer from migraines and allergies, too. Also, because they're indulgent, Aries need to be careful of easily gaining weight. It's a good thing he's so active!

Spirituality

Aries is likely to sample a little of everything before deciding on which spiritual belief fits best. He might live in an ashram, delve into paganism, or even try out a more conventional religion. While involved with a particular spiritual path, he will be passionate about it. But unless his passion is sustained, an Aries will eventually get bored and move on to something new.

Taurus

THE BULL (APRIL 20–MAY 20)

Element: Earth

Quality: Fixed

Keywords: Endurance, perseverance, stubbornness

Planetary Ruler: Venus

Rules: Neck, throat, cervical vertebrae; natural ruler of second house

While Aries is out pioneering and discovering new lands, Taurus is settling and cultivating the land and using his resources for practical purposes. His stubbornness and determination keep him around for the long haul on any project or endeavor.

Taureans are the most stubborn sign in the zodiac. They are also incredibly patient, singular in their pursuit of goals, and determined to attain what they want. Although they lack versatility because of the fixed nature of the sign, they compensate for it by enduring whatever they have to in order to get what they want. Long after other contestants have fallen out of the race, Taurus individuals are still in the running. As a result, they often succeed where others fail.

Most Taureans enjoy being surrounded by nice things. They like fine art and music, and many have considerable musical ability. They also have a talent for working with their hands—gardening, woodworking, and sculpting.

It takes a lot to anger a Taurus person, but once you do, clear out. The "bull's rush" can be fierce. But thanks to Venus ruling this sign, Taurus people are usually sensual and romantic. They are also physically oriented individuals who take pride in their bodies.

Taurus Woman

She's loyal and dedicated to whatever she loves most. Her central interests reflect her particular tastes in art, color, and decor. She enjoys beauty, whatever its guise. If she's into clothing, then she dresses well and tastefully. If sports and physical activity are her passion, she pursues them diligently and with tremendous patience.

Since the Taurus woman is Venus-ruled, she's a romantic. Court her with flowers, moonlit walks on the beach, and poetry. She's a generous, ardent lover, who probably has a love of music. She may even play an instrument or sing. If you want to change her opinion on something, though, go about it in a gentle way. Don't ever back her into a corner. She'll dig in her heels and refuse to budge!

As an Earth sign, she likes to putter in the garden and perhaps grows and cultivates herbs. She benefits from any time spent outdoors doing something she finds pleasurable. Animals are important to her and if she has pets, they reflect her own tastes in beauty.

Taurus Man

Like his female counterpart, the Taurus man works hard and patiently at what he loves. His patience and perseverance make him good at finishing what other people have started. This guy isn't impetuous. Considerable thought goes into most things that he does. It's not that he's cautious; he's merely purposeful. If he doesn't understand the reason for doing something, he won't do it, and nothing you say will change his mind.

FACT

Taurus's romantic nature may not always show up in flowers and gifts, but he does others things that tell you he cares. In return, he enjoys a good massage; likes having his neck rubbed and adores sitting with a nice glass of wine and his honey in front of a fireplace.

Both men and women in this sign can be jealous and possessive. But this tendency is mitigated considerably if the Taurus man knows you're as sincere as he is. He may have a deep connection with nature and the natural world that manifests in camping and solo sports. If he works out in a gym, he probably does it alone, without a trainer. He may be into yoga, alternative medicine, and health foods.

Work

Taureans excel at work that requires persistence, stability, and relentless drive. They're able to take abstract ideas and make them concrete and practical. This means they're good at behind-the-scenes work, especially if the work is artistically creative—writing, costume design, gourmet cooking, musical composition, or anything to do with nature. You won't find a more tireless worker in the zodiac.

Finances

Despite the Taurean need for material security, they enjoy spending money. But the spending is rarely frivolous because Taurean tastes are quite specific and usually refined. Books, art, travel, and shamanic workshops may offer security for the Taurus.

Physical Traits

Taureans are recognizable by their necks, which are often thick and sturdy. They tend to be attractive people with broad foreheads and many retain their youthful appearances long after the rest of us begin to show our age. They benefit from a daily regimen of physical exercise and should be moderate in their consumption of fattening foods. This, of course, is undoubtedly true for all signs, but particularly true for the bull who has a slower metabolism.

Spirituality

Taurus, due to the fixed, Earth temperament of the sign, often seeks spiritual answers in nature. While camping, hiking, or engaging in some sort of physical activity outside, she connects with the deeper levels of self. Music and the arts can have the same effect on a Taurus.

Gemini

THE TWINS (MAY 21–JUNE 21)

Element: Air

Quality: Mutable

Keyword: Versatility

Planetary Ruler: Mercury

Rules: Hands, arms, lungs, nervous system; natural ruler of the third house

After Aries and Taurus have discovered and cultivated new land, Gemini ventures out to see what else is there and seizes upon new ideas that will expand their communities. Their innate curiosity keeps these people on the move.

Geminis, because they're ruled by Mercury, tend to use the rational, intellectual mind to explore and understand their personal worlds. They need to answer the single burning question in their minds: Why? This applies to most facets of their lives, from the personal to the impersonal. This need to know may send them off to foreign countries, particularly if the Sun is in the ninth house, where their need to explore other cultures and traditions ranks high.

ALERT!

Geminis are changeable and often moody! Their symbol, the twins, means they are often at odds with themselves—the mind demanding one thing, the heart demanding the opposite. To someone else, this internal conflict often manifests as two very different people. As a Gemini's significant other, you might reach a point where you wonder which twin you're with!

These individuals are fascinated by relationships and connections among people, places, and objects. Their rational analysis of everything, from ideas to relationships, drives them as crazy as it drives everyone else around them. When this quality leads them into an exploration of psychic and spiritual realms, it grounds them. In romance, the heart of a Gemini is won by seduction of the mind.

Gemini Woman

At first glance, she seems to be all over the place. She can talk on any number of topics and sounds like she knows what she's talking about, until you discover that her knowledge on most things is, alas, superficial. But if you hit on one of her passions, her knowledge is deep and thorough. She excels at communication; the form this talent takes depends on other aspects in her chart.

In her twenties, she tends to be flirtatious and flighty, unable or unwilling to commit to a relationship. On the one hand, this girl loves her freedom; on the other, relationships are important to her. If she marries young, she may marry at least twice. In her thirties and forties, she begins to settle in. By this time, she has made a kind of peace with herself. She has a better understanding of her moods, needs, and emotions. By fifty, the Gemini woman knows whom she is; now she must begin living that truth.

If you want to change this woman's attitude or opinion, you have to prove that your attitude or opinion is more logical. Remember that her concept of logic may differ from yours. She's simultaneously a control freak and easy going. If you make her think she has her way, she'll be perfectly content.

Gemini Man

He's quick, witty, and enigmatic. Just when you think you've got him figured out, he says or does something that blows your concept of who he is. Don't expect a courtship from this guy; he doesn't possess the sensual appreciation of beauty that a Taurus man has. But if you appeal to his intellect—if you court him mentally—he might dedicate his next book to you.

The Gemini man makes a good editor, writer, or orator. He may hold down two jobs and is certainly capable of working on more than one project at a time. Once he commits to something though, whether it's a profession or a relationship, he needs to know that he is appreciated.

QUESTION?

How do you solve the Gemini man riddle?
Like his female counterpart, the Gemini man often seems to be two people inhabiting one body. One twin is attentive to your every need and whim. But the other twin couldn't care less. You won't change this particular quality. It's inherent. You simply have to get accustomed to it.

Work

Geminis excel in any line of work that provides diversity. It doesn't matter if it's with the public or behind the scenes, as long as it isn't routine. They make good counselors because one of the twins is always willing to listen. Their love of language gives them a talent for the written word. Acting, politics, libraries, research: all these fields fit Gemini. The bottom line is simple: boredom to a Gemini is like death.

Finances

How a Gemini handles money depends on which of the twins holds the purse strings at the time—the spendthrift or the tightwad. Either way, Geminis enjoy spending money on the things they love, such as books, movies, theater, and travel.

Physical Traits

Gemini generally are slender people, filled with nervous energy. All this energy can be difficult to rein in sometimes, particularly on nights when they work late and their heads race with ideas. Geminis benefit from breaks in their established routines and need physical exercise to ground their thoughts. They are prone to respiratory and nervous ailments.

Spirituality

Geminis are so restless mentally that they generally don't do well within organized religions, unless they've chosen that path for themselves. They sample spiritual belief systems the way other people sample new foods. However, once a Gemini finds a spiritual path that makes sense, she generally sticks with it.

Cancer

THE CRAB (JUNE 22–JULY 22)

Element: Water

Quality: Cardinal

Keyword: Nurturing, emotional drive

Planetary Ruler: Moon

Rules: Breasts, stomach, digestive system; natural ruler of the fourth house

Once Aries, Taurus, and Gemini have discovered, settled, and expanded their new land, Cancer comes along and tames it—civilizes it. These people need roots, a place or even a state of mind that they can call their own. They need a safe harbor, a refuge in which to retreat for solitude.

Imagination, sensitivity, and the nurturing instinct characterize this sign. Cancerians are generally gentle and kind people, unless they're hurt. Then they can become vindictive and sharp-spoken. They forgive easily, but rarely forget. Cancerians tend to be affectionate, passionate, and even possessive at times. As parents, they may be overprotective. As spouses or significant others, they may smother their mates with love and good intentions.

FACT

Emotionally, Cancerians act and react in the same way the crab moves—sideways. They avoid confrontations and usually aren't comfortable in discussing what they feel. They're reluctant to reveal who they are and sometimes hide behind their protective urges, preferring to tend to the needs of others rather than to their own needs.

Cancers are intuitive and can sometimes be psychic. Experience flows through them emotionally. They're often moody and always changeable; their interests and social circles shift constantly. Once a Cancer trusts you, however, he lets you in on his most private world.

Cancer Woman

At first she seems enigmatic, elusive. She's so changeable in her moods that you never know where you stand with her. Beneath her gentle and sympathetic nature, beneath her bravado, she's scared of being pinned down and insecure about who she is.

If a Cancer woman doesn't have children of her own, she probably has some sort of connection with children. Animals or people in need are like her own children—she likes to extend herself emotionally. Somehow, her nurturing instinct finds expression through giving to other living things, including plants.

She needs roots—her own home, preferably near water—where she can establish a base. She nurtures everything—animals, her own children, waifs, and orphans of all shapes, sizes, and species. This woman is emotion distilled into its purest form. She feels first, then thinks. Sometimes she's a psychic sponge, absorbing every emotion around her.

Cancer Man

Like the female Cancer, the male has expressive eyes that communicate a kind of forlorn nostalgia for things past. He's kind, affectionate, and nurturing, but only to a point. When he feels his personal space has been infringed upon, he retreats just like the crab—rapidly to the side. Then he buries himself in sand by retreating to his special place—his own home. Like the female Cancer, he is often nurturing and gets along well with children.

This guy is hard to figure out. Sometimes he courts you with flowers and candlelight; other times he's sacked out on the couch lost in his own gloom. Your best course of action is to let him be. Don't prod him when he's in this kind of mood. You won't get anywhere with him even if you do.

If he's interested in spiritual issues, chances are he's in deep. In this sign, you're likely to find psychic healers and clairvoyants—people who use their intuition in highly developed and sophisticated ways.

Work

Cancerians may be happiest when they work from their own homes. Due to the intensity of their feelings, they do well in medicine, working directly with patients. For the same reason, they also make good psychic healers, counselors, and psychologists. Teaching children, publicity and marketing, being involved in sociology or anthropology, running a daycare center, or even taking care of other people's homes are also good fits for the Cancerian personality.

Finances

Cancers aren't lavish spenders except when it comes to their homes and families. Then, nothing is too expensive. Otherwise, they tend to be big savers. As teens, they stash their allowance in cookie jars; as adults, they stick their money in long-term CDs.

Physical Traits

This sign is more recognizable than some of the others because Cancerians have round faces. The entire body, in fact, may be rounded, though not necessarily overweight. Cancerians benefit from water sports, a day at the beach, or anything having to do with water. There's usually some lightness in the eyes—even if they're brown. Many Cancers also have eyes the shape of a cat's.

ALERT!

If any Cancers have hang-ups about their earlier lives, particularly childhood, hypnosis might be a good way to dislodge and work through the past. It's important that a Cancer not cling to past hurts and injuries, because these emotions eventually lodge themselves in the body and create health problems.

Spirituality

Introspection is the key with Cancers, and it doesn't matter if it's provided in the guise of organized religion or an alternative belief system. When they feel a particular set of beliefs is a fit, they stick with it, explore it, and draw upon their innate intuition to understand it.

Leo

THE LION (JULY 23–AUGUST 22)

Element: Fire

Quality: Fixed

Keywords: Action, power

Planetary Ruler: Sun

Rules: Heart, back, and spinal cord; natural ruler of the fifth house

Leos roar. They love being the center of attention and often surround themselves with admirers. To remain in the proud kingdom of a Leo, her admirers have to think like she thinks, believe what she believes, and hate and love whom she hates and loves. To a Leo, this is loyalty. In return, Leo offers generosity, warmth, and compassion.

ALERT!

Don't ever argue to change the opinions and beliefs of a Leo! You won't succeed, and the Leo will just get annoyed with you! As a fixed sign, Leos stand firm in their belief systems. They have found what works for them and don't understand why their beliefs might not work for someone else. In general, though, they are optimistic, honorable, loyal, and ambitious.

Leos have an innate dramatic sense, and life is definitely their stage. Their flamboyance and personal magnetism extend to every facet of their lives. They seek to succeed and make an impact in every situation. It is no surprise that the theater and allied arts fall under the rule of Leo.

Leo Woman

She's up front about what she feels and invariably is disappointed when she finds that other people may not be as forthright. You'll never have to guess where you stand with a Leo woman unless there's something in the aspects of her chart that says otherwise. She can't "pretend." She can be diplomatic, but, if her heart isn't in it, she isn't capable of deceiving someone into thinking it is. She loves flattery and over-the-top romantic courtships. She is an ardent lover.

ESSENTIAL

The Leo woman exudes confidence, and because of this, other people place their trust in her. And that's no mistake: Leo is loyal, to a fault. She needs to be at the helm in her workplace—a managerial position will do, but CEO would be better. She dislikes playing second fiddle on any level and would rather work from home than have to contend with working for employers whom she doesn't respect.

In a marriage, don't expect her to be content with staying home, unless she's running her business from there. If she's a mother, she's not just a mother. She has a career, hobbies, and passions. Because Leo also rules children, she may be involved somehow with children, even if she doesn't have her own.

She likes nice clothes and probably dresses with flair and style in bright, bold colors. Remember that she's an actress and adept at creating certain impressions and moods through the way she looks and acts. She's a chameleon. She likes order in her world, but it has to be her order.

Leo Man

Give him center stage, and he's at his best; tell him what to do, and he's at his worst. Once you accept that about the Leo man, he's easy to get along with because you really want to like this guy. He's warm, outgoing, and fun. Kids love him because in many ways he's like they are—full of magic.

People are attracted to him because they sense his leadership abilities. They like his frankness, abundant energy, and ambition. If you're a Leo's significant other, get used to sharing him with his "court," whomever they might be. Rest assured, though, that if your Leo commits to you, he means it.

Work

A Leo excels at work in front of the public. He's a great actor, orator, Speaker of the House, or CEO—a menial job won't do. Leos are good at teaching because the classroom becomes their stage, and their students become their audience. They make excellent writers, editors, and journalists. They also tend to be good with animals and enjoy training, caring for, and loving them.

ALERT!

Neither the male nor the female Leo do well in subservient jobs. They're born leaders. Give them distinction and the power to command, and they do the job exceptionally well. However, they'll growl and become belligerent if they're forced to cower to someone whom they don't like!

Finances

If Leo wants it, Leo buys it. If he can't afford it, he charges it. If his charge cards are maxed out, then he hocks his Rolex or his collection of baseball cards to buy it. Saving for a rainy day just isn't in the picture because, for a Leo, there aren't any rainy days! There are, of course, exceptions to all these generalities. A Moon in an Earth sign, combined with a Leo sun, would mitigate the flamboyance, particularly if the Moon were in Capricorn. But these are just details.

Physical Traits

Jacqueline Kennedy Onassis was the physical epitome of a Leo female with her compelling eyes, thick hair, and regal bearing. Leos generally benefit from low-fat diets because one of the weakest parts of their bodies is the heart. Exercise, even if on the light side, is needed to channel some of their abundant energy.

Spirituality

Most Leos were probably once sun-worshipping pagans in past lives. Now they're sampling everything else along the spectrum. Unless aspects in the chart indicate otherwise, a Leo isn't likely to stay within the confines of organized religion unless it suits him. If he does it out of obligation, then, in his mind, he's doing it for his kids. A Leo's greatest spiritual contribution comes when he expands beyond the parameters of the self and reaches for the universal.

Virgo

THE VIRGIN (AUGUST 23–SEPTEMBER 22)

Element: Earth

Quality: Mutable

Keywords: Order, detailed, dedication

Planetary Ruler: Mercury

Rules: Intestines, abdomen, female reproductive system; natural ruler of the sixth house

The popular image of a Virgo is a picky, critical, and compulsively tidy person. This is misleading. If one or all of these traits manifest obviously, then the natal chart reveals other aspects that enhance this characteristic.

Virgos are like Geminis in terms of mental quickness and agility. Due to their attention to detail, they tend to delve more deeply into subjects they study. Even though they are career-oriented people, they seem to be more interested in doing their jobs efficiently and well. They're happiest when engaged in something that benefits society at large. In other words, duty is important to Virgos.

ESSENTIAL

Virgos tend to be attracted to people who are intellectually stimulating or eccentric in some way. Their standards are high when it comes to romantic relationships, and unless the mental connection exists, the relationship won't last long. In their twenties, many Virgos fall for those who aren't quite good enough for them. They find critical partners or those who don't appreciate them fully—an unhealthy match.

Since Virgos, like Geminis, are Mercury-ruled, they need outlets for all their nervous energy. Running, martial arts, or workouts at the gym are recommended. Writing, pets, reading, and extra education can also serve this purpose.

Virgo Woman

Physically, she's distinctive in some way—intriguing eyes, exquisite facial bone structure, or meticulous grooming. She possesses a certain vibrancy and energy that other people sense even when she's not trying to project an image. In romance, she is attracted first when a mental spark exists. As the mental camaraderie deepens, so do her emotions.

The Virgo woman, like her male counterpart, is often insecure and tends to fret over everything. This trait usually evens out as the Virgo woman matures. It can be irritating to a significant other, particularly when her fretting turns to a constant critique of everything other people say and do.

FACT

A Virgo woman is usually aware of health and hygiene issues, especially when it concerns cutting-edge research. She may not always apply what she knows to her own life, but she has the knowledge. She's also aware of the world and pays attention to business and political issues. She can be a whiz at creating new business ventures if she puts her mind to it.

A Virgo woman enjoys spending money on items like books and pieces of art that strike her fancy. She's sensitive to her surroundings, so her home is always comfortable. If she's a mother, she's conscientious, tactful, and loving. She usually has a soft spot for animals, too.

Virgo Man

He looks good and possesses an indisputable presence. He's mentally quick, intellectually curious, and is an excellent worker. His humor is often biting but rarely malicious.

He can be quite fussy about his personal environment. This is the kind of man who insists on having his own bathroom or, at the very least, his own side of the bathroom counter. If he cooks, then he probably is quite good at it and possessive about the kitchen while he's creating. Like the female of the sign, the Virgo man enjoys pleasant surroundings and usually owns several special items that he keeps for nostalgia's sake.

He's prone to taking himself too seriously and benefits from any activity that forces him to lighten up. He's always hardest on himself, overly critical of what he does or doesn't do and can be quite critical of others as well. He rarely seeks praise for his efforts and, in the less evolved Virgo man, won't give praise even when it's deserved.

Work

Virgos sincerely strive for perfection in their work and careers. They do best when working for others—social work, in hospitals, clinics, hospice programs, or with their children. The challenge in every area of a Virgo's life is to serve without self-sacrifice. Their striving for perfection compels them to evolve and change.

Finances

When Virgos are big spenders, they usually pull back at some critical point and question what they buy and why. What need does it fill? If they are tight with money, then something happens that impels them to loosen their hold—to spend money for enjoyment. Virgos follow an arc of evolvement toward perfection in everything they do. They analyze patterns in their lives and seek to change those that don't work.

Physical Traits

They usually have slender builds and are physically attractive. There may be a sharpness about their features. Since Virgos fret and worry so much, their physical ailments usually manifest first in their stomachs: colic in infancy, stomach upsets as a youngster, ulcers as an adult. But because Virgos are generally fussy about their diet and health, they grow into their own bodies with innate wisdom.

Spirituality

The evolved Virgo is capable of great vision and an intuition that often borders on prescience. They are likely to sample different spiritual beliefs until they find one that appeals to their eminently practical side.

Chapter 3

Sun Signs: Libra–Pisces

Now that you've learned about the first six Sun signs, read on to discover characteristics of the other six. As previously mentioned, when astrology had a spike in popularity in the 1960s, different Sun signs were pegged with traits that weren't necessarily correct. Scorpios were viewed with some trepidation because they were supposedly vengeful. Capricorns were assumed to be rigid in character. This chapter contains the real deal about the last six Sun signs.

Libra

THE SCALES (SEPTEMBER 23–OCTOBER 22)

Element: Air

Quality: Cardinal

Keyword: Balance

Planetary Ruler: Venus

Rules: Lower back and the diaphragm; natural ruler of the seventh house

Librans seem to come in three distinct types: those who are decisive, those who aren't, and those who seek harmony for its own sake. The typical Libra seeks to mediate and balance. Librans have an inherent need to act democratically, diplomatically, and fairly—always.

ESSENTIAL

In love, Libras are natural romantics and flourish in enduring partnerships. They are fair-minded people, but avoid anything that is grim, crude, vulgar, or garish. Adversely afflicted, they have trouble making decisions and may lose themselves in sensual pleasures. In highly evolved Librans, the human mind finds the perfect blend between balance and discretion.

They love beauty in all its guises—art, literature, classical music, opera, mathematics, and the human body. They usually are team players who enjoy debate but not argument. They're excellent strategists and masters at the power of suggestion. Even though Librans are courteous, amiable people, one should never presume that they're pushovers. They use diplomacy and intelligence to get what they want.

Libra Woman

Watch out: She's a flirt who is seductive and romantic, and she bowls you over with the small luxuries she brings you. If she cooks, she probably does it well, using herbs and seasonings. She sets the mood, too, with candlelight, fresh flowers, and soft music. She's a romantic, tender lover who enjoys companionship and flourishes in partnerships.

Her home reflects her refined tastes in art, books, and good music. She may not be extravagant and probably doesn't squander the money she has, but she derives enormous pleasure from whatever she buys. If she likes opera or the ballet, she attends regularly; these extravagances feed her soul. She may play a musical instrument and may have a fondness for chess.

Libra Man

He needs companionship, just like his female counterpart, and generally works better as part of a team. But he also needs to retain his individuality in any partnership, which may be quirky at times. Once you've won his heart, he's loyal and considerate and seeks to perfect the union.

He enjoys pleasant, harmonious surroundings in his work and personal environment. He often finds himself in the role of peacemaker simply because he seeks balance in all things. He shares many of the same artistic interests as his female counterpart.

ALERT!

A Libra man rarely expresses anger. He'd rather work around whatever problems crop up. But if he lets loose, he leaves nothing unsaid! Every transgression and hurt is spelled out. Although his anger passes quickly, such outbursts leave him shaken and sometimes ill.

Work

The Libra's obvious choice for a profession is an attorney or judge because of his finely tuned sense of fair play. Librans generally excel in any profession that calls for an acutely balanced mind and sensitivities. They make good editors, musicians, accountants, artists, and parents. The work itself is less important than what it teaches Libras about making decisions, in spite of their ability to see all sides of an issue.

Finances

A sense of balance allows Libras to strike the right note between spender and miser. Libras tend to save, but they enjoy spending when they can afford it. Most Libras know their limit.

Physical Traits

As a Venus-ruled sign, these people are usually physically distinctive in some way—compassionate eyes or well-formed bodies. They tend to be slender, very attractive, and seem to know instinctively how to bring out the best in their companions. Since Libra rules the lower back and diaphragm, unvented emotions manifest first in those areas of the body. Libras benefit from physical exercise, particularly anything that strengthens the back and maintains general flexibility.

Spirituality

Evolved Libras understand instinctively that they must unite human duality with divine unity. They seek idealized balance; the perfect equilibrium. For some, this is accomplished within the parameters of organized religion. For others, spirituality is sought through community efforts or in their immediate family.

Scorpio

THE SCORPION (OCTOBER 23–NOVEMBER 21)

Element: Water

Quality: Fixed

Keywords: Regeneration, transformation

Planetary Ruler: Mars and Pluto

Rules: Sexual organs, rectum, and reproductive system; natural ruler of the eighth house

Note the sharp point at the tip of the glyph that represents this sign. Symbolically, it's the scorpion's stinger, which characterizes the biting sarcasm often associated with Scorpios. These people are intense, passionate, and strong-willed. They often impose their will on others. In less aware people, this can manifest as cruelty, sadism, and enmity; in the more evolved Scorpio, this characteristic transforms lives for the better. Like Aries, Scorpios aren't afraid of anything. But they have an endurance that Aries lacks that enables them to plow ahead and overcome whatever opposition they encounter.

E ALERT!

Scorpios don't know the meaning of indifference. They tend to live in black and white worlds, dealing with either/or issues. They either approve or disapprove, agree or disagree. You're either a friend or an enemy: there are no shades of gray. Once you've gained a Scorpio's trust, you've won his loyalty forever—unless you hurt him or someone he loves. Then they can become vindictive enemies.

Scorpios possess an innate curiosity and suspicion of easy answers that compels them to probe deeply into whatever interests them. They dig out concealed facts and seek the meaning behind facades. Most Scorpios are exceptionally intuitive, even if they don't consciously acknowledge it. The more highly evolved people in this sign are often very psychic, with rich inner lives and passionate involvement in metaphysics.

Scorpios are excellent workers: industrious and relentless. They excel at anything associated with the eighth house—trusts and inheritances, mortuaries, psychological counselors, and the occult. Sometimes they're more passionate with their work than they are with the important people in their lives.

Scorpio Woman

She smolders with sexuality. This is a woman who turns heads on the street, who walks into a room filled with strangers and instantly grabs attention through nothing more than the power of her presence. If you seek to win a Scorpio woman's heart, you'd better be up front and honest right from the beginning. If she ever catches you in a lie or if you hurt her, she'll cut you off cold.

She's a passionate lover and can be jealous and possessive. You won't ever figure out what she's thinking or feeling just by the expression on her face, unless she's angry—then watch out! Her rage takes many forms—an explosion, sarcasm that bites to the bone, or a piercing look that makes you shrivel inside.

If her intuition is developed, it borders on clairvoyance. This inner sense often shines forth in a Scorpio woman's striking eyes. As a mother, the Scorpio woman is devoted, loving, and fiercely protective. She strives to create a comfortable and loving home for her kids that can also be a refuge from the outside world.

Scorpio Man

Like the female of the sign, he's intense, passionate, and very private. There is always something compelling about a Scorpio man—his eyes, the way he dresses, or the enigma of his presence. He isn't just a flirt. He often comes on like a locomotive with sexual energy, radiating so powerfully that he's difficult to ignore even if you aren't attracted to him.

The Scorpio man often has a marvelous talent of some kind that he pursues passionately, but which may not figure into his income. In others words, his talent is his avocation—music, art, writing, acting, astrology, or tarot cards. Or, he may pour his considerable talent into nurturing his own children.

Many Scorpio men (and women) enjoy sports. They have a distinct preference for more violent sports like football and hunting. Their choice of sports is sometimes a reflection of a personal struggle with emotional extremes.

Work

They make excellent actors, detectives, spies, even teachers. There's just no telling where all that rawness of perception can take a Scorpio. One thing's for sure, though—his work follows his passion.

Finances

Scorpios are masters at using other people's money to build their own fortunes. This is as true of a Mafia don as it is of a Wall Street entrepreneur. Scorpio attaches no moral judgment to it; this is simply how things are. In return, Scorpios can be extravagantly generous in charity work or anonymous donors to worthy causes. Your Scorpio may even rewrite the last act of your rejected screenplay and get it to sell big-time.

Physical Traits

All Scorpios seem to share the same compelling, intense eyes. Regardless of body height or size, they generate a powerful sense of presence and usually have low, husky voices. Due to the unusual will power inherent in the sign, Scorpios often work to the point of exhaustion. Any illness usually has a strong emotional component.

Spirituality

Some Scorpios take to organized religion like a duck to water. They like the ritual and the sense of belonging. Others, however, delve into unorthodox belief systems seeking spiritual answers. Whatever form spirituality takes for a Scorpio, he or she brings passion and sincerity to the search.

Sagittarius

THE ARCHER (NOVEMBER 22–DECEMBER 21)

Element: Fire

Quality: Mutable

Keywords: Idealism, freedom

Planetary Ruler: Jupiter

Rules: Hips, thighs, liver, and hepatic system; natural ruler of the ninth house

These people seek the truth, express it as they see it—and don't care if anyone else agrees with them. They see the large picture of any issue and can't be bothered with the mundane details. They are always outspoken and can't understand why other people aren't as candid. After all, what is there to hide?

This is a mentally oriented sign where logic reigns supreme. But the mentality differs from Gemini, the polar opposite of Sagittarius, in several important ways. A Gemini is concerned with the here and now: he needs to know how and why things and relationships work in his life. A Sagittarian, however, focuses on the future and on the larger family of humanity. Quite often, this larger family includes animals—large, small, wild, or domestic—and the belief that all deserve the right to live free.

Despite Sagittarians' propensity for logic, they are often quite prescient, with an uncanny ability to glimpse the future. Even when they have this ability, however, they often think they need an external tool to trigger it such as tarot cards, an astrology chart, or runes. Many Sagittarians reject the idea of astrology, as well—they rely solely on practicality and inherent intuition.

They love their freedom and chafe at any restrictions. Their versatility and natural optimism win them many friends, but only a few ever really know the heart of the Sagittarian.

Sagittarius Woman

She's hard to figure out at first. You see her in a crowd and notice that she commands attention. She's humorous, vivacious, and outspoken. One on one, she's flirtatious. But the moment you mention having dinner or catching a movie, she's gone. It's not that she's coy; it's simply that you're just a face in the crowd.

ESSENTIAL

If you catch Sagittarius woman's attention, it's because you talk well and quickly about something that interests her. Animal rights, for instance, or paradigm shifts in worldwide belief systems, will definitely be topics of concern. This lady thinks big and if you want to win her heart, you'd better think just as big.

Sagittarian women excel in jobs and careers that don't confine them. If they have children, they allow their offspring such great latitude that to other people it may appear that they're indifferent. This is hardly the case. A Sagittarian mother is loving and devoted, but believes that her children should find their own way. She offers broad guidelines and her own wisdom but doesn't force her opinions.

Sagittarius Man

He's a charmer, flirtatious and witty; the kind of man everyone loves to have at a party. He's also candid and opinionated, with firm ideas on how things work and should be done. His frustration is that ideas that often seem so obvious to him seem oblique to other people. He fails to understand that not everyone sees the world as he does.

His vision is broad and often grandiose. He does everything in a big way and is rarely satisfied with what he achieves. On his way to attaining a particular goal, he gets carried away with the momentum he has built up and ends up taking on more than he can handle.

The less evolved men of this sign sometimes lose sight of the difference between need and greed. They want everything, and they want it immediately. This is as true in business as it is in romance. Sagittarian men often have more than one relationship going on at a time, which suits their need for freedom. For this reason, Sagittarius is also known as the bachelor sign.

FACT

Sagittarius man, like his female counterpart, enjoys traveling—particularly foreign travel—and is too restless for a sedentary lifestyle. During his free time, this man is out horseback riding, maybe practicing archery or white-water rafting. He's always moving and aiming toward the future.

Work

Constraint isn't in the Sagittarian vocabulary. Or, when it is, the word and the reality influence other people's lives, not the Sagittarian's. They work best in jobs and fields where they have complete freedom to call the shots: an owner of an airline, CEO, small business owner, entrepreneur, actor, writer, or traveling salesman. The point isn't the work so much as the freedom of the work. That is always the bottom line with Sagittarius.

Finances

A Sagittarius has plenty of options about where to spend his or her money—travel, education, workshops, seminars, animals, or books—and that's often the problem. How can they narrow their choices? What should they buy first? More than likely, they will toss all their choices into the air and seize the one that hits the ground first.

Physical Traits

Many people born under this sign are tall and wide through the shoulders. They may have a tendency to gain weight because they indulge their appetites. Jupiter, the planet of expansion, rules this sign and often expands the physical body as well. Their faces tend to be oval and elongated.

Spirituality

As the natural ruler of the ninth house, which governs philosophy, religion, and higher education, Sagittarians generally sample a vast array of spiritual beliefs. Once they find a belief system that suits them, they generally stick with it. In this way, they are much like their polar opposite, Gemini. The difference, though, is that Sagittarius delves more deeply into spiritual matters.

Capricorn

THE GOAT (DECEMBER 22–JANUARY 19)

Element: Earth

Quality: Cardinal

Keywords: Materialism, self-discipline

Planetary Ruler: Saturn

Rules: Knees, skin, and bones; natural ruler of the tenth house

Capricorns are serious-minded people who often seem aloof and tightly in control of their emotions and their personal domain. Even as youngsters, there's a mature air about them, as if they were born with a profound core that few outsiders ever see.

This sign's nickname, the goat, represents Capricorn's slow, steady rise through the world. They're easily impressed by outward signs of success, but are interested less in money than in the power that money represents. Like Scorpio, they feel the need to rule whatever kingdom they occupy whether this is their home, work place, or business. Like Scorpios, they prize power and mastery over others, but they tend to be subtler about it.

QUESTION?

What's a relatively unknown fact about Capricorns?
They're natural worriers. Even when they've taken all the precautions they can possibly take, Capricorns fret that they've forgotten something. They can benefit from the idea of "perfect faith"—that whatever they do will work out fine. Unfortunately, it's hard to convince a Capricorn to just sit back and not take action, even when there's nothing to be done immediately.

Capricorns are true workers—industrious, efficient, and disciplined. They deplore inertia in other people. Their innate common sense gives them the ability to plan ahead and to work out practical ways of approaching goals. More often than not, they succeed at whatever they set out to do.

In a crowd, Capricorns aren't particularly easy to spot. They aren't physically distinctive the way Scorpios are, and they aren't the life of the party like Sagittarians. But they possess a quiet dignity that's unmistakable.

Capricorn Woman

At first glance, she appears to be tough as nails—a determined, serious woman who seems to know where she has been, where she is, and where she's going. But when you get to know her, you'll discover she's not tough at all—she's merely guarded and reserved. Don't expect her to welcome you into her life with open arms. You have to prove yourself first.

ALERT!

As a mother, she's devoted and often runs her home with the efficiency of a business. Due to the Saturn influence on this sign, the Capricorn woman can sometimes be too rigid with her spouse and children. She expects a lot and, supported by other aspects in her chart, may enforce her will to the point of dominance.

This woman has certain parameters and boundaries that she simply won't cross. She isn't the type to throw herself recklessly into a casual affair. Once you've proven you're worth her while, she'll open up emotionally, and her depth may astonish you. She plays for keeps in love. She has a soft spot for animals, which often bring out the best in her because she opens to them emotionally.

Capricorn Man

He's well prepared for any journey he undertakes, and it doesn't matter whether the journey is physical, emotional, or spiritual. He doesn't like surprises. He shies away from getting involved in people's lives, and this detachment allows him to focus on his goals. As a boss, he can be dictatorial. As an employee, you won't find a harder worker. He enjoys the company of vivacious women, perhaps because they make him feel lighter and less driven. Once he's committed, he tends to be monogamous. Life seems to improve for him as he ages because he has learned that discipline is not nearly as important as compassion.

Work

Capricorns excel in any profession that is structured, such as engineering, medicine, editing, politics, ceramics, building, architecture, and leatherwork. Their strong desire to succeed is colored by traditional values and a conservative approach. In some Capricorns, these traits make them exceptionally good workers who progress slowly and successfully toward their goals. With other Capricorns, the tradition and conservatism hold them back.

Finances

Thriftiness is the hallmark for Capricorn finances. They build their finances the same way they build their careers: one penny at a time. They do seek status and the acquisition of material goods that reflect what they seek, so they may go through periods where they overspend.

Physical Traits

Capricorns aren't the body-builder types. But because they are Earth signs, they generally appreciate the benefits of exercise and have something physical that they do regularly. Their knees tend to trouble them. Because the sign is sometimes repressed emotionally, Capricorns benefit by venting what they feel, which in turn improves their physical health.

Spirituality

Capricorns flourish within structured and firmly established parameters. Ritual speaks to them and inspires them. They bring the same serious efficiency to their involvement with spiritual beliefs as they do to other areas of their lives. In less evolved types, the expression of spiritual beliefs can manifest as dogma. In the highly evolved Capricorn, the soul clearly understands its purpose in life.

Aquarius

WATER BEARER (JANUARY 20–FEBRUARY 18)

Element: Air

Quality: Fixed

Planetary Ruler: Uranus

Keywords: Altruism, individuality, freedom

Rules: Ankles, shins, and circulatory system; natural ruler of the eleventh house

Aquarians are original thinkers, often eccentric, who prize individuality and freedom above all else. The tribal mentality goes against their grain. They chafe at the restrictions placed upon them by society and seek to follow their own paths.

Aquarius is the sign of true genius because these people generally have the ability to think in unique ways. Once they make up their minds about something, nothing can convince them to change what they believe. This stubbornness is a double-edged sword; it can sustain them or destroy them. When the stubbornness manifests in small rebellions against the strictures of society, energy is wasted that could be put to better use.

Even though compassion is a hallmark of this Sun sign, Aquarians usually don't become emotionally involved with the causes they promote. Their compassion, while genuine, rises from the intellect rather than the heart. The Uranian influence confers a fascination with a broad spectrum of intellectual interests.

Aquarius Woman

Even when you know her well, she's hard to figure out because she's so often a paradox. She's patient but impatient; a nonconformist who conforms when it suits her; rebellious but peace-loving; stubborn and yet compliant when she wants to be.

She likes unusual people and has a variety of friends, both male and female. Economic status doesn't impress her, so her friends tend to come from a broad spectrum of backgrounds. Like the people she associates with, the Aquarian woman has many interests. She may dabble in tarot or astrology, have a passion for invention or writing, or may even be a budding filmmaker. Whatever her profession, it allows her latitude to do things her way.

In romance, the only "given" with this woman is that she's usually attracted to someone who is unusual or eccentric in some way. Even if the significant other appears to be conventional, he isn't. She's a good mother, and she allows her children the freedom to make their own decisions, revels in their accomplishments, and never lets them down.

Aquarius Man

He's often as inscrutable as his female counterpart and for the same reasons. He wants companionship, but not at the expense of his individuality. Even when he marries, he retains his independence to often irritating extremes. He might, for instance, fly off to some exotic place, leaving his wife or significant other to tend to his affairs at home.

The Aquarian man is fascinated by unusual people and places. Even though his attention is focused on the future, he may be interested in the mysteries of ancient cultures—how the pyramids were built, the true nature of Stonehenge, or the disappearance of the Anasazis. His travel to foreign cultures is often connected to these interests.

Aquarian men and women are both natural revolutionaries. If the restrictions placed on them are too confining, they rebel in a major way. But both need a place to which they can return, a sanctuary where they can refresh themselves. When the Aquarian man returns from his exotic journeys, he's eager to indulge himself in his family. As a parent, he may seem remote at times and perhaps somewhat undemonstrative, but his love for his offspring runs deep.

Work

Aquarians work best in avant-garde fields: film, the arts, cutting-edge research in electronics, computers, or psychology. Many have raw psychic talent that can be developed into clairvoyance, remote viewing, and precognition, and most are very intuitive. The main element they seek in their work is freedom.

Finances

Aquarians are generous with their families and loved ones and that compassion extends to the larger scope of humanity as well. They stash money away, but the accumulation of wealth isn't the point; their freedom is.

Physical Traits

The typical Aquarian is tall and slender with a complexion that is lighter than that of her ethnic group. With Uranus ruling the sign, Aquarians have a sensitive nervous system and can be easily excited. Their minds are incessantly busy, and they should guard against exhausting their energy reserves.

Spirituality

The revolutionary nature of the sign definitely extends to spiritual issues. Even if an Aquarian is born into a family that follows the dictates of an organized religion, he or she probably won't stick to it. Aquarians insist on finding their own path and seek a broader spiritual spectrum that honors "the family of man."

Pisces

THE FISH (FEBRUARY 19–MARCH 20)

Element: Water

Quality: Mutable

Keywords: Compassion, mysticism

Planetary Ruler: Neptune

Rules: Externally, the feet and toes. Internally, Pisces rules the lymphatic system; natural ruler of the twelfth house

Pisces need to explore their world through their emotions. They feel things so deeply that quite often they become a kind of psychic sponge, absorbing the emotions of people around them. Because of this, they should choose their friends and associates carefully.

People born under this sign usually have wonderful imaginations and great creative resources. They gravitate toward the arts, in general, and to theater and film, in particular. In the business world, they make powerful administrators and managers because they are so attuned to the thoughts of the people around them.

FACT

Pisces, represented by the fish swimming in opposite directions, can be ambivalent and indecisive simply because they're so impressionable. In highly evolved types, mystical tendencies are well developed, and the individuals possess deeply spiritual connections.

Pisces people need time alone so that they can detach from the emotions of people around them and center themselves. They are very impressionable. Without periodic solitude, it becomes increasingly difficult for them to sort out what they feel from what other people feel. They also tend to be moody because they feel the very height of joy and the utter depths of despair. Love and romance are essential for most Piscean individuals. These fulfill them emotionally, and Pisces generally flourish within stable relationships.

Pisces Woman

She's mysterious, with an air of complexity about her, as if she knows more than she's telling. Sometimes she even comes off as a snob, but it's just her regal composure showing. Her eyes are large, gentle, and almost liquid with compassion. The lady is all feeling and possesses a quiet strength that hints at inner depths.

ALERT!

Don't ever be dogmatic with a Pisces woman! She refuses to be limited or restricted by anyone or anything that might inhibit her freedom of expression! This is reflected in her job, her home, and her relationship with her family and friends. This tendency may sometimes work against her, but she doesn't care. It's against her nature to be otherwise!

Even though she needs companionship, Pisces woman also craves her solitude. It's as essential to her well-being as harmony is to a Libra's. When she doesn't have her time alone, she may be prone to alcohol or drug abuse. Properly channeled, her energy can produce astonishing works in art, literature, and music. In this instance, she becomes a mystical channel for the higher mind. As a mother, her psychic connection to her children allows her to understand what they're feeling even when they don't understand it themselves.

Pisces Man

His quiet strength and self-containment fascinate women. He's a good listener—the kind of man who gives you his full attention when you're talking. He's also a fine friend to people he trusts and is always there when his friends are in need. But, like his female counterpart, he's a sucker for a sob story; he can't stand seeing tragedies or heartbreaks in others.

In affairs of the heart, the Pisces man is a true romantic, even if he doesn't want to admit it to himself. He likes candlelight dinners and intimate conversation. It may take him a while to fall head over heels in love, but, once he does, his emotions run deep and eternal.

The Pisces man may gravitate toward the arts or, because the sign rules the twelfth house, may work behind the scenes in some capacity. Whatever his path, he needs to learn to balance the demands of his inner life with his responsibilities in the external world.

Work

Pisces do well in anything that is behind the scenes. Due to their dreamy imaginations and mystical leanings, they excel in the arts, literature, and drama, or as monks, mystics and even inventors. Piscean Edgar Cayce is probably the best example of what a Pisces is capable of doing in metaphysics. Piscean Albert Einstein is one of the best examples of Pisces as scientific genius.

Finances

Pisces is usually less concerned about money and material goods than he is about enjoying what he does. Can he transcend himself through his work? Does his tremendous compassion find expression through his work? If not, then he will undoubtedly change his work again and again, until he finds the job or profession that suits him.

Physical Traits

There are two types of Pisces individuals—the whale and the dolphin. The first tends to be physically large—in height and in weight. The second tends to be smaller, more graceful. The whale often looks awkward when he walks, as if his feet are too small for the rest of him. His dolphin counterpart is, in contrast, like a dancer—at home in his body.

The extraordinary eyes that are typical of the Pisces individual are exemplified in the violet eyes of Elizabeth Taylor. Also, since Pisces rules the feet, most individuals with a Pisces Sun, Moon, or Ascendant benefit from foot massage and foot reflexology.

Spirituality

Not all Pisces people are psychic, of course, or mystically inclined. Not all of them want to become monks or nuns, either. But most Pisces people are born with a deep intuitive sense, even if it's latent. And this sense is what connects them to a higher power. It may manifest within the parameters of organized religion—or it may veer into something less structured. Whatever form it takes, though, the intuitive side of Pisces constantly seeks expression.

Chapter 4

Ⓔ **Understanding the Planets**

Intuition can bring any natal chart interpretation into clarity. It is the essential connection that links the pieces into a coherent whole—a living story. Without intuition, you're just reading symbols. Knowledge and understanding of the planets will give you a broad base to start from and a context in which to consider those symbols. For instance, one thing you should know is that planets are the expression of energy. They are classified as benefic or malefic: good or bad. In this chapter, you'll find out about this and other characteristics of the planets.

Planet Basics

On a clear night, go outside and look up at the sky through a telescope. Look at the rings of Saturn, the red dust of Mars, and the stark landscape of the moon. Suddenly, the stories about the Greek and Roman gods will leap to life for you. Your intellect will fuse with intuition; pieces will come together. In a moment of utter clarity, you will understand why Mars is the god of war, why Mercury is the messenger, and why Neptune rules the seas and everything beneath them.

As previously mentioned, planetary energy can be labeled as good and bad. Actually, this is misleading because planetary energy isn't positive or negative. Traditionally, Jupiter is the great benefic, the planet that blesses. Venus comes in a close second. The Sun, Moon, and Mercury line up after that. Saturn is the great malefic, the bad guy of the group whose lessons tend to be harsh. Saturn is followed in this negativity by Mars, Uranus, Neptune, and Pluto.

Inner and Outer Planets

Planets orbit the Sun at different speeds. The closer a planet is to the Sun, the faster it travels through its orbit. The Moon, for instance, travels through the zodiac in about twenty-eight days and spends two to three days in each sign. Mercury orbits the Sun in eighty-eight days. Pluto, which lies the farthest from the Sun, completes its orbit in 248 years. The faster-moving planets—Moon, Mercury, Venus, Mars—are known as inner planets. Jupiter, Uranus, Neptune, and Pluto are known as outer planets.

The inner planets are considered to be personal because they relate to the development of our individual egos, our conscious selves. The outer planets relate to the outer world. Since the outer planets move so much more slowly through the zodiac, their pattern of influence is often felt by an entire generation of people.

The luminaries—Sun and Moon—have transpersonal qualities. The Sun represents not only our ego, but fundamental cosmic energy. The Moon, which concerns our most intimate emotions and urges, links us to what astrologer Robert Hand calls, "One's Ultimate Source."

Planetary Motion

Planetary motion is either direct (D), retrograde (R), or stationary (S). In reality, all planetary motion is direct but relative motion isn't. The Sun and the Moon can never turn retrograde, but all the other planets do. A retrograde planet is one that appears to move backward in the zodiac, but this backward motion is actually an optical illusion. Imagine being in a train as another train speeds past you. You feel as if you're moving backward, when in actuality, you're only moving more slowly than the other train. Retrograde motion doesn't change the fundamental essence of a planet; it merely means that the expression of its energy is altered somewhat.

ALERT!

During a Mercury retrograde, communications tend to get fouled up and travel plans are disrupted. Back up your computer files beforehand! Don't sign new contracts! This is an important time to revisit the past and work on old projects. Get in touch with people you haven't talked with for a while. It's not a time to start something new!

During a Jupiter retrograde, the beneficial aspects of the planet are turned down somewhat. Some astrologers contend that if there are three or more retrograde planets in a chart, certain past-life patterns may prevail in the present life. But even if it is true, our point of power lies in the present, in this life; this moment.

During a retrograde, the nature of that planet is forced inward, where it creates tension and stress. The outlet for this tension is usually worked out in relationships with others.

Planets in direct motion have more influence than retrograde planets. Stationary planets, those that are about to turn direct or retrograde, have greater influence in a chart than either retrograde or direct moving planets. This is due to the concentrated energy of the planet.

Strengths and Weaknesses of the Planets

The strength or weakness of a planet depends on its sign, placement in the houses, aspects, and motion. A planet that occupies a sign it rules is *dignified*—Mercury in Gemini, for instance, or Venus in Libra.

When a planet is *exalted,* its drive and essential qualities are expressed more harmoniously. An example would be the Sun in Aries or the Moon in Taurus. Exalted planets are assigned specific degrees and are said to function smoothly within those degrees.

A plant is in the sign of *detriment* when it occupies the sign opposite that of its dignity. An example is Mercury in Sagittarius. Mercury is in detriment here because it rules Gemini, and Sagittarius is Gemini's polar opposite. In a detriment, the energy of the planet is considered to be at a disadvantage. When a planet lies in the sign opposite that of its exaltation, it's said to be *in fall.* A Moon in Scorpio is in fall because the Moon is exalted in Taurus. Its energy is watered down.

One of the most important planets in a chart is the one that rules the ascendant (or rising sign). This planet is usually, but not always, considered the ruler of the chart. A Libra rising, for example, means that Venus is the chart ruler because Venus rules Libra.

Mutual reception occurs when two planets are placed in each other's sign of dignity. The Sun and the Moon, for instance, are in mutual reception if the Sun is in Cancer or Taurus, and the Moon is in Leo or Aries. This happens because the Sun rules Leo and is exalted in Aries, and the Moon rules Cancer and is exalted in Taurus. When a planet is placed in its natural house of the horoscope (Mercury in the third house, for instance), it's *accidentally dignified* and strengthened.

Sun and Moon: Ego and Emotions

The Sun is the very essence and energy of life—the manifestation of will, power, and desire. It represents the ego, individuality, the yang principle and is the thrust that allows us to meet challenges and expand our lives. The Sun represents a person's creative abilities and the general state of his or her physical health.

The Sun embraces the fatherhood principle and, in a chart, symbolizes a person's natural father and a woman's husband. As natural ruler of the fifth house, it rules children in general and the firstborn in particular. Leo is ruled by the Sun—fire.

The Sun spends about a month in each sign, with a mean daily motion of 59'8". It rules occupations of power and authority—royalty and religious and spiritual rulers. Its natural house is the fifth, and it governs the sign of Leo. It rules the heart, back, spine, and spinal cord.

FACT

Since the Sun also symbolizes authority and power, a strongly placed Sun confers leadership ability. A Sun that is badly aspected or weakly placed lessens the natural vitality and may make it difficult for the person to express basic drives and desires.

The Moon is your emotions—the inner you. It's intuition, the mother, the yin principle. Coupled with the Sun and the Ascendant, the Moon is one of the vital parts of a chart. It describes our emotional reactions to situations, how emotions flow through us, motivating and compelling us—or limiting us and holding us back.

The Moon symbolizes a person's mother and the relationship between mother and child. In a man's chart, the Moon represents his wife; in a woman's chart, it describes pregnancies, childbirth, and intuition. Symbolically, the Moon represents our capacity to become part of the whole rather than attempting to master the parts. It asks that we become whatever it is that we seek.

As Earth's satellite, the Moon moves more swiftly than any of the planets, completing a circuit of the zodiac in less than twenty-eight days. It rules activities and professions dealing with children and those that concern the sea. Its natural house is the fourth and it governs the sign of Cancer. The stomach, breasts, mammary glands, womb, conception, and the body fluids in general are ruled by the Moon.

What is an example of how the Moon defines you?
Your Moon represents your emotions—how you instinctively respond to things. For example, if someone says something nasty to you, how do you react? If your Sun sign is Leo, but your Moon sign is Gemini, chances are that you'll react, immediately, as a Gemini would. After the tension is gone, you'll go back to being your regal, Leo self.

Mercury: Your Intellect

Mental quickness. Verbal acuity. Communication. Your mental picture of the world. Mercury is the messenger; it speaks in terms of logic and reasoning. The left brain is its vehicle. Mercury represents how we think and how we communicate those thoughts. Mercury also is concerned with travel of the routine variety—work commutes, trips across town, weekend excursions, or a visit with siblings and neighbors—rather than long-distance travel.

Restlessness is inherent to Mercury because it craves movement, new-ness, and the bright hope of undiscovered terrains. Mercury often tackles something new before the old has been assimilated. On a higher level, Mercury seeks to understand the deeper connections between the physical universe and the divine.

Mercury orbits the Sun in about eighty-eight days. It goes retrograde every few months, and, during that time, communications and travel plans go haywire. Your computer may go down, lightning may blow out your electricity, or you may spend hours in an airport waiting for a flight that is ultimately canceled. Again, it's best not to sign contracts when Mercury is retrograde.

Mercury rules any profession dealing with writing, teaching, speaking, books, and publications. Mercury is the natural ruler of the third and sixth houses and governs Gemini and Virgo. It rules arms, hands, shoulders, lungs, the solar plexus, abdomen, intestines, the thymus gland, and the nervous and respiratory systems.

Venus: Your Love Life

Romance. Beauty. Artistic instinct. Sociability. Venus governs our ability to attract compatible people, to create close personal relationships, and to form business partnerships. It expresses how we relate to other people one-on-one and how we express ourselves in marriage and in romantic relationships.

Since Venus determines our spontaneous attractions to other people, it's one of the areas to look at when doing chart comparisons for compatibility! When Venus falls in another person's Sun sign, it enhances the initial attraction and bodes well for overall compatibility. Venus, along with the Moon, is associated with material love since Venus gives what it has freely and without strings attached.

Venus is also associated with the arts and the aesthetic sense, and it has enormous influence on our tastes in art, music, and literature. The sign and placement of Venus, as well as its aspects, determine our refinement—or lack of it. This planet also has some bearing on material resources, earning capacity, and spending habits. A strong Venus enhances these things; a poorly placed or badly aspected Venus generates laziness, self-indulgence, extravagance, and discord in partnerships.

Venus orbits the Sun in 255 days. It spends about four weeks in a sign when moving directly and is retrograde for about six weeks. It rules all professions having to do with the arts and music. Its natural houses are the second and the seventh, and it governs Taurus and Libra. It rules the neck, throat, thyroid gland, kidneys, ovaries, veins, and circulation of the venous blood. It shares rulership with the Moon over the female sex organs.

Mars: Your Energy

Dynamic expression. Aggression. Individualism. Sexual drive. Action. Mars dictates our survival energy and the shape that energy assumes as we define ourselves in terms of the larger world. It represents the individualization process, particularly in a romantic relationship. A weak Mars placement in a woman's chart may make her too passive and submissive in a love relationship, especially if her significant other has a strongly placed Mars.

Mars rules athletes and competitions. The true Mars individual seeks to take himself to the limit—and then surpass that limit. He refuses to compromise his integrity by following another's agenda. He doesn't compare himself to other people and doesn't want to dominate or be dominated. He simply wants to be free to follow his own path, whatever it is.

QUESTION?

Is Mars considered "good" or "bad"?
Actually, Mars's energy can be either constructive or destructive; it depends on how it's channeled. Rage, violence, and brutality can manifest if the energy is poorly channeled. When properly channeled, Mars's energy manifests as stamina and achievement.

Mars orbits the Sun in 687 days. It spends six to eight weeks in a sign. When retrograde, it sits in a sign for two and half months. As the god of war, Mars governs the military, rules Aries, and is co-ruler of Scorpio. Its natural houses are the first and the eighth. It rules the head, general musculature of the body, the sex organs in general—the male sex organs in particular—the anus, red corpuscles, and hemoglobin.

Jupiter: Your Luck, Your Higher Mind

Philosophy. Religion. Higher education. Expansion and integration. Growth. Tradition views Jupiter as the great benefic planet, associated with luck, success, achievement, and prosperity. But it can also indicate excess, laziness, and other less desirable traits. The bottom line, though, is that Jupiter's energies are usually constructive.

This planet's energy allows us to reach out beyond ourselves and expand our consciousness. It confers a love of travel and a need to explore religious and philosophical ideas. Jupiter also allows us to integrate ourselves into the larger social order—church or religion, community, and corporation.

Since Jupiter rules the abstract mind, it describes our intellectual and spiritual interests in the most profound sense.

ALERT!

As Jupiter is the planet of expansion, it can influence physical expansion as well. In other words, in terms of the body, Jupiter in your sign can often lead to weight gain. Where Jupiter is in your sign can determine whether or not it will be easier to lose the pounds or to put them on!

Jupiter takes about twelve years to traverse the zodiac and averages a year in every sign. It governs publishing, the travel profession, universities and other institutions of higher learning, and traditional organized religions. Its natural houses are the ninth and the twelfth. It rules Sagittarius. Jupiter oversees the blood in general, arteries, hips, thighs, and feet (with Neptune).

Saturn: Your Responsibilities, Karma

Discipline. Responsibility. Lessons to be learned. Limitations and restrictions. Obedience. Building of foundations. No free rides. Saturn has long been known as the great malefic. While it's true that its lessons are sometimes harsh, it also provides structure and foundation, and teaches us through experience what we need in order to grow. It shows us the limitations we have and teaches us the rules of the game in this physical reality.

Astrologer Jean Avery, writing in *Astrology and Your Past Lives*, says, "The description of Saturn's placement, aspects, and rulerships in the horoscope is most important in the process of uncovering past life experiences." Even if you don't believe in reincarnation, there's ample evidence that Saturn holds a key to what the soul intends to accomplish in this life. People with a well-placed or well-aspected Saturn tend to have a practical, prudent outlook.

As one of the outer, slowly moving planets, Saturn takes twenty-nine-and-a-half years to cross the zodiac. Its natural houses are the tenth and the eleventh. Saturn rules Capricorn. This planet governs the bones and joints, skin, and teeth.

When poorly aspected, Saturn creates rigid belief systems, restricts growth, and closes us off to other possibilities. A delicate balance must be attained with Saturn influences. Even though it pushes us to understand and work with limitations, it can also cause us to settle for too little, or to deny our creative expression because we don't want to see what is really possible.

Uranus: Your Individuality

Sudden, unexpected disruptions. Breaks with tradition and old patterns to make room for the new. Genius. Eccentricity. Astrologer Seven Forrest considers Uranus the ruler of astrology; Robert Hand calls Uranus, Neptune, and Pluto "transcendental planets" that can be dealt with constructively only with an expanded consciousness. Unless we nurture a larger perspective, Uranian disruptions appear to bring unpleasant and unexpected surprises. In reality, these disruptions liberate us, revolutionize the way we do things, and blow out the old so that the new can flow in.

Uranus, like the other outer planets, remains in a sign for so long that its effect is felt on the masses. In the twenty-first century, this planet's influence is visible in the breakdown of old paradigms of belief within most of the large structures we have taken for granted: health care, medicine, science, religion, lifestyle, education, and social programs. We are at the beginning of a new century with old structures crumbling around us. But in the shadows, the new paradigms are forming, bubbling with vitality, gathering momentum. This is all part of the Uranian influence.

In a horoscope, Uranus dictates the areas of our life in which these disruptions occur and how we utilize this energy. Do we feel it? Think about it? Seize it? Pull it deep within us so that this becomes rooted in who we are? Are we so afraid of it that we deny it? Uranus also indicates the areas in which we are most inventive, creative, and original.

This planet takes eighty-four years to go through the zodiac. Its natural house is the eleventh, and it rules Aquarius. Traditionally, before the discovery of Uranus in 1781, Saturn ruled this sign. But Saturn's rigidity just doesn't fit Aquarius. It governs electricity, inventions, the avant-garde, everything that is unpredictable or sudden.

Neptune: Your Visionary Self, Your Illusions

Hidden. Psychic. Spiritual insights. Illusions. The unconscious. This planet stimulates the imagination, dreams, psychic experiences, artistic inspiration, flashes or insight, mystical tendencies. On the downside, it deals with all forms of escapism—drug and alcohol addiction, as well as delusion (and false idealism).

Neptune, like Uranus, overpowers Saturn's rigidity. Where Uranus disrupts the rigidity, Neptune simply negates it. This planet is considered the higher octave of Venus, and when it operates in the chart of an evolved soul, its music is extraordinary. Edgar Cayce, known as the "sleeping prophet," was such an individual. While asleep, he could diagnose physical ailments for people he'd never met, using nothing more than their names.

QUESTION?

What is the best way to deal with Neptune's energy?
Most of us experience Neptune through synchronous events and flashes of insight that seem to come out of nowhere. Perhaps we lose ourselves in the illusions we've created. The best way to appreciate Neptune's energy is while we are in quiet contemplation—meditation, yoga, listening to music, writing, or through some activity that involves water.

Neptune takes 165 years to cross the zodiac and spends about fourteen years in each sign. The twelfth house is its natural domain and it rules Pisces. It governs shipping, dance, film, and the arts in general, and is associated with mediums, clairvoyants, psychic healers, and both white and black magic.

Pluto: How You Transform and Regenerate Your Life

Destiny. Transcendence. Redemption. Purge. Power. Afterlife. Good and evil. Pluto's influence is never ambivalent or passive. Although it sometimes works in subtle ways, its repercussions in our lives are far-reaching and transformational. Its two extremes are best symbolized by Hitler and Gandhi, each man possessed of a vision that he manifested in physical reality. Both had a mission, a sense of destiny, but one caused massive destruction and the other elevated mass consciousness.

In our personal lives, Pluto's influence works in the same ways. Pluto tears down our habits and belief systems, the very structures that Saturn has helped us build, thus forcing us to transcend the ruin—or to smother in the debris.

A Pluto placement in Sagittarius, in the ninth house of philosophy and spiritual beliefs, would mean you evolve through expansion of your beliefs in these areas. But before you do, Pluto will destroy your old beliefs, collapsing them like a house of cards.

FACT

Pluto, the higher octave of Mars, governs various types of occult practices: black magic, levitation, witchcraft, and reincarnation. On a personal level in a horoscope, Pluto's influence is most powerful when it occupies a prominent place or rules the chart.

Pluto, discovered in 1930, is the most distant planet from the Sun. It exists at the very edge of our solar system—its light is so dim that Pluto seems almost etheric. It takes 248 years to complete a circuit of the zodiac. Popular astrological theory says that Pluto, like Uranus and Neptune, wasn't discovered until humanity had evolved to be able to understand its energy.

"Through it," writes Steven Forrest, "we embody the visions and terrors of humanity. We represent them. We serve as a living symbol of some communal need or fear." Through Pluto, we tap into that which is larger than our individual selves. We tap into the collective mind in all its hypnotizing horror and magnificent beauty.

Since Pluto's discovery, its influence has been observed in only Cancer, Leo, Virgo, Libra, and Scorpio. In the late fall of 1995, Pluto slipped into Sagittarius. The transformation under this influence is apt to be enormous and far-reaching, completing the collapse of old paradigms and belief systems.

Chapter 5

Planets in the Signs

The sign a planet occupies describes how that particular energy permeates your personality and influences your life. If you have eight out of ten planets in fire signs, then you probably have abundant energy and a fierce temper, and tend to initiate action. If you have mostly Air planets, your approach to life comes from a mental standpoint—rationalizing and thinking before acting. This chapter offers the complete story about planets in the signs. Find out where your planets are, using the charts in the appendices, and then read the translations given in this chapter.

The Moon: Instinct

The Moon expresses your emotions, the inner you, that which makes you feel secure.

Aries Moon. Your emotions are all fire. You're passionate, impulsive, and headstrong. Your relationships, especially when you're younger, can be impulsive. Your own actions ground you. You take pride in your ability to make decisions and to get things moving.

Taurus Moon (exalted). You don't like to argue. You need time alone and thrive in your private spaces, whatever they might be. You enjoy being surrounded by belongings that hold personal meaning. Your emotional well-being depends on the harmony of your emotional attachments.

Gemini Moon. You thrive on change and variety. Your emotions fluctuate and sometimes you think too much, analyzing what you feel and why. Your capacity for adaptability, however, sees you through.

Those with their Moon in Gemini don't have trouble expressing their feelings—the difficulty is in understanding what those feelings are. They see all sides to a situation and can feel angry with someone one minute and understanding the next. This drives Gemini Moon crazy, but it's difficult to change.

Cancer Moon (dignified). You have strong family ties and feel a need to nurture or nourish others. At times, you're very psychic; other times you're merely moody. When you're hurt, you tend to withdraw and brood. You don't like emotional confrontations and seek to sidestep them.

Leo Moon. Your emotions are often dramatic. You feel cheerful and optimistic about life in general. You enjoy the limelight and being recognized for what you do and who you are. You take deep pride in your children and family.

Virgo Moon. You tend to be somewhat reticent about what you feel. You're interested in health and hygiene and how these issues relate to you and the people you care for. You feel happy when you're of service to others and take pride in your meticulous attention to details. You can be overly critical of your personal relationships and of yourself.

Libra Moon. Discord makes you feel anxious. You thrive on harmony in your personal environment and need compatible relationships for your emotional well-being. You go out of your way to avoid confrontations. Music, art, ballet, and literature lift your spirits.

Scorpio Moon (in fall). Your emotions and passions run deep. You feel a profound loyalty to your family and the people you love. You possess great strength and are able to draw on it during times of crisis. Your dreams, premonitions, and many of your experiences border on the mystical. You rarely forget it when someone has slighted you.

Sagittarius Moon. You need emotional freedom and independence. You need your own space so you can explore everything that fascinates you—foreign cultures, inner worlds, or the distant future. None of this means that you love your significant other any less; you simply need your freedom. You enjoy animals.

ALERT!

A person with a Sagittarius Moon needs to be respected. He may have a problem with authority—especially at work. It's very difficult for him to bow down to a boss or even a coworker if he doesn't feel the other person is justified in his higher standing.

Capricorn Moon (detriment). You need structure of some sort to feel emotionally secure. This need can show up in any area of your life; it depends on what issues are important to you at a given time. You aren't as emotionally aloof as some people think; you just don't wear your heart on your sleeve.

Aquarius Moon. Your compassion extends to humanity—the beggar on Seventh Avenue, the children dying in Africa, or the AIDS patients whose families have turned against them. You bleed for them. Your home life is important to you, but it's definitely not traditional. You don't recognize boundaries or limitations of any sort.

Pisces Moon. When your emotions flow through you with the ease of water, you feel and sense what is invisible to others. Sometimes, you're a psychic sponge; you soak up emotions from others and may even manifest those emotions. Your compassion sometimes makes you gullible and impractical. Your artistic sensibilities are strong.

Mercury: Communication

The sign Mercury describes how you express your mental habits and how you gather information. This sign also shows how you study and how you communicate your ideas in life.

Mercury in Aries. You have a quick, decisive mind that makes snap judgments. You're often argumentative but intuitive about the dynamics of relationships.

Mercury in Taurus. Yours is a practical, determined mind with strong likes and dislikes. You have intuition about the practical aspects of relationships and love beautiful, flowing language. You can be quite stubborn.

ALERT!

Since someone's Mercury determines how she communicates, you really need to understand that these signs relate to the way a person expresses herself—not necessarily who she really is. If a person is a Leo, but has her Mercury in Virgo, for example, she may be generous, honest, and sweet—but nitpicky in her dealings with people.

Mercury in Gemini (dignified). Marked by a quick, inventive mind, you're up-to-date on current events and have shrewd powers of observation. You have an adaptable, versatile intellect, ease with language, and intuition about the structure of relationships. You also enjoy travel.

Mercury in Cancer. Your sensitive, imaginative mind also has excellent powers of retention. However, your opinions change quickly. You're interested in psychic matters and may have psychic abilities as well. You're intuitive about the inner connections in relationships.

Mercury in Leo (in fall). Great willpower and lofty ideals characterize you. Your intellect can be self-centered, but intuitive. Your mental aspirations may revolve around children, pets, drama, and sports. Your intellectual efforts often carry your personal unique style.

Mercury in Virgo. You have facility with language and as a linguist. Mentally, you display great attention to detail, which can collapse into criticism and nitpicky tendencies. There's a deep interest in mystery, the occult, and magic, and you have excellent intellect overall.

Mercury in Libra. Yours is a refined intellect, capable of broad scope. You are excellent at balancing issues and intuitive about the innate balance in relationships. This is good placement for any artistic pursuit, particularly music.

Libra can talk with anyone, but because this sign is particularly drawn to beauty, he has an easier time chatting it up with someone he finds attractive in any way. A person with Mercury in Libra will get along well with someone who has his Sun in Libra. The same things should interest the two of them.

Mercury in Scorpio. You have a suspicious but deeply intuitive intellect capable of probing beneath the obvious. You also have a mental need to perceive the hidden order of things, to pierce that order, and pull out the truth. You can be sarcastic and wry in communication.

Mercury in Sagittarius (detriment). You're idealistic and intellectually versatile. Mental and intellectual development comes through philosophy, religion, law, publishing, and travel. Your personal opinions sometimes are inflated and become principles rather than just personal opinions.

Mercury in Capricorn. You're characterized by mental discipline and organizational ability. Your intellect is sometimes structured in a way that inhibits imagination. You experience much serious and thoughtful contemplation.

Mercury in Aquarius (exalted). Your intellect is detached from emotion and endlessly inventive. Your mental interests tend to be progressive, unusual, and often eccentric. You exhibit interest in the occult and science.

Mercury in Pisces (detriment). Your psychic impressions are often so pronounced that reasoning ability is clouded. Great imagination and creativity are indicated and much information is culled through intuitive means.

People with Mercury in Pisces are masters at distinguishing fibs from truth, and they're also good at making instant character assessments. However, they generally keep this information to themselves and don't speak up about it.

Venus: Love

The sign in which Venus falls describes your artistic nature and what you are like as a romantic partner, spouse, or friend. Venus's sign also indicates financial and spending habits.

Venus in Aries (detriment). You exhibit aggressive social interaction and passion in romantic relationships. You form impetuous, impulsive ties and are self-centered in love. You show good initiative in making money, but it usually goes out as fast as it comes in. For you, marriage may happen early or in haste.

Venus in Taurus (dignified). Heightened artistic expression. You attract money and material resources easily. You form deeply emotional love attachments. You have strong financial drive. Marriage is sometimes delayed when Venus is in Taurus.

Venus in Gemini. You're flirtatious and exude great charm and wit. You're a good conversationalist, you're popular, and you enjoy reading and travel. You also have a tendency for short-lived relationships, which can occur simultaneously. You're a spendthrift who earns money from a variety of sources. You will have several occupations and, possibly, several marriages as well.

Venus in Cancer. Home and marriage are important and offer you a sense of security. Family ties are strong. You spend money on home and family, but also squirrel it away in savings. You benefit through houses, land, and wide, open spaces. Being near water gives you a sense of tranquility.

QUESTION?

Why is Venus in Cancer a paradox?
Although Venus in Cancer can be clingy and needs security in love, there can be a tendency for secret love affairs. And settling down—though that is what Cancer wants most—is his greatest fear.

Venus in Leo. You're ardent in relationships and have a gregarious nature. You may have a pronounced talent in one of the arts. You like to entertain and gamble and have a strong attraction to the opposite sex. You gain through investments and speculation.

Venus in Virgo (in fall). Secret romances, disappointment through love, and possibly more than one marriage may befall you. You're too analytical and criticize romantic relationships and emotions. You're a perfectionist about artistic self-expression.

Venus in Libra (dignified). You have a kind, sympathetic nature and love the arts, music, and drama. You have a happy marriage with talented children. You earn money through areas that Venus rules and seek harmony in all your relationships.

Venus in Scorpio (detriment). You have a passionate nature and dominant sex drive. For you, marriage can be delayed and relationships are often stormy. Your friends may have mystical and occult talents. You gain financially through inheritances, taxes, insurance, and the occult.

Venus in Sagittarius. You have generous nature and ardent emotions in love. If your relationships threaten your personal freedom, however, your emotions cool rapidly. Love of arts, travel, and animals, with a particular fondness for horses, characterizes you. There can be more than one marriage.

Venus in Capricorn. You exercise restraint in emotions and experience some disappointment in love and romance. Marriage is usually for practical reasons and may be to someone older and more established financially. The partner may be cold and indifferent. Your emphasis is on acquiring financial and material assets.

Venus in Aquarius. You have friends from all walks of life and strange, unexpected experiences in romance and friendships. You have a need for intellectual stimulation in romantic partnerships and exhibit erratic financial habits. You gain through friends, partnerships, and speculations.

ALERT!

It's tough to keep Venus in Aquarius faithful. They like to try new things and experience new people. They love the drama. They may even have an affair just to get attention from a partner who's not spending enough time with them.

Venus in Pisces (exalted). You have a charitable, compassionate nature. More than one marriage is likely for you. Romantic love and emotional attachments are necessary to your well-being. You exhibit great sensitivity to others and psychic abilities are likely.

Mars: *Stamina and Sex Drive*

The planet Mars describes how you use energy in life. It also indicates your physical stamina and the nature of your sexual drive with a partner. Mars is also the expression of your desire for personal achievement.

Mars in Aries (dignified). You go after what you want. Your strong sex drive sometimes manifests selfishly, with little regard for the partner. Initiative and drive are highly developed, but due to haste and impulsiveness, there can be a tendency not to finish what you've started.

Mars in Taurus (detriment). You're not easily thwarted or discouraged by obstacles. Your sheer determination and strength of will are well-developed, but may not be used to the fullest. You prefer purposeful, practical action to achieve what you want. Your sexual nature is sensual, but can be somewhat passive. You find pleasure through your profession.

Mars in Gemini. Energy is expressed mentally, through a keen intellect and versatile mind. You tend to take on too many projects that scatter your energy. Your mental restlessness needs a creative outlet or otherwise you become argumentative. You enjoy travel, science, and law. This is good placement for writing.

Mars in Cancer (in fall). You take everything personally and find it difficult to be objective about issues that are important to you. Your sex drive is overshadowed by deep emotional needs.

Mars in Leo. Passion rules the expression of your energy. You possess good leadership ability, a fearless nature, and a determined will. You need to be appreciated for who you are and as a lover. Mechanical or musical skill may be indicated.

FACT

Financially, Mars in Leo signifies someone who is incredibly generous. If you're looking for someone who will come home with an unexpected gift or skip off on vacation with you at the drop of a hat, Mars in Leo is your partner.

Mars in Virgo. You express your energy through efficient, practical pursuits. You're an excellent worker, particularly if the work involves attention to detail. You apply your will quietly, with subtlety. Your sexual drive may be somewhat repressed, with the energy channeled into work. This is a good placement for work in medicine, healing, or writing.

Mars in Libra (detriment). You benefit through partnerships and express your energy best with and through other people. This placement of Mars is good for a lawyer or surgeon. Marriage may happen later in life. Your children may be gifted. You're a romantic when it comes to sex.

Mars in Scorpio (dignified). Your drive and ambition are legendary. It's difficult and sometimes downright impossible for you to compromise. Secrecy surrounds your personal projects. You make a formidable enemy and ally. Your sex drive is powerful.

Mars in Sagittarius. You have the courage to act on your convictions. This is good placement for orators, crusaders, evangelists, and New Age leaders. You have a passionate sex drive but are often impulsive and non-committal in your relationships. It's a good sign for competitive sports, travel, and adventure.

Mars in Capricorn (exalted). Your worldly ambitions may take you into public life. You're able to plan well and to work practically to realize your ambitions and goals. You tend to keep a tight rein on your sex drive and may get involved with people who are older than you are.

Mars in Aquarius. Your unique approach may brand you as an eccentric. You act independently to achieve your goals, which are often directed toward humanity in general. Your approach to sex is apt to be rather unemotional.

Mars in Pisces. This placement can go one of two ways. You're either inconsistent in what you seek to achieve or you're able to pull together various facets of a project and make them work. Sex drive is intimately linked with emotions. This is excellent placement for a detective or occult investigator. You try to avoid conflict and confrontations.

Jupiter: Moral and Spiritual Beliefs

The sign in which Jupiter falls describes how you seek to expand your understanding of life, the benefits you receive, and how you express your intellectual, moral, religious, or spiritual beliefs. Jupiter is the furthest of the outer planets, which relate to the larger social world.

Jupiter in Aries. You're zealous in your beliefs and are convinced you're right, whether you are or not. Everything for you is personal and immediate. You expand your life through personal initiative, seizing opportunities when you see them or creating your own opportunities. You gain through travel, children, law, and friends.

Jupiter in Taurus. Your approach is practical. You seek to apply spiritual and philosophical principles to daily life. You gain through children and marriage and greatly love your home. Fixed in your religious or spiritual views, your generosity to others is a result of their need rather than your sympathy.

Jupiter in Gemini (detriment). The hunger for knowledge and the acquisition of information and facts expand your world. You need to communicate what you learn through writing, speaking, or maybe even film. Your travels are usually connected to your quest for understanding larger philosophical or spiritual issues. Benefits come through publishing, education, and psychic investigations.

Jupiter in Cancer (exalted). You hold onto the spiritual and moral ideals of your parents and pass these teachings down to your own children. Your spiritual beliefs are expanded through your compassion for others. Benefits come through your parents, family, and home-related matters.

Jupiter in Leo. Your beliefs are dramatized; you act on them, promote them, live them. In doing so, you attract others who help expand your world. Your exuberance, however, may be interpreted by some as outright pride. You gain through overseas trips that are connected with education, sports, or diplomatic issues.

Jupiter in Virgo (detriment). Through your work ethic and service to others, you expand your philosophical and spiritual horizons. However, your work must be purposeful. You bring a critical and analytical mind to your profession. Travel is primarily related to business. You gain through relationships with employees, and business and professional pursuits.

Jupiter in Libra. You expand your life through your associations with other people and through marriage and partnerships in general. You benefit from the opposite sex. Your sense of fair play and justice are well developed. The risk with this placement is that you may sacrifice your own interests to maintain harmony.

Jupiter in Scorpio. It's as if you were born with your spiritual beliefs already intact. You expand through your relentless search to understand these beliefs and how they relate to the nature of reality. Your willpower and determination are your greatest assets in overcoming any obstacles in your search. You gain through inheritances, psychic investigation, and any areas that Scorpio governs.

Jupiter in Sagittarius (dignified). Your deep need to understand spiritual and philosophical issues broadens your life. Travel, foreign travel in particular, and education benefit your search. This is a lucky placement for Jupiter and usually denotes success in the area described by the house in which it falls. You benefit through all things associated with Sagittarius.

Jupiter in Capricorn (in fall). Your philosophical and spiritual expansion happens mostly through your own efforts. You seek to accumulate wealth, have a great appreciation for money, and tend to be guarded in your financial generosity. You gain through your father, employers, and commercial affairs.

Jupiter in Aquarius. Your progressive views and willingness to explore all kinds of spiritual beliefs expand who and what you are. Your tolerance for other people's beliefs deepens your understanding of beliefs that differ from yours. Benefits come to you through your profession and through group associations.

Jupiter in Pisces (dignified). Your compassion, emotional sensitivity, and imagination expand your philosophical and spiritual foundations. Benefits come through psychic and occult investigations and anything to do with behind-the-scenes activities. Look toward the sign and house placement of the aspects to Pisces to find out what pushes your buttons.

Saturn: The Karmic Planet

The restrictions and structure inherent to Saturn are expressed through the sign it occupies. The sign shows how you handle obstacles in your life, deal with authority, and how you cope with serious issues. Actually, Saturn is thought to be the "karmic" planet of the zodiac. The house placement is personally significant because it shows what area of your life is affected.

Saturn in Aries (in fall). Circumstances force you to develop patience and initiative. Your impulsiveness needs to be mitigated, otherwise setbacks occur. With this position, there's a capacity for great resourcefulness that, constructively channeled, can lead to innovative creations. On the negative side, you can be self-centered and defensive.

Saturn in Taurus. You feel a deep need for financial and material security. But material comfort is earned only through hard work, discipline, and perseverance. As a result, you need to cultivate reliability and persistence in your chosen profession.

The downside to this placement—Saturn in Taurus—is that there can be a tendency for stubbornness in all issues of life: being right all the time. It's hard for this person to see another side to a story. There may also be an excessive preoccupation with material affairs and goods for this person.

ALERT!

Saturn in Gemini. Discipline and structure are expressed mentally through your systematic and logical mind. Problems must be thought through carefully and worked out in detail; otherwise, difficulties multiply.

Saturn in Cancer (detriment). Your crab-like tenacity sees you through most obstacles and difficulties. You choose a course, which may not always be the best, that doesn't threaten your emotional and financial security. There's a certain emotional restraint with this placement because so much is internalized. Psychic and intuitive resources are sometimes stifled.

Saturn in Leo (detriment). Your ego and need for recognition can be your worst enemies. If you try to solve your difficulties in a self-centered way, you only compound the problem. Cooperative ventures and consideration of mutual needs work wonders for this placement.

Saturn in Virgo. You're such a perfectionist, you tend to get bogged down in details. You need to separate the essential from the inconsequential. An intuitive approach to obstacles and challenges is an enormous help with this placement.

Saturn in Libra (exalted). You overcome obstacles and difficulties by cooperation and a willingness to work with others. The best way to achieve your goals is in partnership with others. You have the opportunity to develop an acute sense of balance and timing with this placement.

Saturn in Scorpio. You handle your difficulties in an intense, secretive manner, which increases the suspicion of those around you. By being more open and up front about what you're doing, you're able to overcome obstacles. Work to discipline your intuition; it can be an infallible guide.

Saturn in Sagittarius. You need to loosen up. Any kind of rigid approach only increases your problems and difficulties. Your best bet is to structure your life by incorporating your ideals into a practical, daily life. Your intense intellectual pride makes you vulnerable to criticism by peers.

Saturn in Capricorn (dignified). No matter what challenges you face, your ambition conquers them. You know that everything has a price and strive to make your contributions to the larger world. You respect the power structures that you see. For you, life itself is serious business. Don't get locked into rigid belief systems; remain flexible.

Saturn in Aquarius (dignified). Your emotional detachment and objectivity allow you to meet challenges head on. Your innovative and unique approach to problems is best funneled through a quiet, practical application to daily life. Your peers help you to learn discipline.

Saturn in Pisces. Astrologers don't look kindly on this placement. But much of what might manifest negatively can be mitigated by practical use of the innate psychic ability of Pisces. Instead of letting yourself become trapped in memories of the past, use past triumphs as a springboard to the future. Your psychic ability is a doorway to higher spiritual truths but must be grounded in some way, perhaps through meditation or yoga.

Uranus: Individuality

Uranus remains in the same sign for about seven years, so its influence in the signs has only a general application. The sign indicates the ways in which your urge for freedom and individuality are manifested. The house placement is more significant on a personal level because it shows what area of your life is impacted.

Uranus in Aries. Your spirit of adventure is quite pronounced and prompts you to seek freedom at almost any price. In its most extreme form, this need for freedom can cause estrangement and a complete severance of ties with your past. You're blunt, outspoken, and can have a fiery temper. You need to develop more consideration for others.

Uranus in Taurus (in fall). You're looking for new, practical ideas concerning the use of money and financial resources, so that the old way of doing things can be reformed. You have tremendous determination and purpose. Carried to extremes, your stubbornness can impede your progress. Your materialistic attachments may limit your freedom of expression and stifle spiritual impulses.

Uranus in Gemini. Your ingenuity and intuitive brilliance impel you to pioneer new concepts in the areas where you're passionate. But your deep restlessness can make it difficult for you to follow an idea through to completion. Self-discipline will help you to bring your ideas to fruition. You travel frequently, seeking exposure to new ideas and people. You have the ability to break out of habitual living patterns and need to draw on that talent to succeed in whatever you're trying to do.

Uranus in Cancer. You pursue freedom through emotional expression and seek independence from parental authority that restricts you in some way. Your own home is unusual, either in decor or in the way you run your domestic life. There can be great psychic sensitivity with this placement, which may manifest as occult or spiritual activities in the home. This placement also carries a certain amount of emotional instability.

Uranus in Leo (detriment). Your route to freedom and independence can touch several different areas: love and romance, leadership, and the arts. Sometimes it can encompass all three. Regardless of how it manifests, you chafe at existing standards, so you create your own.

ALERT!

With Uranus in Leo, the risk of egotism (with this placement) is high! Actually, your best channel for expression is in dealing with issues that affect universal rather than personal concerns. This is highly recommended.

Uranus in Virgo. You have original and unique ideas regarding health, science, and technology. You seek your independence through meticulous intellectual research in whatever you undertake. There can be erratic health problems with this placement, which may spur you to look into alternative medicine and treatments.

Uranus in Libra. You seek independence through marriage and partnerships. As a result, there may be a tendency for disharmony in your personal relationships. Your unconventional ideas about law and the legal system may prompt you toward reform in that area. This placement can also produce gifted musicians.

Uranus in Scorpio (exalted). Your independence comes through drastic and profound change in whatever house Uranus in Scorpio occupies. This is an intensely emotional placement, with an innate psychic insight that allows you to perceive the nature of all that is hidden. Your temper can be quite fierce, and you may feel compelled to bring about change regardless of the consequences.

Uranus in Sagittarius. Your individuality is expressed through unique concepts in religions, philosophy, education, or spirituality. You seek out the unusual or the eccentric in foreign cultures in an attempt to incorporate other spiritual beliefs into your own. You have a deep interest in reincarnation, astrology, and other facets of the occult.

Uranus in Capricorn. This generation of people (born 1989–1994) will bring about vital changes in government and business power structures. They won't dispense with the past traditions entirely, but will restructure old ideas in new ways. Their ambitions are as strong as their desire to succeed. Look to the house placement to find out which area of life is affected.

Uranus in Aquarius (dignified). You don't hesitate to toss out old ideas and ways of doing things if they no longer work for you. You insist on making your own decisions and value judgments about everything you experience. Your independence is expressed through your impartial intellect and an intuitive sense of how to make connections between seemingly disparate issues.

FACT

Future trends are born in this placement. Actually, Uranus rules Aquarius. Since Uranus deals with personal identity, it's only natural that Aquarius is always redefining himself. He marches to the beat of a different drummer and longs to be noticed for being "unique."

Uranus in Pisces. You bring about change and seek independence through heightened intuition. You have the capacity to delve deeply into the unconscious and receive inspirations through your dreams that you can use in your daily life. Be cautious, however, that your idealism isn't impractical; face and deal with unpleasant situations as they arise.

Neptune: Intuition

Neptune spends about twice as long in each sign as Uranus—fourteen years. This makes the sign placement far less important that the house placement, unless Neptune figures prominently in the chart. The sign attests to the capacity of your imagination and your spiritual and intuitive talents. It also addresses the area of your life where you cling to illusions: your blind spots.

Neptune in Aries. This placement fires the imagination on many levels and allows you to act on psychic impulses. Your point of illusion may be your own ego.

Neptune in Taurus. Imagination and spiritual energies are channeled into concrete expression. Your point of illusion can be your own materialism.

Neptune in Gemini. Heightened intuition bridges the left and right brains. Imagination and spiritual issues are channeled through logic and reasoning. Your blindspot may be that you believe you can take on anything. This is a sure route to burnout.

Neptune in Cancer (exalted). The enhanced psychic ability with this placement makes you impressionable. You need to be acutely aware of the fine line between illusion and reality.

Neptune in Leo. Bold creative and artistic concepts characterize this placement. Imagination finds expression in artistic performance. Your ego may hold you hostage.

Neptune in Virgo (detriment). Imagination and spiritual issues are carefully analyzed and fit into a broader, concrete whole for practical use. Strive not to overanalyze.

Neptune in Libra. Imagination and spiritual concepts find expression through beauty and harmony. Misplaced idealism can accompany this placement.

Neptune in Scorpio. Great imagination allows you to pierce the depth of esoteric subjects. You may be blind, however, to your own consuming interest in psychic matters. This placement can also induce drug and alcohol abuse and a sexual identity crisis.

Neptune in Sagittarius. Your intuition allows you to understand broad spiritual issues and to fit them into your personal search for truth. Your blind spot may be your need for creative freedom. In a broad, generational sense, this placement can give rise to religious cults.

Neptune in Capricorn (in fall). Spiritual ideals and concepts are given a practical structure in which to emerge. The risk lies in being so practical that the voice of the imagination is stifled.

Neptune in Aquarius. In a societal sense, heightened intuition and spiritual enlightenment bring about vast and innovative changes and discoveries under this influence. The blind spot—in terms of personal issues—is in learning to apply this energy to your own life.

Neptune in Pisces (dignified). A vivid imagination allows you to connect to deeper spiritual truths. The risk with this placement is becoming separated from reality and losing yourself in a world of illusion.

Neptune in Pisces is very difficult in terms of love. This is an idealistic placement—and has trouble seeing a partner for who he truly is. Instead, she sees him as she wants him to be.

Pluto: Transformation

First, Pluto sweeps in and collapses the old. Then it rebuilds, transforms, and regenerates. The sign it's in describes how your personal transformations are likely to happen; the house placement explains which area of your life is affected. Due to the length of time it spends in a sign, which varies from about twelve to thirty-two years, its personal significance lies primarily in the house it occupies. The definitions that follow apply in broad terms to the larger world.

Pluto in Aries. It begins the reform, but doesn't have the staying power to finish what it starts. This transit will begin in 2082 and end in 2101. Perhaps the Aries pioneers will be heading out into the solar system to explore new frontiers on other planets.

Pluto in Taurus (detriment). It resists the initial change, yet slides in for the long haul once the process has started. Pluto goes into Taurus in 2101 and stays there for thirty-one years; the Taurean energy will help settle the new frontiers.

Pluto in Gemini. Regeneration manifests through the dissemination of ideas and through communication. In 2132, Pluto will go into Gemini for thirty years. New forms of communication and new ways to disseminate information will be found under this influence.

Pluto in Cancer. Regeneration comes through deep emotional involvement with the home and all that involves the home and homeland. Pluto in this sign will domesticate new worlds.

Pluto in Leo (exalted). Regeneration manifests dramatically through power struggles on an international level. The last time Pluto was in Leo, a power struggle led to World War II. Hopefully, when this transit comes around again, war will be obsolete, and Leo's power struggles will have to take place on other levels.

Pluto in Virgo. Purging occurs through a careful analysis of what is and isn't essential. Under the last transit in Virgo, great advances were made in medicine and technology. Given the rapid change in both fields, there's no telling where the next transit through Virgo may lead!

Pluto in Libra. Regeneration comes through a revamping of views toward relationships, marriages, and partnerships. By the time this transit comes around again, marriage and family may bear no resemblance at all to what they are now.

Pluto in Scorpio (dignified). This is the eleventh-hour placement of Pluto, which prevailed from 1983 to 1995. We suddenly realized that global warming wasn't just a buzz word; it's a fact. AIDS became a terrible reality. Alternative medicine became the most popular kid on the block. Gender, racial, sexual, and legal issues—everything pertinent to our survival as a society and a species—was on the evening news.

Pluto in Sagittarius. In this sign, the transformation will either succeed or fail. If it succeeds, then it's quite possible that we'll be bound as nations through our spiritual beliefs rather than our profit-and-loss statements. If it fails, chaos ensues.

Pluto in Capricorn. With typical Capricorn practicality and discipline, the pieces that Sagittarius spat out will be sculpted and molded into something useful. This will be the reconstruction period of the Aquarian Age. Kinks will be worked out, rules established.

FACT

During Pluto's last appearance at Capricorn, the United States was founded and the Declaration of Independence was signed. The next appearance of Pluto in Capricorn will roll around again in 2017! Things get accomplished when Pluto is in Capricorn.

Pluto in Aquarius (in fall). In 2041, the new order will be ready for Aquarius's humanitarian reforms.

Pluto in Pisces. This begins in 2061, nearly fifty-six years in the future. Who besides Nostradamus would presume to predict what might happen? One thing is sure, though. With Pluto in Pisces, we'll at least have a deeper understanding of who and what we are and what makes us all tick.

Chapter 6

Reading a Birth Chart

A birth chart is a symbolic represen-tation of how the heavens viewed the moment you were born. It's like a map because there is a particular way to read it and it can function as your guide. It's also a blueprint of certain personality characteris-tics. In this chapter you'll learn how to eval-uate your own birth chart and let it guide you in your life. Your intuition will help you do this. You can also evaluate friends' birth charts and teach them to interpret different facets of their own lives.

Ascendant Emphasis

The ascendant (AS), or rising sign, is one of the most important features of a natal chart. It's determined by your time of birth. The ascendant determines which planets govern the twelve houses and rules the first house of Self. It's the first of the four angles in a chart that you look at in any interpretation.

The horoscope circle is divided into twelve equal parts, numbered counter-clockwise. These are the houses that represent certain types of activities and areas of life. The lines that divide the houses are called cusps. The horizontal line that cuts through the middle of the chart is the ascendant. When evaluating a birth chart, notice how planets fall in relation to the horizon or ascendant. A balanced chart has an equal number of planets above and below the horizon.

In **FIGURE 6-1**, six of the ten planets are placed above the horizon. Of the four that lie under the horizon, Mars (♂) and the Moon (☾) are only one and two degrees away from the horizon (the descendant). This is close enough so that their energy is felt in the seventh house as well as the sixth.

With a predominance of planets above the horizon, most experiences for this person are expressed openly. Not much is hidden. This hemisphere is concerned with conscious thought. As astrologer Steven Forrest notes in *The Inner Sky*, "A visible event marks every important developmental milestone on her path. The event may be a move to another city. A marriage. A journey to the East. . . . For such a person there is a perceptible life ritual signaling every major evolutionary step."

The birth chart in **FIGURE 6-2** is almost the complete opposite of the one in **FIGURE 6-1**. In **FIGURE 6-2**, all the planets except one are under the horizon. A person with this type of placement is less obvious in what he does and more circumspect. As Forrest writes in *The Inner Sky*, "emotion and intuition flavor all his perceptions. . . . His life is a search for an inner state."

ALERT!

Some astrologers say that people who have most of the planets above the horizon tend to be more outgoing, affable, and generally sociable than those who don't. In other words: the first is active, the other is intellectually passive. But this isn't necessarily true! The horizon placement of planets has more to do with how you approach and assimilate experience.

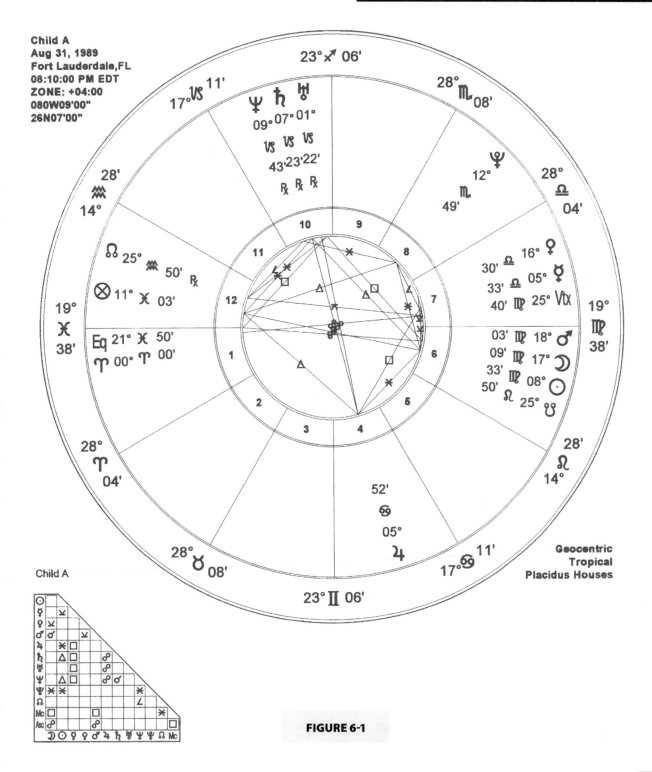

Child A
Aug 31, 1989
Fort Lauderdale,FL
08:10:00 PM EDT
ZONE: +04:00
080W09'00"
26N07'00"

Geocentric
Tropical
Placidus Houses

Child A

FIGURE 6-1

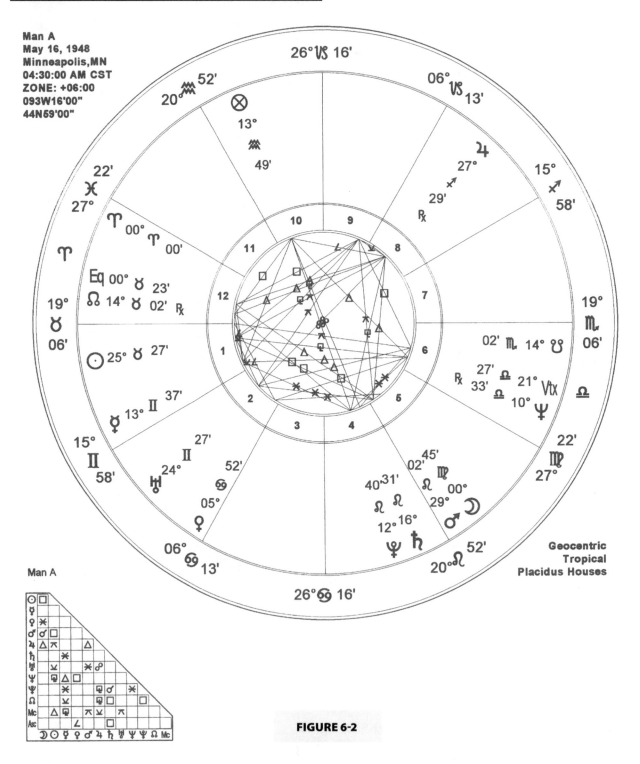

Man A
May 16, 1948
Minneapolis, MN
04:30:00 AM CST
ZONE: +06:00
093W16'00"
44N59'00"

Geocentric
Tropical
Placidus Houses

Man A

FIGURE 6-2

The imaginary line that divides a chart vertically is called the **MC–IC** or vertical axis. The space to the left of this axis is called the eastern hemisphere; this is where planets are rising. This includes houses one, two, three, ten, eleven, and twelve. The space to the right of the vertical axis is called the western hemisphere; this is the twilight where planets are setting. It includes houses four, five, six, seven, eight, and nine.

People with the majority of their planets to the left of the axis tend to be self-determined; they act on their own choices. Astrologer Robert Hand, however, notes: "The planets in the east should not be ones that, like Saturn, tend to frustrate action, or, like Neptune, weaken the basis on which one should act."

When a majority of the planets lie in the western hemisphere, an individual considers her choices before acting. Opportunities may be somewhat restricted by the society in which the person lives.

The Midheaven and the IC

The Midheaven or **MC** is the highest point in a chart. In **FIGURE 6-1**, this point is 23✗06; in **FIGURE 6-2**, this point is 26♑16. The **IC** lies opposite the Midheaven in the same degree.

Even though the Midheaven doesn't provide much information about the personality, it is vital in understanding someone's life because it pertains to social roles, your public life, your relationship with authority, and status. Since it rules the cusp of the tenth house, which is concerned with an individual's professional life and career, the Midheaven also helps define what a person does for a living.

"Perhaps the most important attribute of the Midheaven," writes Robert Hand, "is that it helps to identify what people need to do with their lives in order to grow." In other words, if the **MC** defines the externalization of the self, then the **IC**, as its opposite, represents the internalized self. The **IC** concerns the roots laid down in early childhood.

Any planet that is placed closely to the cusps of the first, fourth, seventh, or tenth houses—the four angles—manifests with considerable strength. In the chart in **FIGURE 6-1**, such planets would be Mars (♂) at 18♍03 and the

Moon (☾) at 17♍09. Both are nearly conjunct the descendant or seventh house cusp. In the tenth house, Uranus (♅) at 1♑22R is within seven degrees of the Midheaven at 23♄06, close enough to be particularly significant.

In the chart in **FIGURE 6-2**, the Sun (☉) in the first house exerts a particularly strong influence.

The Houses, Defined

The sign in which a planet falls tells us how we express who and what we are. The houses explain the conditions and areas in our lives where that expression occurs. Without them, we only have part of the picture. This is what makes your birth time so important to a natal chart; the time you were born personalizes your horoscope.

If you don't know your time of birth, your chart can be rectified according to particular events in your life. Beginning with the ascendant, each house falls within a particular sign. That sign is governed by a particular planet, which rules that house. The planet that rules a house exerts an archetypal influence over the affairs of that house, which are interpreted as psychological and personality characteristics. In the chart in **FIGURE 6-2**, Taurus (♉) lies on the ascendant so it rules the first house of Self. Since Taurus is governed by Venus, that means everything associated with the first house focuses on aesthetics, sociability, relationships, and tastes in art and literature.

In this same chart, the second house of money and material concerns falls in Gemini (♊), ruled by Mercury. Everything that deals with second house affairs will be colored by communication and versatility, the characteristics of Gemini and Mercury.

In traditional astrology, "angular" houses indicate action, and planets placed in these houses motivate you to action. "Succedent" houses tend to be viewed as resource houses, the things that stabilize our lives. "Cadent" houses represent diversification. But not all astrologers agree with this.

FACT

Houses are classified into three types. *Angular* houses are the first, fourth, seventh, and tenth houses. *Succedent* houses are numbers two, five, eight, and eleven. The *cadent* houses are three, six, nine, and twelve.

Astrologer Robert Hand, for instance, believes these classifications are outmoded. He views houses in groups of threes. In his system, houses one, five, and nine are personal houses; houses two, six, and ten are practical; houses three, seven, and eleven are social; houses four, eight, and twelve are unconscious houses.

What the Houses Represent

Astrologers generally agree that the houses represent spheres of activity, experience, action, and areas of life impacted by the placement of planets. But they differ a bit more when it comes to how the houses are divided.

Astrologer Robert Hand notes: "At least one modern writer has proposed a twenty-four house system. And the Irish sidereal astrologer Cyril Fagan has unearthed ancient references to the *oktotopos*, an eightfold division numbered clockwise form the Ascendant instead of counterclockwise as we are used to." The situation becomes especially muddled when you toss in the ancient Greek traditions and modern Hindu astrology.

ESSENTIAL

The trick is to work with the traditional meanings, then allow your intuition to guide you. You may find, for instance, that you read the mother in the tenth house and the father in the fourth; or that in the horoscope for a man, the mother is in the fourth, but for a woman, the father is in the fourth. The point is to develop a system that works for you by studying your own chart first.

As you delve into your own chart and the charts of family and friends, you'll develop your own opinions on what the houses mean and how they should be grouped. For now, try to stick to the traditional meanings. Here is a list of keywords for the twelve houses:

- **House 1:** *Personality.* The Self, beginnings, physical health, early life, physical appearance
- **House 2:** *Finances.* Personal material resources, assets, expenditures, attitudes toward money

- **House 3:** *Communication.* Intellect and mental attitudes, short journeys, brothers and sisters, neighbors, relatives
- **House 4:** *Home.* Family life, domestic affairs, mother or father, early childhood conditioning, your roots, the end of your life, real estate
- **House 5:** *Children and Creativity.* Pleasurable pursuits, creative outlets, children (the firstborn in particular), love affairs, sex for pleasure
- **House 6:** *Work and Health.* Working conditions and environment, competence and skill, general health
- **House 7:** *Partnerships and Marriage.* Partnerships in general, marriage, open conflicts, our identification with others
- **House 8:** *Death and Inheritances, the Occult.* Transformation of all kinds, regeneration, sexuality, taxes, death, psychic ability
- **House 9:** *Higher Mind.* Philosophy and religion, law, long journeys, higher education, publishing, foreign travel and interests, ambitions, in-laws and relatives of the marriage partner
- **House 10:** *Career.* Profession, status, mother or father, worldly ambitions, public life, people in power over you, status
- **House 11:** *Friends.* Group associations, hopes and wishes, ambitions and goals, your network of friends
- **House 12:** *Personal Unconscious.* Institutions, confinement, that which we haven't integrated into ourselves, karma

A Look at Each House

If you operate from the premise that the soul chooses all facets of the circumstances into which it is born, then your chart becomes the voice of your soul speaking to you. Since there are twelve houses, and each house is well-defined in the coming pages, you need to study your chart to find out about yourself, as well as about those who you partner well with and can rely on.

First House (Ascendant): Your Mask

Natural sign: Aries
Natural ruler: Mars
All of us are mixtures of intellectual and emotional needs, talents, memories, desires, dreams, fears, and triumphs. These characteristics are

streamlined and rolled into our personalities, the face we present to others, our masks. The first house is our social mask.

This house, ruled by the ascendant, also governs our physical appearance and the general state of our physical health. The head and face are governed by the first house. (When looking for health issues in a chart, always look to the first house, as well as to the sixth and the eighth.) In this house, the source of illness can be due to an inability to impact the world in the way or to the degree that we want. Consider the following descriptions of the ascendant in each of the signs as personality signatures.

Aries. People under this sign have a need to succeed at everything. They're impulsive, impatient, driven, fiercely independent, and decisive.

Taurus. People under this sign are marked by determination, patience, practicality, and appreciation of beauty. It takes a lot to anger them, but once they're provoked, watch out! People with Taurus rising are often physically attractive and identifiable by short, strong necks.

Gemini. People under this sign need versatility and diverse experiences. These people are mentally quick and perceptive. They are often slender, with long arms and fingers, and walk quickly.

Cancer. People under this sign drive to establish some sort of foundation or home base that defines who they are. They're intuitive and capable of deep feeling. With Cancer rising, the face is often round. They tend toward stoutness in middle age.

Leo. Think drama, pride, and ambition with this rising sign. People under this sign have an excellent ability to organize and direct others, and understand children very well. Physically, these people are handsome and large-boned with thick, beautiful hair.

Virgo. People under this sign possess keen powers of observation and have a fastidious nature. They generally are dedicated to service of others, have a concern for health, and can be very intuitive. Slender bodies and oval faces with a certain softness and charm mark these people.

Libra. People under this sign define themselves through social relationships. They seek harmony and fairness in all they undertake and often are so concerned with being fair that they are indecisive. Physically, Libra rising often produces nearly perfectly formed bodies and physical beauty.

Scorpio. Born under this sign, these people exhibit intensity, passion, strong sexuality, and a profound perception into the secret nature of life.

They are deeply intuitive and possess the ability to drastically alter their personal environment. They tend to have dark hair that is wavy and thick and prominent brows.

Sagittarius. These people have an adventurous spirit, bluntness in speech, and deep independence. They have excellent foresight, a respect for all spiritual thought, and a love of animals. Their bodies are usually tall and slender, with a stoop to the shoulders.

Capricorn. They're concerned about status, self-discipline, and ambition. Impulsive activity is generally restrained. They're good at recognizing and defining the overall structure of a problem or challenge. Physically they can be thin and bony, with prominent features.

Aquarius. They are humanitarians, and also possess unusual or eccentric modes of self-expression. People with this rising sign tend to go against the established order and seek their own truths. They have strong, well-formed bodies, with a tendency to plumpness in middle age.

Pisces. Few rising signs possess more emotional sensitivity and profound perception. People under this sign are often mystically inclined and impressionable, with multifaceted self-expression. They have exquisitely shaped hands and feet and usually have compelling eyes.

Second House: Your Material Goods

Natural sign: Taurus
Natural ruler: Venus

If the planets are aspects to the ascendant and the first house creates issues about self-esteem and self-doubt, the second house can be where we attempt to work them out. This can manifest in any type of behavior that draws attention to our personal material resources. In other words, our self-doubt impels us to prove our own worth through money and possessions.

FACT

The second house deals with money and moveable property (not real estate) and our attitudes toward wealth and material possessions. This house also tells us something about our earning capacity, how we meet our financial obligations, and how we save and budget.

Third House: Your Mind

Natural sign: Gemini
Natural ruler: Mercury

A lot of issues are lumped into this house: the intellect, communication, brothers and sisters, short journeys, conscious thinking, neighbors, and relatives. But this house actually represents daily activities in our lives, things we do automatically. The mental energy is analytical.

A short journey is a commute to work as opposed to a trip to Europe. Brothers, sisters, neighbors, and relatives refer to our experience of these people, not with the people themselves. It implies an unconscious ease that exists between people who have something in common.

Fourth House (IC): Your Roots

Natural sign: Cancer
Natural ruler: Moon

This house symbolizes emotional and physical security. For all of us, this begins with our family, homes, parents, and our sense of belonging.

Some discrepancy exists among astrologers as to whether the fourth house represents the mother or the father. It is often used to symbolize the primary nurturing parent; the primary provider and authoritarian figure is found in the tenth house. Over the course of a lifetime parents often exchange roles, but generally one will be more nurturing and the other more authoritarian. In later life, this house indicates how we support others.

Quite often, in doing family charts, the Sun sign of a parent or even a grandparent appears on the cusp of the fourth or tenth house. Or the Moon shows up in this house, in the parent's Sun sign. Sometimes, you may find that the Sun sign of a woman's spouse appears on the **IC.** When rectifying a chart, this is one of the things to look for.

In the fourth house, we also find issues related to real estate, the collective unconscious, and information regarding the last twenty years or so of a person's life.

THE EVERYTHING ASTROLOGY BOOK

Fifth House: Your Pleasures

Natural sign: Leo
Natural ruler: Sun

Pleasure is the core meaning of the fifth house, but because pleasure is something different to all of us, this can include creativity, children, love affairs, sex, gambling, meditating, running, parties, a nature walk, celebrations, gazing at a piece of art, or reading a book.

The children part of this house also refers to the act of creating them. In this sense, Saturn placed here can indicate a possible stillbirth, abortion, or miscarriage, possibly involving the firstborn. But it can just as easily indicate a restriction or limitation on the pursuit of pleasure—someone too serious to have fun. The interpretation would depend on whose chart you're reading and the aspects to the house.

Sixth House: Health and Work

Natural sign: Virgo
Natural ruler: Mercury

Centuries ago, one of the definitions of this house concerned servants: handmaidens, stable boys, cooks, and maids—in other words, the chattel. In today's world it refers to the way we extend ourselves for others, and the services we perform without any thought of remuneration. It also refers to our general work conditions.

Health issues are also included here. But the illnesses associated with the sixth house are often linked to your work or job. Anything that stifles growth and self-expression—overwork, despising what you do, working just to pay the bills—can lead to illness.

Ultimately, the illness may trigger a transformation in consciousness that forces you to take a vacation, quit your dead-end job, or re-evaluate what you're doing. When that happens, health and hygiene awareness usually increases. In the healing period, it's important to follow your own intuition.

Seventh House (Descendant): Partnerships

Natural sign: Libra
Natural ruler: Venus

This house is about marriage and close partnerships of all kinds. It concerns how you relate to a significant other and how, in doing so, you often deal with an unexpressed aspect of yourself.

QUESTION?

What is special about the seventh house?
This house refers to a partnership founded on mutual chemistry, on "magic." While planets found in this house generally don't describe the significant other, they do, however, indicate a great deal about the type of person that would suit you.

When you love someone, you identify with that person. This is the kind of intimate relationship the seventh house addresses—a relationship that implies commitment. It can also refer to business partnerships where a commitment is made.

Eighth House: Your Instincts

Natural sign: Scorpio
Natural ruler: Pluto and Mars

This house is loaded. It's obsessed with death, sex, and taxes—with the occult tossed in just to muddle things. More specifically, it also includes death benefits, insurance, the partner's earning capacity, alimony, joint finances of any kind, and the recycling of goods.

Traditionally, it's known as the house of death. If that strikes you as bleak, then think of the eighth house as one of transformation. Death is one kind of transformation; sexuality is another; psychic and occult matters are yet another. The house is emotionally loaded because it deals with issues that most of us don't like to dwell on. This emotional impact, however, is why eighth-house events often feel fated or destined. This house relates to the internal energy that seeks outward growth, expansion, and experience.

Ninth House: Higher Mind

Natural sign: Sagittarius
Natural ruler: Jupiter

As the opposite of the third house, the ninth concerns higher ideals, the higher mind, philosophy, religion and spirituality, the law, foreign cultures, and long journeys. Through the ninth house we seek to understand the whole picture and our place in it. We reach out to experience and then try to assimilate the experience into a worldview, a belief system. This can be done through reading, education, and travel—all ninth-house pursuits.

FACT

Some astrologers assign higher education to the ninth house, but all educational pursuits fit into this house. The planets found here bear their unique individual stamp on how we experience and assimilate associated issues. The bottom line is that, through this house, we break out of old thought patterns and habits and take chances.

Tenth House (Midheaven): External Achievements

Natural sign: Capricorn
Natural ruler: Saturn

Where the sixth house covers what you do to earn a living, the tenth concerns your career or profession, work that provides a social role in the larger world. It's the work with which we identify ourselves and by which others identify us.

Clerical work, for instance, probably falls into the sixth house unless the individual identifies closely with the job. But if the clerical worker is a nationally known antique car collector who identifies and is identified in that field, then this would fall into the tenth house. This house also represents the authoritarian parent as well as our experience of authority figures.

Astrologer Robert Hand notes that the tenth house often indicates the direction in which a person must evolve toward transcendence. "The tenth can be a calling beyond the mere calling of how we make a living . . . how an individual can grow on the spiritual as well as the mental plane."

Eleventh House: Friends and Ambitions

Natural sign: Aquarius
Natural ruler: Uranus

This house is about manifestation, about the power of manifestation through a group or collective consciousness. It took me a long time to understand about this.

In the eleventh house, we don't just get along with certain types of people; there are some people with whom we click immediately. Part of their belief system overlaps and parallels our own. With these people, we have an especially strong affinity and from this affinity rises a certain kind of power: the group of collective mind, the mind that works toward a common end, a shared ideal, and a particular goal.

This house can entail all kinds of networking: group charity work, a theater group, a sewing circle, a writers' group, a group of astrologers or psychics, or bridge players. It also entails computer networking. In each group, the collective mind helps us to stabilize our goals.

Signs and planets in this house offer clues about the types of friends and associations that not only benefit us but whom we might benefit as well. As astrologer Steven Forrest writes: "Establish goals. Find people who support them. Then live in the present moment. That is the secret of successful eleventh house navigation."

Twelfth House: Your Personal Unconscious

Natural sign: Pisces
Natural ruler: Neptune

This house is typically considered to be negative and dark, the psychic garbage pail of the zodiac. In Medieval times, it was known as the house of troubles and indicated possibilities of imprisonment, illness, secret enemies, poverty, and dire misfortune. While such possibilities exist with this house, its core meaning is deeper.

The twelfth house represents the personal unconscious, the parts of ourselves that we've disowned—all that is hidden from our conscious perception. Here lie the dregs of early defeats and disillusionments, which ultimately were repressed and not integrated into the rest of our personality. Here, too, are aspects of ourselves that for one reason or another we don't want to express openly to others. These hidden parts of ourselves often come out later in life, surfacing as fears, weaknesses, or phobias that work against us.

Sometimes, these repressed aspects find expression in our most intimate relationships. The daughter of an alcoholic parent, for instance, may find herself confronting her childhood experiences in her relationship with an alcoholic spouse.

On a higher level, the twelfth house can embody spiritual, psychic, and mystical experiences that deepen our connection with the divine.

Evaluating and Interpreting Your Chart

When evaluating the house in a chart, consider these guidelines:

1. Note the ascendant. What element is it in? What does the sign immediately tell you about the individual? Where does the ruling planet fall?
2. Note the cusps of the fourth house (the **IC**), the seventh house (the descendant), and the cusp of the tenth (the Midheaven or **MC**). What do these signs immediately tell you about the person? What do the planets in these houses tell you about the person?
3. What houses do the Sun and the Moon occupy? Are they above or below the horizon? In the western or the eastern hemispheres? In which elements?
4. Note any house where there's a cluster of planets. A house that holds more than one planet indicates activity in that area. It holds a clue as to the soul's purpose in life.
5. Are there any houses that hold three or more planets within three degrees of each other? This cluster is called a *stellium* and indicates intensely focused activity in that particular house.

6. Which house holds the Part of Fortune? Where are the Moon's nodes? The placement of these three points provides valuable information about the soul's purpose.

7. Does the chart have a singleton, one planet that stands alone? An example is in the chart in **FIGURE 6-2**, with Jupiter sticking up there all alone in the eighth house.

8. What intuitive feelings do you get from the chart?

9. What is the chart's general shape?

Astrology is as much an art as it is a science. As with any art, the best impulses and ideas begin somewhere deep inside. They bubble up from the unconscious, make connections with the right brain, and suddenly leap into your conscious awareness as a flash of intuitive insight. These flashes of insight are invaluable when interpreting an astrology chart.

When you have a birth chart in front of you, allow your intuition the freedom to make connections you might not perceive with your conscious mind. Sometimes, those connections are the only ones that matter to the other person. Don't allow the science part of astrology to become dogma. Learn the basics, assimilate them, and then let your intuition speak to you.

When you intuit something, you feel a "click" or an "aha" as you experience it. It's like following a hunch, and it just feels right. The sensation is different for everyone, but it does seem to register somewhere in the body while it's happening. It may be a tightening in your stomach, a sudden pulsing at your temple, or a flash of heat in your hands and fingertips. Once you experience it, you never forget it. Remember to follow your intuition after you have all the facts. It won't let you down.

Chapter 7

Signs and Children

Believe it or not, many mothers choose to discover (or plan out) their child's sign before the child is born (or conceived). If you know a bit about your own compatibility with other signs, it's easy to decide which sign you'd like your baby to be born under. Children are their Sun sign's purest form. However, the way we present ourselves to others is usually displayed by our ascendant—our rising sign. Your child will be a blend of the two, but his ascendant becomes more evident as he gets older. Read on to learn about your child's natural-born sign.

Your Aries Child

On a playground filled with children, an Aries child is easy to pick out. Most likely, he's organizing the others—telling them what to do, what they should play, what they should think, and, basically just directing the action. He's a natural-born leader with smarts, talent, and tons of boasting power. And, if he's not this way yet, trust that he'll grow into it.

In fact, if he's still in his exploratory stage, he could also be off venturing with several of his buddies—perhaps, turning over rocks in search of "cool" bugs. What he does isn't important; the thing is: he's always off doing *something*. He's very independent, too, so it wouldn't be surprising if he enjoyed a bit of time by himself. One thing's for sure, though: an Aries child knows how to get himself into trouble. He should be watched.

E ALERT!

An Aries child, just like the adult Aries, fears nothing. This can be overly disconcerting for any parent. In fact, this recipe for disaster is sure to send any over-protective parent into occasional fits. Watch your Aries child closely but still let him be himself. Too much criticism can stifle this born-to-be creative genius.

Creative and inspiring, an Aries child can be uplifting for any mother. However, when the child doesn't get her way, watch out for huge temper-tantrums. They're explosive. Even as adults, Aries tend to be big babies sometimes. With that in mind, it's easy to imagine that when they're actually babies, the "I want! I want!" attitude is in its purest form. But when an Aries child is feeling good, he's fun-loving, sweet, and tender. If your Aries child is nurtured—but not overly spoiled—your little one will turn out to be a romantic, chivalrous man or a sweet, charming woman.

Your Taurus Child

This child may be a loner or she may just prefer one or two friends to a group of buddies. When she plays, she has fixed ideas about how the play should proceed. She has her own script and won't be persuaded to change it unless she understands the reason why and agrees it's the best way to play the game. In fact, just like the stubborn bull she is, she sometimes has problems with authority and a strange, idealistic view of the way things need to be done.

> You may want to forget the "time out" method for a Taurus child. Why? He or she will simply outwait you! With a Taurus child, sometimes it's better to explain what it is that you object to and why; then ask for a promise not to repeat the act again.

Taurus children are famous for their sense of patience. This can work for you or against you. They'll never tire of wanting what they want. They're not likely to give up easily, even if their attachment is one that is completely unhealthy for them. This manifests itself in Taurus adults as unhealthy romantic attachments that they just can't seem to shake, no matter what they do. Yes, they're idealists. And they suffer from "good girl" syndrome—whether they want to be one or they want to marry one.

Encourage Taurus children to explore their own creativity: art, music, drama, or simply an appreciation of these things. They benefit from the rhythms of nature, from being outside and also from engaging in physical activity. When a Taurus child gets tense, it shows up in the neck area. Therefore, she benefits greatly from massage and physical exercise. Meanwhile, you'll want to show off your Taurus child—she's charismatic, charming, and loyal.

Your Gemini Child

As toddlers, Gemini children's personalities are marked by impatience. They don't bother learning to crawl—they're trying to walk as soon as their legs are strong enough to support them. Once they learn to communicate, they challenge you at every step with questions. They must know the reason for everything.

Gemini children are fascinated by the mundane; they can find humor in the ridiculous. They also have an affinity for the overdramatic. Gemini children are born actors and will probably amuse you at every turn.

E ALERT!

It may be tough to win the loyalty of a Gemini child, but this is not the parent's fault. Though generally warm, sweet, and sensitive, these children can turn on a dime. They can be charming one minute and crafty and manipulative the next. Sure, they're cute—just beware their darker side.

These kids are as precocious as Aries children, but inconsistent in the way they express it. Some days a Gemini will lead the neighborhood kids into anarchy; the next day he or she might keep company with a book, microscope, or pet. They like the furry warmth and security of a dog or a cat and enjoy observing how animals live on a daily basis—they're so curious about nature. Just watch out: They may be studying people or pets in order to put the odds in their favor!

As a parent, you can forget trying to pigeonhole your Gemini child. It just isn't going to work. Instead, accept this fact and try to provide a learning environment in which your Gemini can explore who she is. Be prepared for a wild ride but feel good about knowing that your Gemini child is a versatile, incredibly impressive little person!

Your Cancer Child

The Cancerian youngster definitely marches to the beat of different drummer. Don't expect detailed explanations about how your Cancerian is feeling. If she's in the mood, she might tell you how so-and-so hurt her feelings today at school. But if she's not in the mood, nothing you can say will prod her to explain.

This child is often dreamy. She would rather watch television or read a book than run around outside, unless the activity or sport happens to interest her. In a group, she's likely to take the easy way out and go along with the crowd. Or she may remain completely passive about the situation, hiding her real feelings behind blurts of "I don't know" or, worse, "I don't care."

Cancer children usually pick one of their parents as the favorite and then tend to depend more on that one. In fact, they can get overly possessive with one or the other, and it can be difficult for the one parent who may feel left out or pushed away to deal with it. The best way to remedy this is to not cater to the child's need for the one—make sure that your child gets equal time with both parents. At worst—this child is moody. At best, though, she's wonder and incredible sweetness in one beautiful package!

QUESTION?

What is the best way to deal with a Cancer child?
Carefully. The Cancerian child needs to feel that he is an integral part of the family unit and is appreciated. As a child, he needs to nurture and be nurtured. Therefore, as a parent, your best route to communication with a Cancer child is acceptance and gentle guidance. Let his personality come out. Don't try to change him or make him talk.

Your Leo Child

As toddlers, little Leos keep you running. Their abundant energy fuels them from sunrise to midnight, and by the time you fall into bed, you're ragged. As they mature, Leo kids are surrounded by other children, so your house is likely to be the gathering place for your Leo's youthful tribe. Leos are bossy, but your Leo child is sensitive, too, and this can sometimes be a problem in terms of communication. You'll have to really pry every once in a while, in order to get him to elaborate on his feelings.

Leos have big hearts. Leo children instinctively understand which other children are similar to them, yet they don't care. They'll make friends with anyone who is "a good person," in their eyes. This has a negative side: They can be easily influenced by the wrong crowd because they always see the good in everyone.

ALERT!

Leo children tend to be very rebellious. Sometimes they do things just to see what they can get away with and how far you'll let them go. Some Leo children even do awful things just to get your reaction. The best way to deal with this is to tell them you're disappointed, but you *know* they'll make the right decision. Reverse psychology works.

The innate generosity of this sign manifests itself early. Leo kids feel compassion toward people less fortunate than they are. They're likely to bring home strays of all shapes and sizes. They also tend to be fearless, accept every dare, and take risks that will turn you gray before your time. One thing is for sure: Life with a Leo child is never boring!

Your Virgo Child

You'd better know how to think quickly when you're around a Virgo child. They're impatient, and they possess boundless energy. They love to learn, and their curiosity prompts them to poke around in everything. When they feel passionate about something, they bring the full power of their entire being to that particular endeavor.

This child is inclined to fluctuating moods in the same way that Cancer children are. But for a Virgo, the cause of the fluctuation originates first in the mind rather than in the emotions. If they can't understand something, their frustration mounts until they either explode or work to finally understand the problem. Their attention span improves with age and maturity. The compassion that marks them at a young age usually deepens with time. They also love animals.

As the parent of a Virgo child, provide him or her with books, learning tools, and plenty of positive feedback and praise. Virgo babies and children are amazing at learning new languages. Start them off early. They're like sponges—waiting to soak up all they can take in!

Also, Virgo children do tend to be a bit cleaner than other children. Even as babies, they have a sense of personal space and, more than likely, would rather their room be clean and tidy than messy and cluttered. It's actually important for a Virgo child to have this kind of beauty around her.

They also love music, dancing, and even conversation with strangers once they warm up. Human interaction is more essential to their development than watching television or a video. Meanwhile, you'll be amazed at what a genius your Virgo baby is! Make sure to stimulate her mind and she'll be a calm and happy child.

Your Libra Child

Chances are good that you won't find a Libra baby or child rolling around in a sandbox or looking for bugs. Their sensibilities are usually too refined for that. The typical Libra child is more likely to be reading a book or listening to music in the comfort of his own room. They're like little adults even at a young age.

Libra children enjoy group activities and get along well with others kids in a group. They usually have one special friend with whom they confide. Don't be alarmed, though, if your Libra toddler has an imaginary friend that she talks about and plays with, too. This is common with Libra babies. In fact, many creative people had imaginary friends as youngsters. This use of the imagination distinguishes and enriches their personalities.

ALERT!

Never shout at a Libra child. She's extremely sensitive. She will cower, concede, and then resent you for it. Instead, just tell her what behavior you object to and extract a promise that the problem won't be repeated. With a Libra child, this is the method that works best.

Libra children are well known for their sense of fair play. Though they love to be in the spotlight—an only child especially—they're quickly brought around to a sense of right and wrong if they're taught this at a young age. They learn how to share long before other children do. You'll find them negotiating peace on the playground—if they dare to get involved.

Many Libra children may start trouble and then take off before the going gets rough. At this point, though, their curiosity is unimaginably high, and they'll go off to a safe spot and watch the chaos unfold at a distance. Libra children have a good sense of character and are people watchers. They love to try to understand human nature. As children, they are sweet and kind.

Your Scorpio Child

From infancy, these children are usually distinctive in some way. They form their opinions early, based on what they experience and observe. Their intensity and depth of emotions is legendary, even at an early age. They can have outbursts of temper when they don't get their way or terrible bouts of crying when their feelings are hurt.

Scorpio children can be manipulative. They're sometimes sneaky and incredibly secretive. It's tough to know which way they're going so you'll have to keep tabs on your Scorpio child. Unfortunately, they're so intense—even as children—that they can be prone to depression or self-pity. It's highly unlikely that your Scorpio child will be superficial on any level, even if he puts up a wall to others and appears to be so.

ESSENTIAL

As the parent of a Scorpio child, there are times when you'll be completely puzzled over your child's behavior. Don't leave it alone. Investigate. Instead of trying to guess what's wrong, just be forthright and ask. Your child's response may astonish you.

Scorpio children flourish in an environment that is rich with variety, but they definitely need their own space. Deep, bold colors are good choices for their bedrooms. Dark browns, reds, and oranges make a Scorpio child feel safe and secure. There should be many books around—including those intended for older children. Scorpio kids are very bright. They may never get around to reading, but they'll be happy to know the books are there for them.

Scorpio children are masters at human behavior and exhibit deep knowledge and wisdom long before you'd expect it. Scorpios are all about transformation. As a parent, a Scorpio child will change your outlook on life forever!

Your Sagittarius Child

From the time they are old enough to have friends, the phone will never stop ringing for your Sagittarius child. These kids possess such optimism and vivacity that other kids are drawn to them. Sagittarius children are always the center of attention. They're wise and helpful—even if they have a serious problem with authority.

ALERT!

Getting a Sagittarius child to do what you want him to do may be an uphill battle! He's likely to give in only when he feels like it. If you punish him, he'll take it in stride, and you may not even be sure you got your point across. With all Fire sign children, reverse psychology works well.

A Sagittarius child's candor may be welcome with friends but it may not sit well with you or with other adults. Both Sagittarius children and adults say it like it is. They have a refined sense of sarcasm and wit and call it as they see it—even if that's bound to hurt someone's feelings. They're direct, but generally lack tact.

On the other hand, a Sagittarius child may refuse to surrender his opinion to anyone. Sagittarius children make decisions on who is "worthy" of their attention. If another child or adult has lost a Sagittarius child's respect, this child won't give him the time of day. Yet Sagittarius kids are also warm, loving, and generous with those they deem important.

As a parent of a Sagittarian child, your best approach is to establish the parameters of authority early. Always allow your child the freedom to say what she thinks and believes, even if you don't agree. The Sagittarian child needs to know she won't be reprimanded for standing up for what she believes.

Your Capricorn Child

Capricorn children can converse as easily with other kids as they can with adults. They seem wise beyond their years—and they are. In fact, they're sometimes more at ease with adults. In some respects, Capricorn children actually regard the adults in their lives as equals. However, this doesn't mean that they never act like kids. When they loosen up, they can be wild and unpredictable, silly and goofy. But they're probably almost never reckless.

Capricorn children need boundaries. They feel safer and more secure with a schedule and a plan. If they're allowed to do anything they want at any time, they will feel uncomfortable. Substance and purpose is needed for ambitious Capricorn children. Give them chores they'll enjoy every once in a while.

Like their adult counterparts, Capricorn children attack whatever they do with efficiency and patience. They often exhibit deep compassion for less fortunate people. As the parent of a Capricorn child, you may even have to teach him to lighten up! But, also, you'll relate well with your wonderful Capricorn child. They're very bright and warm-hearted!

Your Aquarius Child

Aquarius children don't recognize barriers of any kind among people, so their friends span the gamut of the social and economic spectrum. They tend to be extroverts, but can also be content in solitary pursuits. They can be as stubborn as Taurus children, particularly when it comes to defending something they believe in.

While Leo has a habit of fighting for the real underdog, Aquarius sometimes picks the wrong side to support. Though her intentions are good, she sometimes chooses the wrong battle to fight. She's worldly at a young age, but an Aquarius child can also be quite gullible.

Aquarius, though outwardly gregarious, likes freedom and time spent alone. She tends to be a bad judge of character because she always finds the good in everyone. Even as a child, she plays with everyone and is a loyal friend. However, once someone has wronged her, she won't hesitate to cut this person out and eject him from the sandbox.

Even though these kids get along well with their peers, Aquarius children aren't followers. They aren't afraid to disagree with the consensus opinion. Within a family structure, they need to have the freedom to speak their own minds and know that their opinions will be heard. They may chafe at rules that are too rigid and strict—and they simply detest criticism. It cuts them to the core.

Remember, too, that Aquarius will take things in stride but that freedom with careful consideration works best. They have to know that you care but aren't on top of them all the time. Do this, and you'll have a generous, bright, and charming Aquarius child!

Your Pisces Child

In a crowd, the easiest way to pick out a Pisces child is by her smart, discerning eyes. Her gaze seems wise and almost ancient. Little Pisces girls sometimes come off as snobs to others who don't know them well; Pisces boys can come off as stuck-up or all knowing. These traits are innate. They simply have a certain inbred regality, like little princesses and princes. They have a cool sense of style and good bearing, and an equally keen imagination.

In fact, it sometimes seems that a young Pisces is not listening to you; it's not true! A Pisces child hears everything and will surprise you when she revives the subject at any given time. If you tell your child you're not feeling well, for instance, she's likely to ask you a few hours later or the next day how you're feeling. Even as children, Pisces is caring and sweet. His mind is always working. He thinks too much and worries a lot, contributing to his idealism and desire to make the world a better place.

Pisces children tend to have vivid dreams. Many Pisces children also show an early interest in psychic phenomena. If the mystical tendencies are nurtured and encouraged, a Pisces child can grow into a true medium, psychologist, clairvoyant, and/or healer.

These children feel everything with such intensity that a cross look is probably all a parent needs to keep them in line. If you raise your voice to a Pisces child, it's the equivalent of a physical assault. Their feelings are easily hurt. However, if other children challenge them, they will stand up for themselves.

Pisces children are truly paradoxes—equally strong and insecure. They long to find their own way and yet, once they do, they are sought out constantly by other children for pep-talks and good advice. Pisces is nurturing, sweet, and always knows what to say to everyone. Her sense of diplomacy is the stuff of legends—even with her parents. You'll feel lucky to have a Pisces child at your side!

Chapter 8

Aspects

To find the aspects in a birth chart, astrologers measure the geometrical distances between the different points. The most important aspect is the *conjunction*, which is the perfect distance that is created when two planets occupy the same degree (see Chapter 9). The *opposition*—created when two planets are 180 degrees apart—is also an essential aspect to know. In this chapter, you'll learn all about aspects, orbs, and other bits and pieces of the astrology puzzle.

Understanding Aspects

As geometric angles between planets, aspects seem rather simple and straightforward. However, they influence everything. Aspects result from the division of the 360 degrees in the horoscope circle. In **FIGURE 8-1**, the North Node (☊) is separated from Pluto (♇) by about ninety degrees: a square. The square is an aspect.

Symbolically, angles are the network of arteries and veins that link energies between the houses and the planets. They indicate connections between our inner and outer worlds. The square between the North Node and Pluto creates tension—a springboard for growth.

Traditional astrology considers aspects, like planets and houses, in terms of good and bad, difficult or easy. The terminology is actually misleading. Aspects, like planets, are merely representations of certain types of energy. Energy itself is neutral. What we do with the energy is either beneficial or not. Again, it comes back to free will.

Glance at the chart in **FIGURE 8-1** again. The North Node (☊) in 14♉02 in the twelfth house and Pluto (♇) at 12♌40 in the fourth house are about 88 degrees apart; a square is 90 degrees. Does that mean they don't form a square? Not at all. Astrologers work with "orbs" of influence, which means there are several degrees of latitude allowed when the aspect isn't exact.

Orbs

The problem with orbs is that astrologers don't generally agree on how many degrees should be allowed for each type of aspect. In *The Inner Sky*, astrologer Steven Forrest writes: "No orb can be defined rigidly. To attempt to nail them down is like trying to determine the exact day on which your kitten became a cat. It doesn't work."

Astrologer Robert Hand considers smaller orbs to generally be more accurate, but is rather philosophical about the whole issue. In *Horoscope Symbols*, he writes: "What the question boils down to is not how far out of

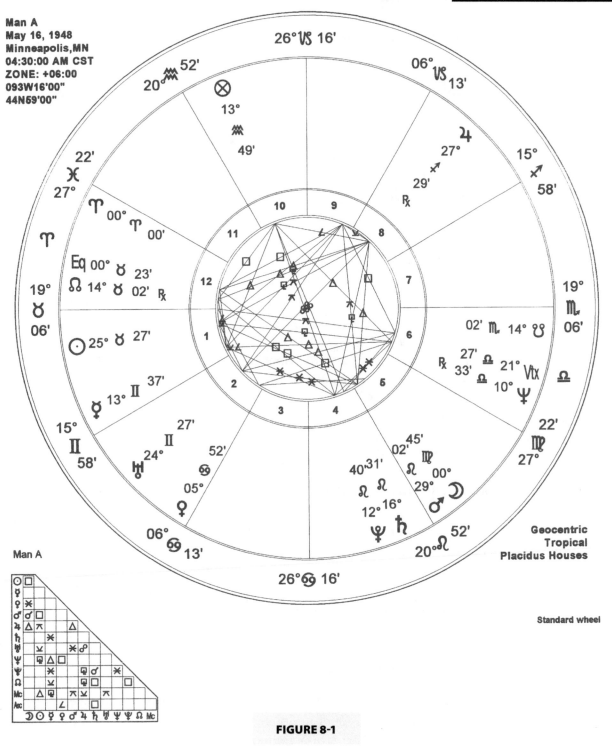

Man A
May 16, 1948
Minneapolis, MN
04:30:00 AM CST
ZONE: +06:00
093W16'00"
44N59'00"

Man A

Geocentric
Tropical
Placidus Houses

Standard wheel

FIGURE 8-1

orb an aspect can be and still have an effect, but rather how subtle a linkage one will accept as significant." In other words, with practice, you'll arrive at your own sense of how large or small an orb should be.

FACT

Astrologer Robert Hand tends to use relatively small orbs: five degrees for all major aspects. One of his exceptions to this rule is to use orbs wider than five degrees when a chart doesn't have many tight-orb aspects. This was his solution to the problem.

Rose Lineman and Jan Popelka, writing in *Compendium of Astrology*, use an eight-degree orb for conjunctions and oppositions and smaller orbs for other aspects. Steven Forrest favors orbs of up to five degrees. Although he feels that orbs of six and seven degrees should still be considered, he believes their impact is considerably less. In Forrest's opinion, orbs of eight or nine degrees hardly count. But if an aspect involves the Sun or the Moon, he recommends allowing a wider orb by one or two degrees.

Planets and Orbs

In the past, astrologers assigned particular orbs to particular planets. A Jupiter aspect, for instance, was allowed an orb of ten degrees, which is very wide, considering that the ten degrees applies on either side of the actual degree. In this system, Mercury, Venus, Mars, Saturn, Uranus, Neptune, and Pluto were permitted an eight-degree orb. The Sun got twelve degrees for an orb and the Moon eight.

Most astrology software programs work with orbs between six and eight degrees. If there aren't any tight orbs in the chart, allow orbs of five or six degrees for all aspects. Hand's orbs tend to be smaller than the norm because he uses Midpoints when interpreting a chart.

Aspects Versus Midpoints

A Midpoint is the halfway mark between any two planets. Hand, like many other astrologers, considers midpoints nearly as important as the aspects themselves. He writes: "I use midpoints because they often give information that would not otherwise be available in the chart. Without them, I have seen important characteristics of a person and events in a life completely overlooked."

ALERT!

Learn about the aspects, but don't worry if it doesn't click right away. It takes time to understand these things. To simplify matters, you can choose to focus on one particular area. For example, astrologer Grant Lewi only stuck to the broad strokes in horoscope interpretation. The Sun, Moon, and major aspects were enough for him.

The bottom line is that you can talk to ten different astrologers and get ten different answers on the issue of orbs. This is one of many gray areas in astrology that your own experience will determine for you. Think of this book as a reference manual to guide you as you learn what you'll be personally comfortable with.

Why All the Details?

For decades, many people publicly denied or ignored astrology, though many considered it more closely in secret. Many astrologers focused on its science, rather than its art, believing that the scientific side made it more legitimate. For this reason, the study of astrology became quite complex over the years; it now includes so many rules, parameters, and minute details. This explains also why you can often find entire books on a single planet in the astrology sections of bookstores.

Science or Art?

This is a very common question in the study of astrology. Take Mars, for instance. Once you get through its influence in mythology, folklore, popular fiction, and the movies, the only thing left to explain is the meat: its influence in a chart. The rest is just filler to justify a book on the subject.

Unfortunately, this practice tends to make astrology seem dull and boring. It also misses the point. What matters in the interpretation of a birth chart is the entire chart. The whole is definitely greater than the sum of the parts, in this case. Also, by attempting to interpret increasingly smaller pieces of a chart, your intuitive voice gets lost. The science of astrology comes from the left brain; its art is from the right brain. The interpretation should be a bridge between the two.

The Aspect Grid

Look at the chart in **FIGURE 8-1.** In the lower left-hand corner, there is a grid with the planet symbols lined up along the edges. The squares of the grid contain the aspect symbols. This is called an "aspect grid" or Aspectarian. Most astrology software programs include them, so you can tell at a glance what aspects a chart contains.

Locate the Sun symbol (☉) along the bottom of the graph. Now locate the **MC** along the left side of the graph. To find out what aspect the Sun and the **MC** make, follow the Sun column up two squares until it's directly opposite the **MC**. You'll see a trine (△).

FACT

The traditional aspects have been in use at least since the second century A.D. They're called "classical" or Ptolemaic, after the Greek astrologer Ptolemy (Claudius Ptolemaeus). These aspects are the conjunction, sextile, square, trine, and opposition. They are considered the major or hard aspects and are also the most powerful.

Defining Aspects

There are numerous minor aspects to consider in a birth chart, but they have far less influence than the major ones. The minor aspects can also be a bit confusing when you're just starting out. So, it's recommended that you don't use them until you've mastered the major aspects. Concentrate on those discussed in the following few pages for now.

Conjunction, a Major Hard Aspect, o Degrees

This is the simplest aspect to identify, but it's also one of the most complex because of the intensity and power involved. Whenever you see two or more planets piled on top of each other, usually, but not always, in the same house, their energies fuse and intensify. If the orb is exact or within one degree, the impact is considerable.

Let's say that Saturn and Pluto are conjunct in the tenth house, within six degrees of each other. Saturn seeks structure and Pluto seeks revolution and transformation—the purposes of the two planets are at odds. This conjunction can be disruptive because the structure of a person's career (tenth house) continually undergoes transformation.

This actually means that just when Saturn had found a structure that works (but one that may also limit or restrict the individual in some way), Pluto comes along and blows it apart. Through this process, circumstances seem to force the individual to expand or change her professional approach. This has a direct effect. Since the conjunction in this example is six degrees, the impact is considerably less than that of a precise conjunction.

In the child's chart in **FIGURE 8-2**, Mars (18♍03) and the Moon (17♍09) are conjunct within one degree. Since this conjunction involves the Moon (emotions) and is conjunct—within one and two degrees—of the descendant, it's particularly powerful. It influences both the sixth and seventh houses and energizes and intensifies emotions.

A Sextile, a Major Soft Aspect, 60 Degrees

This usually represents a free flow of energy between the planets involved. It symbolizes ease and lack of tension, and provides a buffer against instability. But when there's an excess of sextiles in a chart, the individual may be too passive.

In the child's chart in **FIGURE 8-2**, there are sextiles to Pluto—the Sun, Moon, and Neptune. These aspects all have to do with the regeneration of energy through inner resources and the inherent potential to use Plutonian energies in a positive way.

Square, a Major Hard Aspect, 90 Degrees

The keyword with this aspect is friction. But the energy that accompanies the friction tends to be dynamic and forceful, galvanizing an individual to action. Squares force you to develop and evolve. They are expressed internally through the lens of our subjectivity.

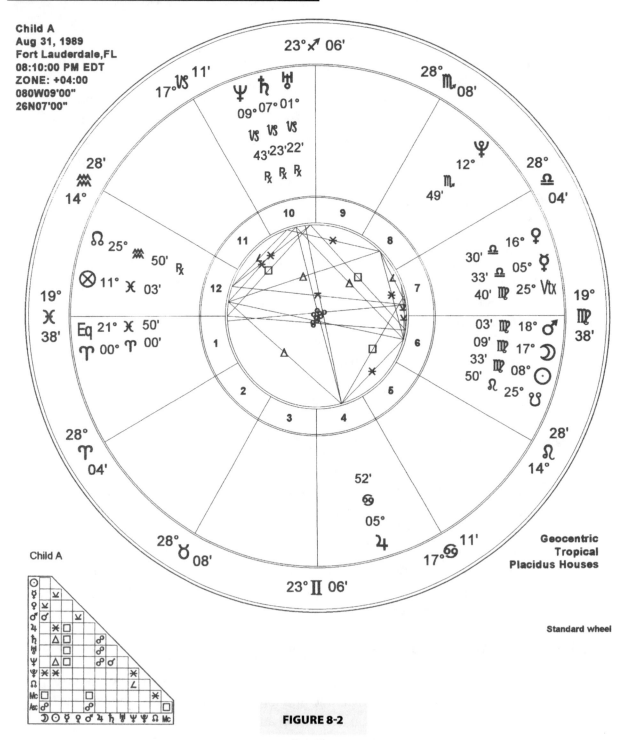

Child A
Aug 31, 1989
Fort Lauderdale, FL
08:10:00 PM EDT
ZONE: +04:00
080W09'00"
26N07'00"

Child A

Geocentric
Tropical
Placidus Houses

Standard wheel

FIGURE 8-2

ALERT!

The important detail to remember about a square is that the tension can't be ignored or repressed. If you don't deal with it, the same pattern of friction will repeat over and over again until you tackle it. As Steven Forrest writes in *The Inner Sky,* "The friction produced in a square exerts relentless developmental pressure on each of the planets."

Look again at the chart in **FIGURE 8-1**. There's a square between the Sun (25♉27) and Mars (29♌02). The orb is about four degrees, certainly tight enough to have an impact. In this case, the ego represented by the Sun is never satisfied with personal achievements, so the Mars energy makes this person restless and sometimes argumentative. But if the Mars aggression is channeled constructively, the square can lead to success.

Trine, a Major Soft Aspect, 120 Degrees

Like a sextile, the connected energies in this aspect work together harmoniously. The inner harmony related to trines often acts as a buffer against turmoil, just as sextiles do. But again, if there are too many trines in a chart, passivity may result.

When trines involve an event, it comes about on its own accord and not because the individual has taken action to make it happen. In the child's chart in (**FIGURE 8-2**), the Sun in the sixth house (08♍33) is trine to Saturn (07♑23R) and Neptune (09♑43R) in the tenth house. Both aspects are tight, within one degree of the Sun's eight degrees, so they exert considerable influence in the chart.

The aspect to Saturn allows the child to set realistic goals and attain them. The aspect to Neptune gives her deep compassion for other people, as well as psychic ability. Taken together, the trine attracts the right opportunities for the advancement of her goals.

Opposition, a Major Hard Aspect, 180 Degrees

This aspect forces change through conflict. Sometimes this aspect represents traits that we project onto others because we haven't fully incorporated them into who we are.

Oppositions often involve polarities: Gemini-Sagittarius, Taurus-Scorpio. This means their elements differ—air to fire, Earth to water—but complement each other. They may also share qualities, as in the two earlier examples. Gemini and Sagittarius are both mutable signs; Taurus and Scorpio are both fixed. This gives some basis for compromise.

Imagine an opposition as Siamese twins with different agendas. Twin A wants to stay home and read; Twin B wants to party. How can such different needs, in general, be resolved? The bottom line is that these differences may never be resolved. Or they may take a lifetime to work out. One thing is for sure with oppositions: resolving differences ultimately will enrich your life.

Special Aspect Patterns

Several aspects can combine to create particular patterns that change or enhance the original aspect. There are five such patterns you should look for when interpreting any birth chart: stellium, T-square, grand square, or grand cross, grand trine or cosmic cross, and kite.

Stellium

This is a cluster of stars within the same sign or house or within a certain orb in adjacent houses. The key here is to pay special attention to any sign or house that contains three or more planets. In **FIGURE 8-3**, note the stellium of five planets in the first house. Four of the planets—Sun (☉), Jupiter (♃), Venus (♀), and Mercury (☿)—are in Aquarius. Even though the Moon (☽) is in Pisces, it's conjunct the Sun at a five degree orb, so it should be considered in the overall impact of the stellium.

Some astrologers contend that a stellium consists of three or more planets in the same house or sign. Other astrologers say you have to look for four or more planets. Well-known astrologer Alan Oken allows a ten-degree orb for planets in adjacent signs.

In the eighth house, there are three planets: Mars (♂), Neptune (♆), and Saturn (♄). The planets are in Libra and Virgo and aren't conjunct, unless you take into account a wide seven-degree orb between Mars and Neptune. But toss in the South Node (☋), and we find that eight out of the ten planets and two out of the three points fall within two houses. Now these three planets in the eighth house—even though they aren't conjunct by sign or degree—assume a vital importance.

At a glance, the stellium in the first house immediately tells us the individual's perception of the world is heavily colored by subjectivity. She probably has a clear sense of herself—who she is and where she's going. Her interaction with the world is expressed through the affairs of the eighth house. Not surprisingly, this woman was an attorney for many years and is now a family court judge.

T-Square

This pattern is formed when two or more planets are in opposition and square a third planet. The third planet becomes the center of tension and represents the challenge the individual faces. It's often found in the charts of prominent individuals.

In the horoscope in **FIGURE 8-2**, Jupiter in the fourth house opposes Saturn, Neptune, and Uranus in the tenth house at orbs of two to four degrees. These planets, in turn, square Mercury in the seventh house. This forms a T-square to Mercury.

Grand Square or Grand Cross

This pattern is an extension of the T-square. Created by four squares and two oppositions, the pattern has at least one planet in each of the quadruplicities: fixed, cardinal, or mutable. This pattern is one of extreme tension. But when the energies are used correctly, it can lead to great strength.

Grand Trine or Cosmic Cross

Look for three planets that occupy different signs of the same element at 120-degree angles. This auspicious aspect in a chart indicates tremendous creativity expressed through the element of the trine. Too many trines in a chart actually indicate that the individual may lack focus and ambition.

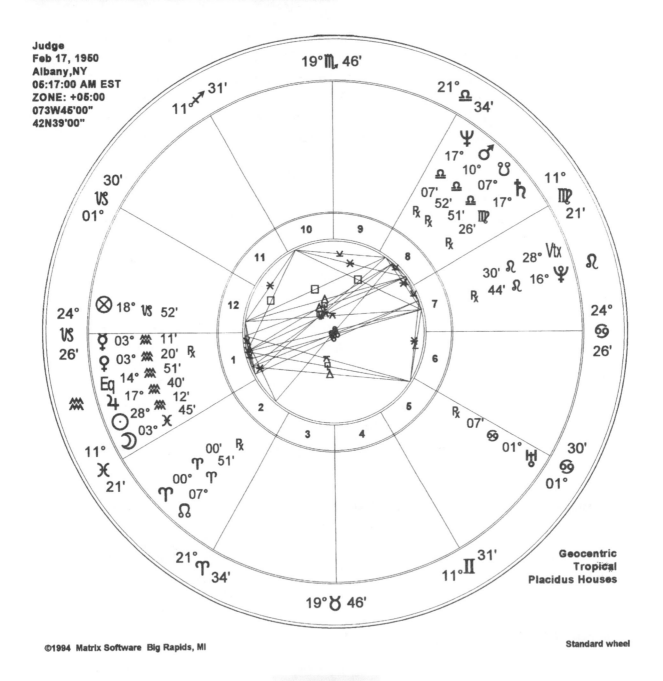

Judge
Feb 17, 1950
Albany,NY
05:17:00 AM EST
ZONE: +05:00
073W45'00"
42N39'00"

19°♏ 46'

11°♐ 31'

21°♎ 34'

30'
♑
01°

Ψ
17° ♂
♎ 10° ☊
07' ♎ 07' ♄
52' ♎ 17'
℞ ℞ 51' ♍
26'
℞

11°
♍
21'

24°
♑
26'

⊗ 18° ♑ 52'
☿ 03° ♒ 11'
♀ 03° ♒ 20' ℞
51'
Eq 14° ♒ 40'
♃ 17° ♒ 12'
⊙ 28° ♒ 45'
03° ♓

30' ♌ 28° Vtx
44' ♌ 16° ♆
℞

24°
♋
26'

11°
♓
21'

℞ 07' ♋
01° ♅

30'
♋
01°

00' ℞
♈ 51'
00° ♈
07°
♈ ☋

10   9
11   8
12   7
1   6
2   5
3   4

21°♈ 34'

11°♊ 31'

Geocentric
Tropical
Placidus Houses

19°♉ 46'

©1994 Matrix Software Big Rapids, MI

Standard wheel

FIGURE 8-3

A Water trine enhances psychic ability, receptivity, and compassion. A Fire trine increases initiative and drive. An Earth trine brings material abundance. An Air trine intensifies intellectual ability and expression.

Kite

This pattern is an extension of the Grand Trine. A fourth planet forms an opposition to one corner of the triangle, thus sextiling the other two corners.

Applying Versus Separating Aspects

Due to the different rates at which planets move, some aspects in a chart are applying or forming, and others are separating or moving away from an exact aspect. Applying aspects have more impact than those that are separating.

When an aspect is forming, it means that conditions, events, circumstances, emotions, or states of mind become evident as a person moves through life. Separating aspects pinpoint elements of an individual's experiences that are part of his nature at birth and may include karmic conditions and relationships.

In the chart in **FIGURE 8–3**, Mars (♂) is forming an aspect to Neptune (♆) because it is the faster-moving planet. In the chart in **FIGURE 8–2**, the Moon in the sixth house is forming an aspect with Mars because the Moon is the faster-moving planet.

In terms of their speed, from faster to slower, the planets line up with the Moon leading the procession, followed by Mercury, Venus, Sun, Mars, Jupiter, Saturn, Uranus, Neptune, and Pluto.

Exercise: Reading Aspects

The chart of Janet Doe in **FIGURE 8-4** belongs to a well-known celebrity, whose name you'll find at the end of this exercise. Using what you've learned up to this point, study the chart, then jot down your immediate impressions. Don't get bogged down in detail; just take note of what is obvious. Use the following questions as guidelines, and don't cheat!

1. What is the focal area of this person's life?

2. How does this individual transform himself or herself?

3. In what area is this person most lucky?

4. What house has the greatest concentration of planets?

5. What do the conjunctions indicate?

6. Are there any stelliums?

7. In what area does this person find restrictions and need structure?

8. What do the Midheaven and **IC** signs tell you about this individual?

9. How many trines are there?

10. How many squares?

11. Are there any sextiles or oppositions?

The chart of Janet Doe in Figure 8–4 belongs to Madonna.

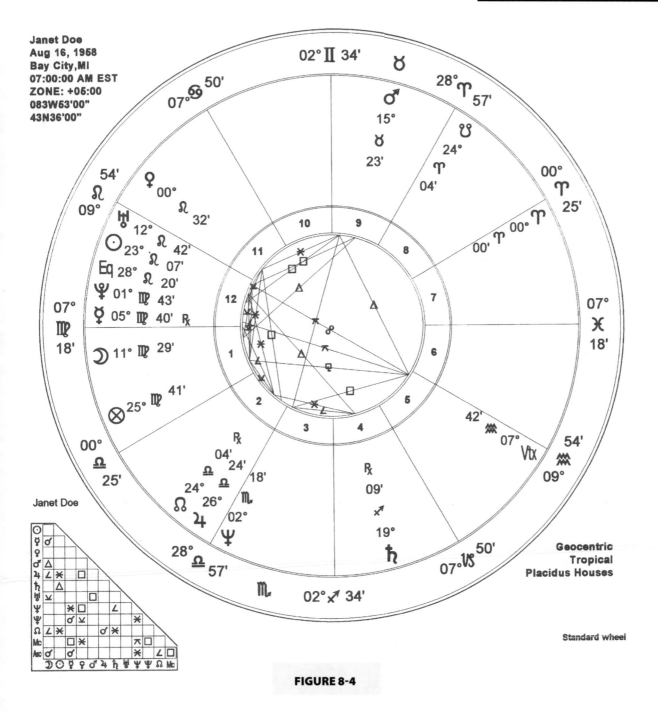

FIGURE 8-4

Chapter 9

E Conjunctions: 0 Degrees

Conjunctions are the easiest aspects to identify in a chart because the planets are clustered together. They don't have to be in the same sign. Two planets must be within 8 degrees of each other (10 degrees with the Moon or the Sun). This is also called a hard aspect. When interpreting conjunctions, remember that they fuse and intensify planetary energies. Relate the conjunctions to the houses in which they are found. Then dig deeper to find out more about yourself!

Conjunctions of the Sun

Conjunctions of the Sun act as a magnifying glass to intensify and focus solar energy. The essence of a conjuncting planet doesn't just blend with that of the Sun; it unites with it, enhancing and strengthening its (solar) energy.

ESSENTIAL

There are at least two schools of thought on conjunctions of the Sun. The first holds that the planet's energy is burned up by the Sun. The second theory is that the solar energy becomes a perfect vehicle for the manifestation of that planet's energy. Both theories can apply—it depends on the overall chart.

If a planet lies within half a degree to four degrees from the Sun, it's said to be *combust*. This means exactly what it sounds like: The planet's energy breaks down and is essentially absorbed by the solar energy. If a planet is less than half a degree from the Sun, it's said to be *cazimi*.

Sun Conjunct Moon. You get what you want through a perfect blend of will and ego. Your creative urges spring from deep instinctive levels. Your self-motivation can be impulsive, which may create problems for you. You have strong ties with your family, spouse, and home.

Sun Conjunct Mercury. Your will is focused through your intellect. You don't just sit around talking about ideas; you act on them. Mercury is never more than twenty-eight degrees from the Sun, so a conjunction is the only major aspect that occurs between these two planetary bodies.

Sun Conjunct Venus. You're definitely a lover: A lover of life, beauty, music, and art; a lover of love. You gain through speculation, unless the fifth and second houses are poorly aspected. In a man's chart, this conjunction can indicate an effeminate nature; in a woman's chart, she's the social butterfly. You have a terrific way with kids and possess the gift of bringing happiness to others. On the downside, you may have a tendency toward laziness and self-indulgence. (This is the only aspect Venus can make to the Sun because it's never more than forty-eight degrees from the Sun.)

Sun Conjunct Mars. You charge through obstacles and meet challenges with all the subtlety of a T-Rex. You're aggressive, self-motivated, and bold.

You're also outspoken and blunt, which sometimes proves to be an advantage, but usually gets you into trouble. You need to practice self-control so that your abundant energy can be channeled in more advantageous ways.

Having the Sun conjunct Mars can give you a real competitive streak. Some might think you're too aggressive and urge you to calm down when you're playing sports. Sexually, it can make you adventurous and daring—you'll try anything once!

Sun Conjunct Jupiter. This aspect works like a magnet that attracts what you need exactly when you need it. Even in adverse times, you're naturally lucky. You're a lavish spender, but also generous and magnanimous with people you care about. Your self-confidence and self-reliance always bring you more than you need. You gain through your father.

Sun Conjunct Saturn. This aspect either provides the structure and discipline you need to achieve prominence, or it oppresses you so deeply that you always feel a tinge of melancholy. Responsibility is thrust on you at an early age that might cause you to withdraw into yourself. You are the proverbial lone wolf, independent but often lonely. Your best bet is to turn your considerable intellect away from your own concerns and reach for whatever it is you most desire.

Sun Conjunct Uranus. Think genius. Through flashes of insight and an instinctive understanding of divine laws, you have the ability to venture into unexplored realms and impact the world with what you find. You're high strung and probably try to get by on very little sleep, which only burns you out. You have the ability to succeed at virtually anything you set your mind to.

Uranus deals with the unexpected and marching to the beat of a different drummer. It takes more than eighty years for Uranus to move through the twelve signs of the zodiac. If your Sun is conjunct Uranus, it means that you're an original, creative thinker, though you tend to want everything done perfectly.

Sun Conjunct Neptune. People consider you somewhat mysterious. Your strong mystical bent, used constructively, can trigger enormous creativity. If the conjunction is in Taurus, your mystical side is grounded, and you make the unreal real. The downside to this aspect is scattered mental and emotional energy, a fascination with or overindulgence in drugs or alcohol, and a tendency to daydream.

Sun Conjunct Pluto. Your powerful will regenerates and transforms everything it touches. Sexual and mental energy are usually your vehicles for transformation. In self-aware people, this conjunction may manifest as a pure channel for spiritual energy; in less evolved people there may be dictatorial tendencies.

Sun Conjunct North Node. With this aspect, the South Node is in opposition and should be considered in the interpretation. Your opportunities for self-expression are greatly enhanced and can manifest as leadership. The luck inherent in this aspect is something you've earned through past lives; your efforts were directed toward the world beyond yourself. A solar or lunar eclipse most likely occurred around the time of your birth.

Sun Conjunct South Node. Circumstances in your life either deny or limit your chances for self-expression. The house placement tells which area is affected. This aspect usually indicates past lives in which you, perhaps, pursued your goals at the expense of other people.

Sun Conjunct Ascendant. Imagine vitality at its peak—illness is as rare as water in the Mojave Desert. Even when you do get sick, you recuperate quickly and completely. You possess an intuitive understanding of divine law and have a tremendous capacity for positive influence on the masses.

ESSENTIAL

Here's an extra tidbit: If you know your Part of Fortune and your Sun conjuncts this, then you're in luck—literally. In other words, your luck and success come through personal efforts, in the area represented by the house that the Part of Fortune occupies.

Sun Conjunct Midheaven. You seek fame, acclaim, and the realization of your professional abilities. Politics and public life may figure into the equation. However your fame manifests, it's sure to impact the masses.

Sun Conjunct IC. Family and home are paramount in your life. You have a deep appreciation of your early life, family roots, and values. You may do a lot of entertaining in your home and hobnob with famous people.

Conjunctions of the Moon

Conjunctions of the Moon heighten the emotions and unconscious mind, and represent your subconscious. This aspect always involves women and relationships with women. It also governs instinctive reactions to events and situations indicated by sign and house placement.

Moon Conjunct Mercury. This aspect links the left and right brain, the conscious and unconscious mind. All your thoughts are heavily influenced by your emotions, but your emotions are your conduit to information stored in your unconscious. Your wit is sharp and often biting.

If well-aspected, you have an excellent memory and heightened intuition. If poorly aspected, you are restless and are excessively sensitive to criticism. If your Moon is conjunct Mercury (the way you communicate), chances are that you need to express your emotions frequently and have them validated.

Moon Conjunct Venus. Life is pretty easy for you, especially if you're a woman. You're physically attractive in a way that attracts other people's attention. You're successful in romance and friendships and with women in general. If this is a man's chart, this aspect is all about the kind of sparkling personality that makes other people feel good when they're around you. You may be a little vain and self-indulgent, but so what? You deserve it, right?

Moon Conjunct Mars. Your emotions are intense, and you have a quick, expressive intellect. The combination can result in artistic or musical ability; combined with a Venus conjunction, you may develop into a great artist or musician. Generally, this aspect suggests fortunate financial affairs. In a woman's chart, it means a magnetic personality and a drive to achieve prominence or recognition that is commensurate with a man's. Your aggression and intense emotions sometimes lead to disruptive relationships. Emotions have a strong impact on your health.

Moon Conjunct Jupiter. Your sympathetic and generous nature wins you friends among many different kinds of people. There's a certain nobility about you that people respect and gravitate toward. Women are especially helpful to you. Your health tends to be robust. You enjoy travel, particularly if it's with family members or people who are like kin to you.

Moon Conjunct Saturn. Your nature is rather serious and thoughtful. You're a plodder in whatever you undertake, moving carefully and efficiently through whatever steps are necessary to accomplish your goals. Your bluntness is sometimes hurtful to others, but you don't see it. You tend to be introverted, may be emotionally repressed, and sometimes act as if you're the center of the universe. On the other hand, Saturn here can lend structure to your emotions and channel them for a more constructive use.

Moon Conjunct Uranus. You're a complete original: eccentric, independent, and fearless. You often behave so unpredictably that people don't know what to expect from you. Your imagination and intuition are highly developed and erratic. Your home life is unusual in some way.

Moon Conjunct Neptune. You're psychically attuned to other people, to their emotional environments. In some instances, this trait can be so pronounced that you become a psychic sponge. Depending on other aspects in the chart, there can be mental and emotional confusion or heightened mediumistic tendencies that can provide spiritual insight.

Moon Conjunct Pluto. Clear the decks! Your emotions are so intense that other people may have trouble handling you for long periods of time. And yet others are drawn to your charisma. Your willingness to take emotional risks results in a periodic purging of your most intimate relationships.

ESSENTIAL

Moon conjunct Pluto is often an indication of a true psychic. Edgar Cayce had this aspect in his birth chart. One who has the Moon conjunct Pluto also probably has an abiding interest in life after death, reincarnation, or other metaphysical topics.

Moon Conjunct North Node. You've got your finger on the public pulse and use this to your advantage. Your relationships with women are generally good and beneficial to you in some way.

Moon Conjunct South Node. Your timing isn't good. You somehow miss being in the right place at the right time. This may lead to depression, bitterness, and, ultimately, isolation. But if you can get past your emotional reactions you succeed against the odds. This aspect can be related to past lives in which you, perhaps, abused wealth and power.

Moon Conjunct Ascendant. You empathize with others. Your early childhood experiences are carried with you throughout your life and color your emotional responses as an adult. You have strong ties to your home and family.

Moon Conjunct Midheaven. If you're not living your life in the public eye now, you will at some point in your life. This aspect favors actors and politicians. Women help you achieve your goals.

Moon Conjunct IC. The Moon rules here naturally, so this is an excellent aspect. Your strong family ties support you emotionally. Your intuition is well developed, particularly when it pertains to your children, parents, family, and home. You probably live or would like to live near water.

Conjunctions of Mercury

Mercury conjunctions energize the intellect. They also clarify and validate mental processes. Also, Mercury conjunctions show our true communication skills. Do we communicate well? Do we hide our feelings and then let them out all at once? Are we able to put our thoughts into words for others? Do we insist, or do we make our points quietly, but surely? In this section, find out all you need to know.

Mercury Conjunct Venus. You have literary talent and a deep appreciation of the arts in general. You're a soft-spoken individual, with a facility for communicating your ideas. You never have to raise your voice to make your point. Your popularity is well deserved.

Mercury Conjunct Mars. You want facts, not speculations. You speak your mind, act on your decisions, and enjoy debating about controversial issues. You may have a tendency to allow debate to collapse into heated arguments in which you passionately defend your position, even if it's wrong. This aspect is a good one for investigative reporters.

Mercury Conjunct Jupiter. Your intellectual integrity may already be legendary in your workplace. You can't be pushed or coerced into doing something that isn't right. It's as if you were born knowing right from wrong; there are no gray areas for you. You have a deep interest in religion, spiritual issues, the law, and education. You enjoy the intellectual expansion that comes with foreign travel. You are recognized as an authority in your field.

Mercury Conjunct Saturn. Your innate understanding of structure and form gives you a powerful capacity for visualization. You can see something in its completed form when it's still an abstract idea. This aspect is good for engineers, architects, designers, and builders of all sorts. It may delay recognition in your profession, but your careful planning and foresight wins in the end. You may be prone to excessive worry and occasional bouts of depressions.

Mercury Conjunct Uranus. Genius and originality are your birthright. Your mind moves so quickly that other people have trouble keeping up with you. Your intuitive flashes allow you to perceive things that other people miss. This inspiration provides you with original solutions to issues and problems. You never settle for the traditional route; you have to prove everything to yourself first. If this conjunction is poorly aspected, you may be conceited, stubborn, and hard to get along with.

Mercury Conjunct Neptune. Your imagination is a central and complex part of your life. Through your imagination and psychic receptivity to your immediate environment, you travel into realms that are closed to the rest of us. You may write poetry, music, or mystical fiction, a creatively beneficial outlet for this aspect. You need to express the beauty you see around yourself.

ALERT!

Neptune is the planet of idealism, and it makes us lose sight of what is real. In other words, if you have your Mercury conjunct Neptune, make sure to carefully channel all this psychic input. If you don't, it could hurl you into a world where you could lose touch with reality.

Mercury Conjunct Pluto. You pierce the masks of other people's secrets. Your enormous willpower and resourcefulness allow you to penetrate to the truth of whatever it is you need and want to understand. You would make a terrific detective or scientist who works with classified or secret information. You seem to have an instinctive understanding of energy—what it is, how it works, and how you can use it. The danger with this aspect is potential misuse of power.

Mercury Conjunct North Node. You're in the flow; aware of what the public seeks. You can become an intellectual leader or spokesperson for a particular idea or set of ideals. You evolve through your communication skills.

Mercury Conjunct South Node. Your timing is off. You're either behind the times or ahead of them. This can lead to deep frustration, but that's the easy way out. Persevere and your originality will win out.

Mercury Conjunct Ascendant. You're very bright, high strung, and maddeningly logical. You enjoy writing and are quite good at it. Once you apply your intellect to what you want, you succeed far beyond your own expectations.

If your Mercury conjuncts your Part of Fortune (remember, it's where your luck lies), here's some good advice: Plan well, use your resources, and look to the house the Part of Fortune occupies to understand where to direct your energies.

Mercury Conjunct Midheaven. Career, business, and professional ambition are your areas of interest. Publishing, journalism, writing, any kind of communication profession would suit you.

Mercury Conjunct IC. You come from a well-educated family where intellectual achievements are recognized and honored. You love books and your home is probably filled with them. You may live with a brother or sister.

Conjunctions of Venus

Any planet that conjuncts Venus influences your social behaviors, including your friendships and your acquaintances. This will also tell more about what kind of artistic expression fascinates and defines you. It also gives away your sexual affinities and romantic inclinations.

Venus Conjunct Mars. Sexuality is a big issue for you. Your passionate nature gets you involved in many different types of relationships, not all of them good for you. If this conjunction is poorly aspected, promiscuity may be evident. In extreme cases, there may be involvement in violent crime. But generally, this aspect indicates that you're very attractive to the opposite sex. You're lucky in financial matters, and you enjoy spending money. This is a good aspect for any artistic endeavor: it adds fire, passion, and drive.

Venus Conjunct Jupiter. This aspect sounds like a carnival fortune-teller's line: happiness and financial success. You're cheerful, optimistic, sociable, and kind toward other people. You probably support religious or spiritual causes and help people who are less fortunate than you. Artistic ability usually comes with this conjunction. In self-aware individuals, talent as a peacemaker may be indicated.

ALERT!

On the downside, when Venus conjuncts Jupiter, things can be too easy, which can lead to indolence, self-indulgence, and laziness! If Saturn is prominent in your chart, it will add structure and discipline to the overall horoscope and create a channel for using this aspect positively.

Venus Conjunct Saturn. Romantic relationships are serious business for you. You don't love easily, but once your heart is won, your loyalty is unwavering. Your adherence to tradition, however, may compel you to stay in a relationship long after it no longer works. Divorce is rare with this aspect. If the conjunction is poorly aspected, you could be swayed to marry for money alone.

FACT

Highly talented artists often have their Venus conjunct their Saturn; Saturn gives structure and discipline to creative expression. In other words, Saturn gives you that certain "oomph" to keep learning and advancing in skill. Venus gives you the natural-born talent. Together, they work well.

Venus Conjunct Uranus. Your romantic relationships are unconventional and probably begin and end suddenly. The line between friendship and love can be quite blurred for you at times. Individuals with this aspect should never marry in haste. Your artistic tastes and ability are highly original and unconventional. Your earning and spending habits are marked by the same erratic tendencies as your love life.

Venus Conjunct Neptune. Your physical beauty reflects the mystical and spiritual traits inherent in this conjunction. People are drawn to your gentleness, sensitivity, and elusive spiritual nature. You love music and art that are mystically inspired. You tend to idealize your romantic partners.

Innate healing ability and transcendent knowledge are often evident with this aspect. But unless the individual is self-aware, a pattern of events and circumstances may not develop that pushes the person toward a realization of this talent. On the negative side, you may be disillusioned in love and romance by getting involved, unknowingly, with deceitful people. You trust too much.

Venus Conjunct Pluto. Sexual magnetism and tremendous passion mark this aspect. Quite often, past-life attachments are indicated. In self-aware individuals, this aspect can lead to the height of spiritual love and compassion, which transforms everyone who comes in contact with it.

As with all Venus conjunctions, artistic ability is indicated. But here it's likely to be expressed through drama and music or a combination of the two, like operas and musicals. As with all Pluto aspects, the risk is that the power of the conjunction can be used positively or negatively, to transform or destroy.

Venus Conjunct North Node. You have a knack for being in the right place at the right time. Through social contacts you develop because of this, you attract what you need for personal fulfillment and success.

Venus Conjunct South Node. You feel emotionally isolated much of the time, but it's due to your own behavior patterns. Try to develop a more acute sense of timing in your social interactions; don't bug people when they're preoccupied with something else.

Venus Conjunct Ascendant. Physically you're a knockout, especially if you're a woman. You can charm your way into getting virtually anything you want. If poorly aspected, however, there can be a tendency toward vanity and affected mannerisms.

If your Venus happens to conjunct your Part of Fortune, your love life should be smooth sailing! In fact, it doesn't get much better than this. You benefit financially through marriage and partnerships in general. You gain through love.

Venus Conjunct Midheaven. Social ambition is what this aspect is about. It's a wonderful aspect for artists, publicists, and diplomats. You attract money and power through social contacts and relationships.

Venus Conjunct IC. Your life is about creating, maintaining, and enjoying domestic harmony. Your marriage and family are important to you, as are your parents and early childhood. Your home is artistically decorated. Chances are that you enjoy gourmet food.

Conjunctions of Mars

With Mars conjunctions, think activity: It has to do with your energy levels and the way you deal with work and the people around you. Mars conjunctions will also give away your aggressiveness: Do you take decisive action, or do you lie back and let others push their way to the front of the line? This conjunction will also show what your sexual appetite and tendencies are like.

Mars Conjunct Jupiter. You have few equals in terms of energy and enthusiasm, particularly when you're dealing with something you feel passionate about. Whenever you're told that something can't be done or that you can't do something, you proceed to prove everyone wrong. Your sex drive is as strong as your drive to succeed. Poorly aspected, there can be a tendency to prove you're right at any cost.

Mars Conjunct Saturn. Your physical endurance surpasses that of many of your contemporaries. You work hard and long to achieve what you desire. This aspect is sometimes found in the charts of professional military people. Your sex drive may often be channeled into your work.

Thanks to Saturn's restrictions, you may repress anger and other hostile emotions until you explode, and your attitudes may be somewhat dictatorial. You may also be prone to broken bones.

Mars Conjunct Uranus. You despise boredom and are constantly looking for thrills and chills. Your dare-devil attitude can lead to extremism and rebellion against authority and any restriction of your personal freedom. In daily life, your strong personality may come across to others as too impersonal to make you the popular kid on the block. You're at your best when you follow your intellect rather than your emotions.

Mars Conjunct Neptune. Astrologer Grant Lewi called this the "most powerful magnetic aspect in the horoscope." In self-aware people, it may be exactly that because it unites physical and spiritual energy. In practical terms, this means that psychic healing ability may be evident and that you have the innate capacity to manifest what you desire.

ALERT!

If your Mars conjuncts your Neptune, impractical goals, scattered energy, and peculiar romantic involvements may result. However it manifests in your life, if your Mars conjuncts Neptune, be advised to stay clear of drugs and alcohol and to maintain good health through diet and exercise.

Mars Conjunct Pluto. This aspect gives incredible physical strength and a powerful personal magnetism. How it manifests, however, depends on whether Mars or Pluto is the dominant planet in the horoscope. If Mars is more prominent, then the power is expressed through baser emotions: lust, greed, and achievement at the expense of others.

With Pluto dominant, you have the capacity to transform and regenerate yourself in such a way that your voice becomes that of a spiritual leader. If poorly aspected, however, there's a chance that Pluto will perform his usual shtick and turn everything around. This power may be expressed through cruelty, savage passions, and violence. Be self-aware!

Mars Conjunct North Node. You're in step with the times and in harmony with your personal environment. Your drive to succeed (look to the house placement to find out which area is affected) allows you to overcome any restrictions imposed by the sign and house placement of the South Node.

Mars Conjunct South Node. You're a loner. You may object to the military values of the country in which you live and to many of the current trends. Your sense of timing may be off, and, because of this, you may unknowingly antagonize others.

Mars Conjunct Ascendant. You've got all the Mars traits: aggression, energy, initiative, and impulsiveness. On the downside, you may also be reckless and accident-prone. Your relationships and marriages are emotionally charged. Intense dealings go hand in hand, and it sometimes becomes difficult for the people around you to stay on your dramatic level for long.

If your Mars conjuncts your ascendant, there is a curious side effect. When you're ill, you probably run a high fever. The explanation is this: When Mars is in the opposition position (conjunct the descendant or seventh-house cusp), there is an affinity for high fevers because of its proximity to the sixth house.

Mars Conjunct Midheaven. You're focused on your career and professional achievements and pour a lot of energy into attaining prominence. You're extremely competitive and don't shrink from the task at hand when confronted with setbacks. Good aspects from Jupiter, Saturn, and the planetary ruler of the sign on the tenth-house cusp help you achieve success.

Mars Conjunct IC. Disharmony in the home and family life is indicated unless Mars is well-aspected or you work out of your home.

Conjunctions of Jupiter

The influence of a Jupiter conjunction is felt mostly in the house where the conjunction falls. It's important to look at the aspects made to the conjunction. If they're good, then the terrific, expansive qualities of Jupiter dominate. If the conjunction is badly aspected, then look for extravagance and excess.

Jupiter Conjunct Saturn. This aspect, which comes around about once every twenty years, means you probably have to overcome major obstacles to expand the affairs of the house where the conjunction falls. The two planets are basically in conflict: Jupiter wants to expand, Saturn wants to restrict.

Jupiter Conjunct Uranus. This one rolls around every fourteen years or so. It means that you experience sudden and unexpected opportunities to expand in whatever area the house placement rules. You may travel suddenly. You gain through friends, occult groups, and through progressive, original ideas and methods.

Jupiter Conjunct Neptune. Look for this aspect every thirteen years. You're imaginative, have a distinct spiritual or mystical bent, and possess some sort of psychic talent that you should develop. There can be extreme idealism with this aspect, which must be channeled constructively in order to be put to practical use.

Jupiter Conjunct Pluto. This powerful aspect can work constructively or destructively. You either seek to achieve goals that benefit not only yourself but others as well, or you're a power monger.

With those who are more emotionally mature or self-aware, Jupiter conjunct Pluto is a good reason for learning about and fully developing your spiritual side. Beneficial practices include: yoga, meditation, metaphysical studies, and spiritual healing.

Jupiter Conjunct North Node. This is a terrific aspect, particularly if you're involved with the public. Your beliefs are in tune with current trends.

Jupiter Conjunct South Node. You feel blocked much of the time—restricted or limited—just as you would with a Jupiter-Saturn conjunction. Be careful while traveling abroad. Look to the house placement of the North Node to understand how to overcome the challenges of this aspect.

Jupiter Conjunct Ascendant. Your optimism inspires others, who may look to you as an authority of some kind. Your main passions revolve around education, legal, or spiritual concerns. You enjoy travel, particularly overseas. There's a tendency with this aspect to gain weight.

Jupiter Conjunct Midheaven. This is a fine aspect for achieving professional recognition and success. It's often found in the horoscopes of politicians, attorneys, educators, anyone in the public eye.

Jupiter Conjunct IC. You're a builder—either literally or figuratively. This aspect is good for real estate brokers and anyone in the home construction, improvement, or decoration business. Your early childhood was probably fun and active. You have a solid relationship with your parents. In the latter half of your life, you can expect prosperity and material comfort.

Conjunctions of Saturn

Saturn conjunctions can restrict and limit the flow of energy between planets or can discipline and structure the energies to create a single-minded purpose or goal. Definitely scrutinize the house that holds the conjunction to find out which area of life is affected.

Saturn Conjunct Uranus. This aspect happens every ninety-one years. In evolved individuals, it suggests the ability to funnel original and unconventional ideas into practical use and application. You're able to build on the experiences of past lives to enrich your creativity in this life. This conjunction can be found in the charts of astrologers, mathematicians, and scientists.

ALERT!

On the darker side, the conjunction of Saturn and Uranus can lead to muddled thinking, a temper that flares periodically (and is nearly impossible to control), and a lack of distinction between the real and the imagined. Someone with this conjunction must be self-aware and focused in order to stay clear of these negative influences.

Saturn Conjunct Neptune. You're clairvoyant and possess tremendous spiritual insight. You may practice meditation or yoga or study music or art. Your compassion extends to all living things. This is a lucky aspect, which usually indicates financial fortune. In strong charts, this conjunction often leads to fame and prominence.

Saturn Conjunct Pluto. With this powerful aspect, the intense Plutonian energy is structured through Saturn. This gives concrete expression to your ambitions, for which you're willing to work long, hard, and patiently. If well-aspected, the conjunction can result in truly great accomplishments. This conjunction can be compared to John Fowles's masterpiece *The Magus* because it allows you to work constructively with occult powers.

Saturn Conjunct North Node. You thrive in a conservative environment and follow protocol to the letter. With the South Node opposing, you must work to overcome your prejudices.

Saturn Conjunct South Node. You're too rigid for your own good. It holds you back professionally and personally. Loosen up or decide what it is you want and go after it!

Saturn Conjunct Ascendant. Generally, this aspect makes for a tough childhood. It may mean that at an early age you were forced to face harsh realities and to assume responsibility. Or it may mean you suffered from self-consciousness or lack of confidence at an early age. Life for you is serious business. You're responsible, a hard worker, and conscientious in all you do.

Saturn Conjunct Midheaven. You're headed for the big time, but only through hard work and perseverance. Recognition is likely to come after the age of forty.

Saturn Conjunct IC. Saturn here usually indicates an emotionally detached relationship with your parents. You feel conflicted and torn between your professional ambitions and your duty to your parents and/or family.

Strangely enough, Saturn conjuncting **IC** can lend itself to an odd twist of fate. Saturn is the taskmaster and teaches you lessons you must learn in life. Many people with this conjunct find that, later in life, they're forced to deal with the relationship with their parents—and, perhaps, must take care of one of them due to illness or injury.

Conjunctions of Uranus

Like conjunctions of Saturn, Neptune, and Pluto, conjunctions of Uranus have broad effects on generations of people because they're such slow-moving planets. This aspect of Uranus brings uniqueness and humanitarian ideals to the planets it conjuncts.

Uranus, Neptune, and Pluto are considered higher-octave planets. They're farther away than most other planets. As such, they represent how the soul's individual choices merge and meld with the shaping of nations, cultures, and the family of man.

Uranus Conjunct Neptune. This one occurs every 171 years or so. It occurred most recently in 1994, so children born under this conjunction will make incredible strides in psychic and spiritual development. They may be the ones who take computer technology light years from where it presently is. They will certainly impact life in the twenty-first century.

Uranus Conjunct Pluto. Blame this aspect for revolution. It's responsible for the overthrow of governments and the collapse of outdated belief paradigms. It comes along about every 115 years. It affects people born in 1965–

1966. If you're self-aware, this conjunction brings unimagined occult talent; if you're not, it brings all the negative Pluto power to bear.

Uranus Conjunct North Node. You're quick to spot new trends in science and technology, the arts, films, and any endeavor that deals with the masses. Your best bet is not to resist the flow; if you do, the negative tendencies of your South Node can handicap you.

Uranus Conjunct South Node. Your life is disrupted by changing mores, beliefs, and trends. Unless you roll with the punches, you're in for a tough ride.

Uranus Conjunct Ascendant. You're exceptionally bright. Your IQ may even shoot into the genius range. You're also incredibly eccentric, with unusual tastes. Your early childhood was marked by independence, freedom, and sudden and unexpected changes. You may have moved a great deal. You're tolerant of others, unless they try to restrict you in any way. If badly aspected, you may be intellectually arrogant.

Uranus Conjunct Midheaven. This aspect is good for astrologers, scientists, and occultists, and is marked by unusual work conditions. You do best as your own boss. If well-aspected, overnight success may result. But this can be followed just as quickly by obscurity. Play your cards wisely, carefully, and nurture your intuitive voice.

ESSENTIAL

If you're *lucky* enough to know that your Uranus conjuncts the Part of Fortune, then you know that your luck often comes in spurts, at unexpected moments, and probably when you need it most. If you learn to recognize synchronicities and attempt to understand what they're telling you, you'll stay ahead of the surprise game.

Uranus Conjunct IC. This conjunction is like working for IBM: the initials stand for "I've been moved." Your parents and/or home are peculiar in some way, and there are a lot of odd people coming and going. Electronic gadgets and cutting-edge computer technology may be present.

Conjunctions of Neptune

Neptune conjunctions, like those of Saturn, Uranus, and Pluto, affect generations of people. They enhance psychic and spiritual development, imagination, and intuition. They bolster artistic ability and compassion. These conjunctions are akin to Luke Skywalker's quest in the *Star Wars* trilogy. On the negative side, they bear an unsettling similarity to the darkness of Darth Vader. In other words, Neptune conjunctions can reach mythic proportions.

Neptune Conjunct Pluto. Somewhere in the twenty-fourth century, this conjunction will roll around again. It usually means spiritual revolution and rebirth with Pluto's capacity for constructive or destructive tendencies. It also usually coincides with the rise and fall of cultures and nations. On a personal basis, this aspect is sometimes found in the charts of people who are conflicted with or about their sexuality.

Neptune Conjunct North Node. Relax and follow your intuitive urges. If you do, you'll always be in the right place at the right time and make the right contacts. The challenge with the South Node is to resist the pull of the crowd. Don't get swept along with mass hysteria, whatever it concerns.

Neptune Conjunct South Node. The road with this aspect isn't always easy. You say the wrong things at the wrong times. You have trouble getting your act together. Put one foot in front of the other, maintain your individualism, and never forget that you create your own reality.

Neptune Conjunct Ascendant. In a woman's chart, she's probably a knockout. In a man's chart, he's a charmer through and through; he'll seduce you and spin your head. You've got a lot of psychic talent, but unless you develop and work with it, the talent lies latent. Guard against drug and alcohol abuse.

Neptune Conjunct Midheaven. Your career ambitions may be impractical and unrealistic. If you've got a degree in veterinary medicine, for instance, then at the age of fifty, it would be impractical to take up acting—impractical, but not impossible. And that's the point with this conjunction. Listen to your intuitive voice. Heed its guidance.

Neptune Conjunct IC. On the plus side, your spiritual passions enter your home. You're mystically inclined, with the heart of a pagan who feels a kindred link with the planet and cosmos. On the minus side, your psychic energy can be misdirected and result in hauntings, paranoia, and an obsession with séances and the black arts. You probably live near a body of water, and the larger it is, the better.

Conjunctions of Pluto

All aspects of Pluto bear a disturbing similarity to marriage vows: "for better or worse, until death do us part." The conjunction is no different. With the slowly moving planets, conjunctions tend to affect mass movements, nations, cultures, and the planet. With the rapidly moving planets, Pluto intensifies the energy.

QUESTION?

How does Pluto affect us directly?
Pluto's impact on us depends to a large degree on how consciously aware we are. In other words, the planetary energy tends to hit us in the area of our lives where we most need to change so that we can grow and evolve as spiritual beings. Pay attention to it, and you'll come out ahead!

One of the popular notions among astrologers is that Pluto aspects don't affect you personally unless Pluto is strong in your chart. This is not a hard and fast rule.

When Pluto moved into Sagittarius at the end of 1995, many people went through monumental changes in their lives. Health crisis. Financial crisis. Marriage crisis. Professional crisis. Divorce, bankruptcy, psychological or physical breakdown. Other people sailed through the transition with hardly a ripple in their lives.

Pluto Conjunct North Node. You think you've got it all figured out? Think again. Look deeper. Take nothing for granted. Scrutinize the hidden elements in your life. Seek to understand what isn't obvious, and you'll be way ahead of the game.

Pluto Conjunct South Node. You work alone to transform your life. You may be a part of mass events that wipe your security slate utterly clean, forcing you to start over again and again. And when you finally figure out the pattern, you break it and evolve.

Pluto Conjunct Ascendant. Each of us possesses the capacity for good and evil. The manifestation of one or the other depends entirely on our free will. That's what this aspect is about: free will. The development of clarity, the deliberate use of intuition to manipulate energy, and the image you project into the world define this conjunction. Many people simply can't do what it takes to master the challenges here. They give up too soon, but shouldn't.

Pluto Conjunct Midheaven. You reinvent yourself professionally and publicly, time and again, until you get the message. This powerful aspect leads to fame or notoriety, either/or. That's how Pluto works.

Pluto Conjunct IC. It's not easy, and it's not fun. But one way or another you learn to deal with change and transformation in your home life, or you will repeat this pattern over and over. And that's nothing to write home about.

Chapter 10

Squares: 90 Degrees

Squares tell a great deal about the challenges a soul chooses before it is born into physical reality. They spur us to action because the points of friction they create are difficult to ignore. Squares create a kind of terrible itch in certain areas of our lives that compels us to do something in order to change the status quo. In this chapter, find out everything you need to know about the squares we have in our charts and what they mean.

Sun Squares

Look at your own chart. What planets and houses are involved in the squares? What do these particular planets and houses tell you about yourself? How can you work with the friction to alleviate it? Sometimes a square will spur us on and make us stronger—less lazy and more willing to demand what we can from ourselves. The following are Sun squares. Note that there can never be a Sun square Mercury or Venus.

Sun Square Moon. Your conscious mind constantly battles with your emotions over what you want and how you should achieve your goals. To meet the challenge, you must bring old behavioral patterns that may have originated during your childhood to light.

Sun Square Mars. You're hot-tempered. It takes a lot to make you mad, but when you reach that flash point, you explode. You're also argumentative, passionate, and energetic. If well-aspected by Saturn, this square gives you terrific drive to achieve. Cultivate patience and learn to think before you act.

Sun Square Jupiter. You make a comfortable living, but spend money as fast as it comes in. You overindulge in everything and have great fun doing it. Your excesses may cause you problems of all sorts, particularly through ill health in later years. Your humanity, however, remains constant: you always help people in need. Learn moderation, and you'll overcome the challenges of this aspect.

Sun Square Saturn. You struggle to succeed and yet, at every turn, your efforts seem to be thwarted. But your ambition, pierced by inner friction, drives you forward. You seize on every mishap and somehow turn it to your advantage. The challenge is to recognize the difference between pride and principal. Cultivate optimism and flexibility.

Sun Square Uranus. Your powerful, creative urges often frustrate you because they come in spurts. You must develop perseverance and discipline so you can structure this force and work with it regularly. Your creative desires propel you into erratic love affairs, which usually end because they restrict your freedom in some way.

Sun Square Neptune. Self-delusion may be your undoing. Guard against mystical feelings of grandeur, avoid cults of any type, and seek to cultivate your reasoning, left-brain faculties.

ALERT!

Neptune can play with our heads and draw us into the world of the mystic and surreal. Sun square Neptune is a difficult aspect because it's easy to become prey to fantasies—they're so much simpler than real life. The true test is to avoid the temptation of sliding over to "the dark side." In fact, an affinity for secret love affairs often accompanies this aspect.

Sun Square Pluto. This one is difficult. Pluto creates so much inner friction, your need to achieve overwhelms nearly everything else in your life. But if the friction is turned inward, toward transforming the self, the darker elements in this square are greatly mitigated.

Sun Square Nodes. This aspect forms what is called a T-square. It can be a dynamic aspect, one that propels you forward. But until you understand it, it makes you feel obstructed by circumstances in your life and in society in general. To overcome this, you need to nurture the part of your life described by the house your Sun occupies.

Sun Square Ascendant. You're conflicted about projecting yourself as you really are. It creates problems in your closest relationships because no one seems to understand you. To overcome this, cultivate the area of your life described by the house the Sun occupies.

Sun Square Midheaven. You don't get along with the authority figures in your life. Your professional ambitions may be stymied somehow by your family obligations. Look to the house the Sun occupies to understand how to overcome this challenge.

Moon Squares

Moon squares often indicate unconscious blocks, prejudices, and habits that impede your emotional expression. This can affect your health, particularly in a woman's chart.

Moon Square Mercury. You talk too much. But you're so witty and glib that people usually enjoy your company anyway. The problem, though, is that you may talk about things that would be better kept to yourself. In fact, your nervous chatter gets on people's nerves sometimes. Overcome this challenge by being more circumspect in your speech.

Moon Square Venus. You feel inferior to others, and this prompts you to indulge in all sorts of detrimental habits. You spend your money foolishly, allow yourself to be taken advantage of, and aren't very sociable. With this square, there can be difficulties or delay in marriage. Think before you act, and strive to overcome your feelings of inferiority.

Moon Square Mars. You take things much too personally, which fuels your emotionally volatile nature. Your independence often runs to the extreme, creating problems with your parents when you were younger and with your own family later. Avoid alcohol and drugs. If you need to relieve stress, follow an exercise regimen.

FACT

According to accomplished astrologer Grant Lewi, a Moon square Mars will often manifest itself as early as childhood. Other aspects won't necessarily be so pronounced so early on. This aspect shows itself as precociousness in early childhood.

Moon Square Jupiter. You're a sucker for a sob story. You go overboard with everyone you love and even with people you don't know. But you can afford your extravagances because you believe you'll always have more than you need. The challenge here is to overcome your appetites and excesses.

Moon Square Saturn. Astrologers generally view this aspect unfavorably, saying that it leads to depression, melancholy, and emotional coldness. But Grant Lewi has a different take on it: "This is perhaps the most powerful single aspect you can have in a horoscope. It gives both ambition and the ability to concentrate on it." He acknowledges that it's accompanied by bouts of moodiness and depression. But he believes the aspect is so powerful that, if it's bolstered by any other favorable aspect, "it will produce success along some line or other."

ESSENTIAL

No single aspect makes or breaks a chart. With this square, you need to look at how it fits with the rest of the horoscope. In one person, this square may very well lead to depression and ill health. But in someone else, it can be the trigger that galvanizes the individual to great professional heights.

Moon Square Uranus. You're emotionally restless, flitting from one thing to another in search of the ultimate. The problem is that you haven't defined what the ultimate is for you. Your talents are exceptional and reflect your individualism. External circumstances sometimes toss you a curve ball: a sudden accident or illness or involvement in some natural disaster. These events are your signposts. Once you understand what they're trying to tell you about yourself and your life, you break the pattern.

Moon Square Neptune. You're a daydreamer who spins wonderful tales and fantasies. But you're so impractical, you don't know how to make these flights of fancy into concrete achievements. You feel emotionally confused much of the time. You need to ground yourself, set goals, and get moving with your life. Don't surrender your imagination, instead channel it in constructive ways.

Moon Square Pluto. Don't be so intense! Life isn't always an either/or proposition. You don't have to burn your bridges with your family and intimates just to make a point. Use your psychic abilities and intense emotions to bring about a more gradual change in your life.

Moon Square Nodes. This T-square configuration urges you to overcome emotional or unconscious habits and prejudices. Until you do, you run into problems with women and can't fulfill your ambitions.

Moon Square Ascendant. You have trouble expressing yourself emotionally. As a result, you experience difficulties in partnerships, marriages, and with your family. If you can become aware of your habitual attitudes and patterns of behavior, you're on your way to breaking them and freeing yourself.

Moon Square Midheaven and IC. Domestic problems seem to get in the way of your professional ambitions. This leads to frustration, which only compounds the original problems. The source of the trouble isn't external. It lies somewhere in your unconscious behavioral patterns. In fact, this is what other people respond to.

Moon Square Part of Fortune. Your emotional frustration detracts from the areas of life in which you're lucky. Dig deep within to find the habitual patterns that are holding you back.

Mercury Squares

These squares create friction, intellectually, through all types of communication. They also create friction with siblings and neighbors. Look to the houses and signs to understand where the intellectual abilities aren't being developed to their fullest. Mercury and Venus can only form a conjunction and a sextile because they are never 47 degrees away from each other.

Mercury Square Mars. Your sharp tongue often borders on outright rudeness. It tends to alienate the very people whose support you need. Your mind is equally sharp but as undisciplined as your way of speaking. Take time to gather the facts and plan what you're going to say before you say it. After all, being argumentative doesn't get you very far.

Mercury Square Jupiter. You would make a terrific fiction writer or tribal storyteller. Your mind is rich and imaginative, but your judgment is often flawed because you either misinterpret or don't have all the facts. The best way to overcome the challenges of this aspect is through education, books, and any kind of mental training.

Mercury Square Saturn. You're a thinker with a profound mind able to grasp complex issues. But you think and worry too much, dwelling on past injustices and injuries. This may create negative and prejudicial attitudes that ultimately hold you back. You're not always selfish, but the tendency exists. If it's perpetuated, you may become one of those people who believe the end justifies the means.

In order to overcome the challenge of this Mercury Square Saturn, you need to break with your habitual patterns. In other words, you must release the past. Forgive people who have injured you. Strive to consider other people's feelings before you act. This will make your life so much better.

Mercury Square Uranus. Mentally, you're way ahead of the pack. Your insight can be brilliant and original. Your entire thought process is radical and independent but sometimes so unfocused that your energy ends up scattered and wasted. At times you can be so obstinate about your opinions that it borders on intellectual conceit. You can be tactless, which alienates others. You're always in a hurry to get things done. To overcome this challenge, slow down, think before you act and speak, and try to see things the way the other guy does. Don't jump to conclusions.

Mercury Square Neptune. This aspect favors fiction writing, particularly of the mystical variety. It also gives insight into the motives and behaviors of other people, which is helpful in creating interesting fictional characters. Writing or art are constructive ways to channel the challenges of this square, which lends itself to confused thinking and unreliability. Psychic talent is usually evident with this aspect, but it needs to be developed and funneled constructively.

Mercury Square Pluto. You're able to assess a given situation swiftly and accurately. No one puts anything over on you. You're secretive, but when you've got something to say, you don't mince words. Your willpower is well developed, and you may try to force your ideas on others. You don't take anything anyone says at face value; you need to prove the truth to yourself. To conquer this aspect, you need to be less suspicious of others, to speak your mind more gently, and to turn your willpower toward improving yourself.

Mercury Square Nodes. Think before you speak. Otherwise, you may speak at the wrong time and will be sorely misunderstood. Take a deeper interest in the world you inhabit; an awareness of current trends improves your professional ambitions.

Mercury Square Ascendant. It's difficult for you to express yourself. It's not that you lack talent or don't know what you want to say—it's the way you go about it. You benefit from training in speech and writing, through education, workshops, and anything that provides a structure. This, in turn, improves your relationships with the people in your life.

Mercury Square Midheaven. Your communications skills are flawed, and this creates disharmony at home and on the job. The misunderstandings that result make you miserable. Seek educational training in these areas. Apply your natural talent. The change in your life may shock you.

Venus Squares

These squares generally create friction in relationships. They also affect finances: the way you spend and the way you regard money, in general.

Venus squares can also indicate enhanced artistic ability. They also show you the lessons you need to learn and grow from in love.

Venus Square Mars. Your strong passions are attracted to the wrong kinds of people. You often find yourself in stormy romantic relationships that go nowhere. You use other people for sexual gratification or you are used yourself. Your spending habits and extravagances lead you into financial troubles. To overcome the challenge of this square, you must cultivate temperance and balance.

Venus Square Jupiter. You're seduced by the pleasures in life and tend to be extravagant in everything you do. Your emotions may lack depth, but people are drawn to your expansive, affectionate nature. In a woman's chart, this square spells vanity and expenses in maintaining her physical appearance. In a man's chart, there's a certain egotism with physical appearance. To overcome the challenge of this square, you need to pull back from your life and scrutinize it with detachment.

Venus Square Saturn. Your fear of poverty may be related to past lives in which you had nothing. This fear colors everything you do and feel. Your basic nature alternates between seriousness and a certain melancholy, particularly when you're intimately involved with someone. The bottom line is that you're probably at your best when you're alone. You desperately want a place of your own—a house, land, or a sanctuary. To overcome this challenge, bring your fears to the surface and deal with them.

Venus Square Uranus. Your love life is marked by sudden changes, abrupt beginnings and endings, and unusual, sudden attractions. You're constantly seeking the excitement of new romances, but the second the relationship infringes on your freedom, you split. You need to honestly assess what you're looking for in life and pursue it diligently, and with forethought.

FACT

Here's a strange little astrology tidbit: Many astrologers have claimed that Venus Square Uranus could actually indicate homosexuality if the fifth house is also aspected. But it doesn't always refer to this. It can also indicate some sort of unusual marriage arrangement. Astrologers have long studied these odd patterns.

Venus Square Neptune. Your artistic abilities are excellent and can provide you with a creative outlet for much of the friction caused by this square. Your imagination is fueled by the forbidden, and, as a result, you may get involved in secret love affairs. Bisexuality is a possibility with this aspect, if other factors in the horoscope support it. You need to come to terms with what you need emotionally, and then try to create it in your life.

Venus Square Pluto. Your sexual passions nearly swallow up the rest of your life. You attract people who may be involved in illegal activities. In extreme cases, this aspect indicates prostitution, criminal tendencies, and sex-related crimes. This square doesn't favor harmonious marriages or partnerships.

Venus Square Nodes. In social situations, your emotional reactions are inappropriate. You're the proverbial fish swimming upstream against social norms.

Venus Square Ascendant. You're rarely satisfied with your close relationships or your marriage partner. You need to develop insight into your own motives and needs and strive to communicate those needs.

Venus Square Midheaven. Somehow, your career and home life always seem to conflict with your social and artistic needs and desires. Get rid of the chip on your shoulder, and strive to improve your behavioral patterns.

Venus Square Part of Fortune. Your romantic inclinations and financial habits can cause setbacks in your life.

Mars Squares

This aspect creates friction due to rash and impulsive speech and behavior. It also triggers intense and often focused activity and ambition as well as some sexual concerns. By seizing the energy of Mars and using it constructively, this square can be conquered. It's often found in the horoscopes of successful people.

Mars Square Jupiter. Moderation will take you much farther than the financial and emotional gambles you take now. Slow down and don't count so heavily on your luck, because when it runs out, you'll be up against the consequences of your actions. Your life is screaming for moderation. This aspect, incidentally, is often found in the charts of people who support war.

Mars Square Saturn. Your judgment is flawed. You either overestimate your abilities, your luck, or both. Grant Lewi calls this square "the aspect of fortunes made and lost." Emotionally, your aloofness translates as outright coldness to others. You're seen as austere, and even harsh. Lighten up on yourself, and control your temper. Go out and have some fun!

Mars Square Uranus. Your temper can be so explosive and fierce that it threatens to overtake your entire personality. Sudden, unpredictable events disrupt your plans. There's a thrill-seeking element to this square that manifests itself in dangerous sports and in taking physical risks. If you're not very careful, you can get seriously hurt, or even die from your throw-caution-to-the-wind attitude. Watch out!

Mars Square Neptune. This aspect is often found in the charts of astrologers and psychologists because it allows insight into deep, unconscious patterns. Your active imagination seeks expression through art, music, and dance, all of which are excellent vehicles for the mystical and psychic inclinations of this aspect.

Escapism—addiction to relieve stress and boredom—can be prevalent with Mars Square Neptune. It is highly recommended that those with this square focus on the more healthy practices in life and make sure to avoid alcohol, drugs and even cults. Control and direct your imagination. It's highly attuned. Use it wisely.

Mars Square Pluto. This aspect is a double punch because both planets are associated with Scorpio. Your sex drive and aggression are pronounced. When something pushes one of your buttons, your temper can be explosive. When you refuse to acknowledge the friction of this square, it finds expression in some other area of your life, thus forcing you to change. In self-aware individuals, however, this square provides the impetus for great accomplishments.

Mars Square Nodes. If you control your anger and get rid of your resentment, you're able to use the energy of Mars more constructively.

Mars Square Ascendant. You can't bully your way through life and expect to be viewed as a paragon of gentleness and diplomacy. You need to learn tact and cooperation or your partnerships and marriage will be filled with discord.

Mars Square Midheaven. You bring your work problems home with you, which creates disputes and arguments with your family. Stop being an agitator. Think before you speak.

Jupiter Squares

These squares are similar to those with the Part of Fortune. They tend to hinder the beneficial aspects of the planet. This aspect can also indicate legal problems, obstacles or difficulties in higher education, and all things associated with Jupiter.

Jupiter Square Saturn. Aim higher. Your goals are too limited, narrow, and restrictive. Part of the problem is that you don't imagine yourself achieving more than what you already have. You get discouraged too easily by setbacks and obstacles that you run into. You would certainly benefit from workshops in self-confidence, visualization, and using your imagination to succeed.

Jupiter Square Uranus. Your ideas and imagination are impressive but impractical. You love to gamble in a big way with investments, real estate, or business deals. You would be better off curbing this impulse because you might lose your shirt. You're too impulsive. You may be drawn to eccentric religions or spiritual belief systems. Your restlessness sends you off on countless travels and adventures.

Jupiter Square Neptune. Your wanderlust propels you into foreign countries: the more exotic, the better. If you were born into money, you won't hold onto it for long. You usually promise more than you can deliver, but people like you in spite of it because your nature is generous and kind. To overcome the challenge of this square, you need to cultivate pragmatism.

Jupiter Square Pluto. You're dogmatic about religious and spiritual issues. Your beliefs are so inflexible that you have no tolerance for people who don't believe as you do. Power is vital to your well-being and how it manifests depends on the house placement in your chart.

Jupiter Square Nodes. Your religious beliefs and educational experiences aren't in step with the prevalent societal trends. Take steps to correct this, and your life in general will be much simpler and easier.

Jupiter Square Ascendant. You don't know when to keep quiet. People perceive you as bombastic and perhaps intellectually arrogant. You try to do too much at once and, consequently, end up doing few things well. Learn to focus on one thing at a time and cultivate humility.

Jupiter Square Midheaven and IC. You have a large family and a large home, both of which place heavy financial burdens on you. Strive to be realistic about your abilities.

Saturn Squares

Discipline, patience, and perseverance are the cornerstones of Saturn squares. The friction created isn't easy to deal with, but if you learn the lessons, tremendous inner strength and resilience results.

Saturn Square Uranus. Talk about dichotomy! Saturn imposes discipline, while Uranus screams for freedom. You're constantly confronted with situations that require thought and consideration, but the Uranian influence chafes at the restraints.

With Saturn square Uranus, you're swimming against the current. Balance is necessary and will help you tremendously. Also, your incredible inventiveness and originality with this aspect actually need limitations and discipline to flourish. Control your hot temper if you want to reap the benefits of your madcap creativity.

Saturn Square Neptune. Lack of ambition characterizes this square. It's not that you can't do what you set your mind to; it's simply that you don't feel like exerting yourself. You may try to escape the uglier realities of life through drugs or alcohol or some other form of escapism. Your best bet in overcoming this square is to find something that stirs your passions. Plan on how you can attain it, and go after it.

Saturn Square Pluto. Your hunger for power may be acute. You may be involved in schemes, plots, and intrigues—the stuff of spy novels. Maybe you need the drama; maybe you simply don't know anything else. To conquer the friction of this square, you need to attempt to change.

Saturn Square Nodes. Your selfishness and outdated prejudices hold back your development. Honest self-appraisal helps overcome the challenges of this square.

Saturn Square Ascendant. Others probably see you as somewhat aloof, maybe even cold. This is certainly true when strangers intrude on your time or people make unreasonable demands. It may also be why you choose to limit your close friendships. Learn to structure your time so that your life is more balanced.

Saturn Square Midheaven. Your home life as a child was probably rigid and overly disciplined. As an adult, your responsibilities to your own family and parents may block or delay your career ambitions.

Uranus Squares

These squares affect generations of people. Their impact on personal horoscopes depends on whether Uranus is prevalent in the chart. This also deals with social interactions and the choices of personal freedom. Remember that Uranus deals with original thinkers and the outrageously unique.

Uranus Square Neptune. Think rebellion, pioneers, idealism, and psychic talent. The generation born under this aspect (1950s) faces tremendous social upheaval and emotional confusion. Their lives are disrupted by wars, catastrophes, and major disasters. On a personal level, peculiar circumstances seem to plague your life. Your thinking can be muddled and confused.

Uranus Square Pluto. Worldwide, this suggests upheaval, fanaticism, and massive destruction. Hardly the kind of stuff you want to write home about. The generations born under this aspect (1930s) are now in their sixties and seventies and have faced drastic social upheaval in their lives.

FACT

On a personal level, with Uranus square Pluto there can be a need to reform and change the established order of things in general. Note that this aspect is strange because those who have it may have a strange relationship with money. Even if you're born into money, for example, you may never feel completely secure.

Uranus Square Nodes. You don't think much of traditions. You're a non-conformist at heart, but at times you take it so far you alienate the very people who could be helpful.

Uranus Square Ascendant. You want to be unpredictable and rebellious, but don't expect other people to love you for it. Your personal life would improve immeasurably if you learned to be cooperative with the people you care about. If you don't change, your intimate relationships aren't going to improve at all.

Uranus Square Midheaven and IC. You bounce around a lot by changing jobs and moving frequently. You're forever seeking the elusive job or relationship that won't restrict your personal freedom. Step back, detach, and honestly evaluate what you're doing and why.

Neptune Squares

Like the squares of the other slower-moving planets, Neptune squares affect generations and impact a personal chart primarily if Neptune figures prominently in the chart. Problems arise through idealism and seeing the harsh facts with rose-colored glasses, in order to avoid dealing with reality. Neptune influences can be sadly misleading.

Neptune Square Pluto. There's no getting around it: This is an ugly aspect. It last occurred in the early 1800s and will roll around again in the twenty-first century. It indicates the breakdown of society and the general collapse of the old paradigms and belief systems. Spiritual bankruptcy and moral depravity are in the cards with this one.

Neptune Square Nodes. Cultivate practicality and bring your mystical daydreams back to Earth. Stop drifting and dig in your heels. Set goals.

E ALERT!

Node squares, themselves, act as distractions in whatever areas they affect. They often offer penetrating insights into issues we would rather avoid. With node squares, you tend to blame other people for the things that go wrong in your life. As soon as you understand that you create your own reality, that you are completely responsible for yourself, you'll be on the way to vanquishing distractions.

Neptune Square Ascendant. You don't mean to be deceptive or unreliable, but you often are. As a result, you attract people who reflect these traits in yourself. Be more aware of what you say, what you promise, and how you act. Cultivate honesty in yourself. Don't take criticism so personally.

Neptune Square Midheaven and IC. Your professional and home lives are most likely in a constant state of confusion and turmoil. You need to set goals, which is often the case with these squares. Find your passions and try to channel them more constructively.

Pluto Squares

Expect the usual heavy Pluto stuff with this aspect. With any Pluto aspect, go back to the root meaning of the planet: transformation—the collapse and end of the old and beginning of the new. This also deals with regeneration, rebirth, and tough lessons that need to be learned.

Pluto Square Nodes. By adjusting to the nuances of pop culture and current trends, you overcome the darker aspects of this square. Everything doesn't have to be a life or death issue.

Pluto Square Ascendant. You're too aggressive and demanding in your personal relationships. You would do better trying persuasion than coercion to get what you want. This lesson may hit home when you're not very high on the corporate pecking ladder and have to take orders from others.

Pluto Square Midheaven and IC. You rebel against all authority figures: parents, law-enforcement officials, employers, and the government. You want to reinvent everything, to transform existing institutions, and you probably want to do it out of some lust for power. You need to reassess your life and evaluate where you're going.

Chapter 11

Sextiles and Trines: 60 and 120 Degrees

S extiles—60-degree angles—symbolize ease and provide a buffer against instability. Trines—angles of 120 degrees—are similar but relate more to inner harmony and a state of equilibrium. Sextiles and trines to the Nodes, Ascendant, Midheaven, and **IC** are so similar that it makes sense to discuss them together. In this chapter, find out all you need to know about these intriguing aspects and how they affect you and your life.

Sun Sextiles and Trines

Sextiles to the Sun pinpoint areas in which your abilities can be expressed positively; they often represent opportunities. Trines to the Sun enhance self-expression and generally indicate harmony in the affairs associated with the planets that form the sextile and trines.

Sun Sextile Moon. You get along well with people. Try to help them when you can, and they, in turn, will do the same for you. You're successful working with the public and have the communication skills to do it well.

Sun Trine Moon. You attempt to create the kind of harmony in your home that you knew in your childhood. The smooth flow between your unconscious and conscious desires helps you to achieve what you want and need. If there's any drawback to these aspects at all, it's that, at times, your life is so generally happy that you become apathetic.

Sun Sextile Mars. You have seemingly endless energy. Your creative ideas usually find expression in some form because you're forceful about achieving them. But you don't step on anyone else's toes to accomplish what you want. You respect other people for their talents and abilities.

Sun Trine Mars. Your physical vitality keeps you moving long after your competitors have gone to bed for the night. Your magnetic personality and decisiveness draw people to you. You may follow some sort of exercise program that maintains your stamina and bolsters your already considerable physical strength. Good leadership abilities come with this trine.

Sun Sextile Jupiter. You have high ideals, lofty aspirations, and numerous opportunities throughout your life to manifest what you want. Your self-expression usually comes through the house that Jupiter occupies.

Sun Trine Jupiter. Luck, optimism, and financial prosperity usually accompany this trine. You have tremendous creative potential, but you may not do much with it unless squares and oppositions in your chart create sufficient friction and tension. Your personal integrity is probably without equal.

FACT

Well-known astrologer Grant Lewi made a classic remark about the aspect of Sun trine Jupiter: "No poet with this aspect ever starved in a garret or anywhere else, for that matter." In other words, financial luck and creativity go hand in hand with this aspect.

Sun Sextile Saturn. Your ambition won't ever exclude everything else in your life. You plan carefully, take your work seriously, and structure your life so that everything is judiciously balanced. You achieve through your own efforts.

Sun Trine Saturn. You have great self-confidence, abundant talent, and luck. Your parents or the people responsible for you are probably older than the norm and have shielded you from hardships. Opportunities often come to you. Combined with a Moon/Mars conjunction, those opportunities either drop into your lap out of nowhere or you create them.

Sun Sextile Uranus. Your personality is charismatic, magnetic, and often forceful. You're deeply intuitive, which gives you valuable insight into other people. You don't pay much attention to traditions. You prefer going your own way, even if others consider it eccentric. This aspect is often found in the charts of people who are interested in or practice astrology.

Sun Trine Uranus. You're an original and progressive thinker whom other people want to know simply because you're so different. Things happen around you. Your perception of reality is broad and profound; you never lose sight of the larger picture.

Sun Sextile Neptune. Much of your inspiration rises from the deeper levels of your psyche and flows easily into your conscious thought. It's as if a conduit exists between the psychic activity in your unconscious and yourself—the person who participates daily in the world. Your creativity is considerable and, with a little effort on your part, can flourish and bloom.

Sun Trine Neptune. If you aren't self-employed now, then you should take steps in that direction because you don't work well under others. You need to create and express yourself in some artistic way, and you have profound creative talent that needs to be expressed. If your talent doesn't find expression, the block can create health problems. You're very psychic. In fact, much of your knowledge comes to you this way even if you don't realize it.

With Sun trine Neptune, your sleeping mind is psychically active, with vivid, colorful dreams. The dreams bubble up from the deeper levels of your psyche. Work with them and strive to understand them. They will provide you with an endless supply of answers and guidance.

Sun Sextile Pluto. Deep within, answers and information are available to you. Once you're able to access this profound level, you'll understand why your will is so powerful and how you can use it to achieve what you want. You need to communicate what you know and sense. You evolve through creative expression.

Sun Trine Pluto. You're the person who brings friends and loved ones back from the brink of chaos. You help restore order to their lives. You would excel at any profession where you can do this for other people. Your willpower is considerable; you're a natural leader. Always listen to your intuition before you act.

Sun Sextile or Trine Nodes. You do just fine in most circumstances, with most people. Conditions, overall, in your life are helpful to you. With very little effort, you overcome whatever holds you back.

Sun Sextile or Trine Ascendant. You don't have much of a problem expressing who you are. You're honest in your dealings with other people and don't tolerate dishonesty from others. You're a natural optimist, which helps bring about the many opportunities you experience in life. Your personal relationships are harmonious, and, because you cooperate with others, you're able to achieve what you want.

Sun Sextile or Trine Midheaven and IC. Your family is helpful to your professional ambitions and success. They support your efforts completely, which is part of why both your professional and domestic lives are so harmonious.

FACT

The reason that Venus and Mercury are not listed in this section is that it is impossible for the Sun to form a sextile or trine with these planets. The reason is that both Venus and Mercury are too close to the Sun to make a sextile or trine.

Moon Sextiles and Trines

These aspects deal with the expression of emotion, early childhood, and your relationship with your mother and women in general. They also focus on the harmony within your own home, certain qualities of memory, and intuition.

Moon Sextile Mercury. Your memory is excellent. Your emotions and mind operate together in complete harmony. Your communication skills are highly developed, and you can use them in virtually any profession you choose. This aspect favors writers or others who use communications skills professionally and may also work out of their homes.

Moon Trine Mercury. You have a lot of common sense, and you're a quick learner. Your ability to recall past events is nothing short of remarkable, but you're not hung up in the past. You communicate well, especially with members of your family. This is a good aspect for people who work with their hands.

Moon Sextile Venus. You have abundant charm and a generous nature. Your artistic interests and inclinations are considerable. In a man's chart, you get along well with women and benefit from your partnerships with them. In a woman's chart, you are sociable and affectionate. This also indicates fertility and a fulfilling, happy marriage.

Moon Trine Venus. Financial prosperity and an element of luck go along with this aspect. It indicates that you're charming, refined, and physically attractive. You enjoy being surrounded by beautiful things. You're an optimist, love children, and want or have kids of your own. Harmonious marriage is indicated.

Moon Sextile Mars. You're an emotionally charged individual whose energy and vitality propel you through whatever needs to be done. You may flare up occasionally, particularly if you're provoked, but you generally don't hold grudges. You're known as a person who gets things done.

Moon Trine Mars. You have good control over your emotions and passions and a quick, sharp intellect. Your emotions and your mind are rarely at odds. Your self-confidence and ease with the public is impressive and helps you to achieve your ambitions.

Moon Sextile Jupiter. Your hunches and gut feelings about situations and people are usually right on target. You have an enormous storehouse of experiential knowledge and an excellent memory. You nearly always recognize the good in people.

Moon Trine Jupiter. Unconscious urges may prompt you toward foreign travel where you seek evidence of ancient cultures or your own past-life connections with these places. Your spiritual leanings, whether orthodox or unconventional, form an intricate part of your inner life.

With Moon trine your Jupiter, your optimistic outlook and charitable nature may inspire others to do great things. This aspect also usually indicates a happy, satisfying family life and financial prosperity.

Moon Sextile Saturn. Your patience and insight allow you to understand the inner workings of personal relationships. You're able to structure your unconscious feelings so that you work with them consciously, with awareness. You have excellent business sense.

Moon Trine Saturn. You're reserved and cautious by nature, but you don't allow this to hold you back. You change when it's time to change. You're loyal to your family and friends, who return that loyalty to you. You're able to structure your creative impulses into practical projects.

Moon Sextile Uranus. You embrace change and use it to your advantage. Your heightened intuition allows you to quickly grasp the intricate workings of any situation. You're different from other people, but that has never bothered you.

Moon Trine Uranus. Your magnetic personality attracts stimulating people. You're a progressive thinker whose timing is usually so acute that you know instinctively when to seize an opportunity. The past holds meaning for you only in terms of what you learned from it; the future interests you far more. This aspect often indicates involvement with metaphysical groups. An interest in astrology often shows up with this trine.

Moon Sextile Neptune. Your imagination and psychic ability are equally strong and fuel each other. This is an excellent aspect for fiction writers, physicians, and psychic healers. Your memory may be photographic.

Moon Trine Neptune. Expression in dance, art, music, theater, acting, and writing are particularly strong with this aspect. Your nature is fundamentally spiritual, imaginative, gentle, and compassionate.

Moon Sextile Pluto. Somehow, you're always able to regenerate yourself through your emotions. You draw on the deepest levels of your psyche to find the answers or create the opportunities you need whenever you need them. This aspect suggests great purpose and a sense of destiny.

Moon Trine Pluto. Your emotional intensity is well-controlled and channeled constructively. You use it, consciously or unconsciously, to evolve spiritually. Others recognize this quality in you and gravitate toward you because of it.

Moon Sextile or Trine Nodes. Although you remember the injuries of the past, they don't hold you back. You learned from them and embrace your future. Your instincts rarely fail. Cultivate your inner voice.

Moon Sextile or Trine Ascendant. You're sensitive to criticism, but as you get older you begin to understand why. You have a good sense of the public pulse and take advantage of it. Your sensitivity to other people's feelings helps you to get along with just about anyone. Your family and intimate partnerships are vital to your emotional and physical well-being.

Moon Sextile or Trine Midheaven and IC. Pay attention to the synchronicities in your life; they'll guide you to fulfillment. Women and family members are helpful to your career and support your professional ambitions. The trine usually strengthens the changes for professional success.

Mercury Sextiles and Trines

These aspects provide opportunities for intellectual development and communication skills. They're excellent for professional writers, speakers, and people in public relationships or politics.

Mercury Sextile or Trine Venus. You're gifted in both speech and writing and have refined artistic tastes. Your lively intellect and gentle nature instill your life and relationships with harmony. Mercury and Venus are never far enough away from each other to form a trine.

Mercury Sextile or Trine Mars. Mental energy is what you're about. You're decisive, intellectually quick and agile, and able to finish what you start. This aspect favors professional writers, sports strategists, and professional speakers or politicians.

Actually, the aspect of Mercury sextile or trine Mars is good for anyone involved in organizations. You're good at becoming part of a unit. Strangely enough, many astrologers claim that people with this aspect usually follow some sort of exercise program with a high rate of success.

Mercury Sextile or Trine Jupiter. You respect the truth, whatever its guise. You're an unbiased individual with broad intellectual interests. You teach and are involved in publishing, writing, universities, or religious/spiritual organizations. You enjoy foreign travel because it expands your understanding of the world.

Mercury Sextile or Trine Saturn. You're intuitive but practical. Your mind is finely balanced, your thought processes are structured, and you have the discipline to create whatever it is you want out of life. So go for it.

Mercury Sextile or Trine Uranus. When supported by other factors in the horoscope, these aspects suggest brilliance. Your thinking is well beyond the scope of the present, but you're somehow able to bring your advanced ideas into the here and now and communicate them. Your intuition and psychic awareness are well-developed.

Mercury Sextile or Trine Neptune. Your psychic ability fuses seamlessly with your imagination, allowing you access to deep spiritual realms. Poets sometimes have this aspect as do novelists, shamans, mystics, composers, and spiritual speakers.

Mercury Sextile or Trine Pluto. Words are your gift. You transform and regenerate yourself through your intellectual resources and communication skills. Your profound insight into the nature of reality allows you to achieve luminous success.

Mercury Sextile or Trine Nodes. You've earned an intellectual ease through efforts in other lives. In this life, you use these gifts to overcome any limitations or restrictions that hold you back.

Mercury Sextile or Trine Ascendant. Your wit and self-confidence attract friends and allies who reflect your intellectual interests. You work hard at expressing your creativity, and it's likely that if you persevere, you'll make money at it.

Mercury Sextile or Trine Midheaven and IC. The people you care about most understand exactly who you are and what you're trying to do. They support your professional ambitions and urge you to follow and achieve your dreams.

Mercury Sextile or Trine Part of Fortune. You achieve your greatest success by evolving intellectually.

Venus Sextiles and Trines

These aspects signify opportunities related to social, financial, artistic, and romantic issues. They also indicate expression in these areas, as well as artistic ability.

Venus Sextile or Trine Mars. You get along well with the opposite sex. Your romantic relationships, partnerships, and marriage are harmonious and satisfying. A lot of energy goes into your creative pursuits. You may even work with your spouse or significant other in some sort of artistic endeavor or business.

ALERT!

People with their Venus sextile or trine their Mars enjoy making money almost as much as they enjoy spending it. In fact, this can be a big problem! Spending all the considerable money that they earn can be a huge downfall. The advice here, with this aspect, is that one should probably start stashing some of it away—and stop throwing it to the wind.

Venus Sextile or Trine Jupiter. This lucky financial aspect allows you to attract wealth and ample opportunities for making money. It indicates a happy marriage and prosperous partnerships. You're admired by your peers and recognized in some way for your artistic ability.

Venus Sextile or Trine Saturn. Your social activities revolve around your business concerns. You're thrifty about money, but not penurious, and have numerous business opportunities to increase your financial base. You don't jump into partnerships, especially romantic relationships. But when you do commit, the marriage is stable though not particularly demonstrative.

Venus Sextile or Trine Uranus. You're very attractive to the opposite sex and get involved in a variety of stimulating romantic affairs. You fall in love quickly, but your affairs end just as abruptly, usually without rancor on either side. You benefit through involvement in groups, which may include e-mail news groups and online chat groups. Unusual people are attracted to you.

Venus Sextile or Trine Neptune. Compassion, artistic ability, and spiritual depth are indicated by this aspect. There are usually karmic ties with the marriage partner, who is apt to be gentle and refined. This aspect quite often suggests great wealth, especially when combined with any Venus or Mars conjunctions with Jupiter. There's usually considerable clairvoyant ability with this aspect.

Venus Sextile or Trine Pluto. Love is your vehicle for transformation and regeneration. You listen to your intuition and follow its guidance, particularly in romantic issues. You have a strong sex drive. This aspect also is often indicative of an inheritance and of material benefits in general.

FACT

With Venus sextile or trine Pluto, love and serendipity tend to take hold. For instance, when you do commit to someone, it's because you share a mutual depth of love and have many interests in common, but there may be a sense of destiny connected with the relationship, too.

Venus Sextile or Trine Nodes. Through your social contacts, you find the opportunities you need when you need them. You're very conscious of proper social conduct and protocol, which allows you to overcome the restriction of the South Node.

Venus Sextile or Trine Ascendant. Your physical beauty is enhanced by innate grace and charm, particularly in a woman's horoscope. You probably have considerable musical or artistic talent.

Venus Sextile or Trine Midheaven and IC. Through your physical graces and social contacts, you further your ambitions. Your home reflects your personal harmony and beauty and is often a social meeting place. For artists, this aspect usually indicates professional recognition.

Venus Sextile or Trine Part of Fortune. Financial prosperity and recognition of some sort comes through your social contacts.

Mars Sextiles and Trines

These aspects help channel energy and drive in positive, constructive directions. The planets and houses that are aspected indicate the areas of development that are enhanced.

Mars Sextile or Trine Jupiter. Physical strength, a muscular body, and integrity are indicated by this aspect. Your optimism and enthusiasm infuse your ambitions and provide you with many opportunities to realize your dreams. These aspects usually suggest eminent achievements in your chosen field.

Mars Sextile or Trine Saturn. You're a relentless worker, particularly in the pursuit of your ambitions and dreams. You're able to structure your considerable energy and creative ability to achieve what you want. Your sex drive is strong, but more controlled than in most Mars aspects.

Mars Sextile or Trine Uranus. Your courage and daring extend to all areas of your life. In your profession, you don't hesitate to try progressive but unproved methods to attain results. Once you reach one goal, you embark on a new journey with new goals.

With this aspect, in your personal life, you're an explorer in the truest sense of the word. In other words, the need to explore affects your sex life and your need to travel. People with this aspect are usually sexually uninhibited and enjoy exotic travel to foreign countries—off the beaten path.

Mars Sextile or Trine Neptune. You're compassionate, gentle, and blessed with spiritual insight. You would benefit from meditation, yoga, bodybuilding, and a vegetarian lifestyle. Your acute psychic ability alerts you to opportunities in finances and the arts that enhance your professional ambitions. You're secretive but honest. Your creativity may manifest in dance, music, or competitive sports.

Mars Sextile or Trine Pluto. With this aspect, the house ruled by Pluto in the chart will pinpoint the area of life most likely to be affected. Your enormously powerful will can bring about immense and drastic change in your life through which you evolve spiritually. Your insight into deep mysteries about the nature of reality is keen and profound. In self-aware individuals, these aspects indicate metaphysical knowledge that can be used to benefit humanity.

Mars Sextile or Trine Nodes. Your timing is usually on target. This aspect favors politicians and celebrities whose lives are public. Your dynamic personality attracts people who aid you in your endeavors.

Mars Sextile or Trine Ascendant. Your directness impresses other people. You're physically strong and your health is good.

Mars Sextile or Trine Midheaven and IC. You have numerous opportunities to advance yourself professionally. Your career is solid and dynamic and so is your home life. You may work out of your home.

Mars Sextile or Trine Part of Fortune. Your drive to achieve pays off because your ambitions are directed, funneled, singular. Your physical stamina and health are generally strengthened with this aspect.

Jupiter Sextiles and Trines

These aspects usually imply success and prosperity in the areas governed by Jupiter: law, publishing, religion and spiritual issues, higher education, foreign travel and cultures. The trines in particular are like built-in safeguards that mitigate other less fortunate aspects to Jupiter.

Jupiter Sextile or Trine Uranus. This is a karmic aspect in that you receive unexpected windfalls of money or opportunities. Your insight is highly developed and alerts you when to seize opportunities that other people miss. You travel suddenly and unexpectedly and have unusual experiences abroad that expand your perceptions of what is possible.

FACT

Those with Jupiter sextile or trine Uranus usually have defined views of the world. Their political beliefs lean toward the very liberal. Their spiritual inclinations, too, are more unconventional and metaphysical than orthodox and conservative.

Jupiter Sextile or Trine Neptune. This mystical aspect often finds expression in spiritual studies and attainment. The knowledge, thanks to the expansive nature of Jupiter, is usually shared with others. Spiritual practices like yoga and meditation may be practiced. In evolved people, this aspect can indicate a benevolence that approaches that of a Mother Teresa.

Jupiter Sextile or Trine Pluto. This is one instance in which the darker attributes of Pluto are absent. Your tremendous willpower and finely honed psychic ability indicate that you can emerge as a spiritual leader. You act on your spiritual convictions and are capable of instigating the kind of change that affects the masses.

Jupiter Sextile or Trine Nodes. Whatever direction your life takes is in keeping with your soul's intent. You have opportunities to correct the excesses or mistakes in past lives.

Jupiter Sextile or Trine Ascendant. This aspect attracts the things we all seek: good luck and health, happy marriages, and prosperous partnerships. Your optimism and humor attract loyal friends and supporters.

Jupiter Sextile or Trine Midheaven and IC. This is another one of those incredible aspects that indicates outstanding professional success and a happy domestic life. If you've got this aspect, consider yourself blessed.

Jupiter Sextile or Trine Part of Fortune. This aspect suggests material benefits, spiritual insight, and happiness according to the sign and house placements.

Saturn Sextiles and Trines

Considering the nature of Saturn, these aspects to the planet are always welcome. They enable you to structure your energy around realistic and practical goals, bring stability to your life, and often result in tangible rewards.

Saturn Sextile or Trine Uranus. Due to the conflicting natures of these two planets, most aspects between them create a tug-of-war. This struggle for power is absent with a sextile and trine between the two. The unique inventiveness and brilliance of Uranus is molded into practical expression by Saturn. You respect conventional thought, but aren't limited by it.

Saturn Sextile or Trine Neptune. The dreamy, imaginative, and spiritual qualities of Neptune are brought down to Earth with this aspect. You're able to put your spiritual knowledge into action through humanitarian efforts on a small or large scale.

Those with this sextile or trine believe that every species, regardless of its order on the food chain, lives to realize its greatest potential. For them even the lowly black snake in the garden deserves its freedom.

Saturn Sextile or Trine Pluto. This aspect funnels all that Plutonian power into a positive, practical structure that you can use. Your ambitions are tempered by your innate understanding that if you're to effect change, you must do it through careful planning. It's quite likely that if you adhere to your path, you'll achieve a prominent and powerful position in your life.

Saturn Sextile or Trine Nodes. Your efforts are rarely without purpose. You find the proper vehicle for their most practical expression and, in doing so, overcome the limitations of your South Node.

Saturn Sextile or Trine Ascendant. You possess a quiet dignity. Even though you may marry later in life, you marry for keeps. Any partnership you enter is usually beneficial to your long-range goals.

Saturn Sextile or Trine Midheaven and IC. You attain professional success through hard work and careful planning. Your home life is satisfying and orderly.

Saturn Sextile or Trine Part of Fortune. This aspect brings status, success, and good fortune.

Uranus Sextiles and Trines

If you're quick, if you're prepared, you'll be able to take advantage of the opportunities that show up with this aspect. Think of them as psychic gifts, things you've earned from previous lives: a glimmering insight, a flash of inspiration, a psychic hunch that pays off big time.

Uranus Sextile or Trine Neptune. On a broad basis, this signals a fertile time for psychic and spiritual development and humanitarian reforms. If Uranus or Neptune is prominent in your horoscope, then you're most likely spiritually aware. You're probably very psychic, with a mystical imagination that connects you to the deeper levels of reality.

Uranus Sextile or Trine Pluto. Under this aspect, great forces are harnessed and channeled. Atomic and nuclear power, space exploration, quantum physics, and the nature of reality all come into play. On a personal level, you abhor social injustice and strive to live your own life free of bias with your sight on the future.

Uranus Sextile or Trine Nodes. By following your path of humanitarian ideals and progressive thought, you evolve spiritually.

Uranus Sextile or Trine Ascendant. You're one of those magnetic personalities who attracts the unusual and often bizarre. You set trends and are constantly moving forward. You probably marry quite suddenly, and your significant other is as unusual as you are.

Uranus Sextile or Trine Midheaven and IC. You're not interested in following the crowd; instead, people tend to follow you because of your uniqueness. Unusual career opportunities come your way when you least expect it. Your home is unusual in some way, with many interesting people coming and going.

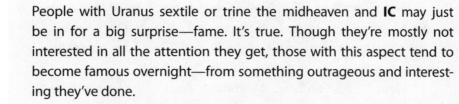

People with Uranus sextile or trine the midheaven and **IC** may just be in for a big surprise—fame. It's true. Though they're mostly not interested in all the attention they get, those with this aspect tend to become famous overnight—from something outrageous and interesting they've done.

Neptune Sextiles and Trines

These aspects emphasize imagination, artistic and psychic ability, and spiritual evolution. They affect large numbers of people.

Neptune Sextile or Trine Pluto. The personal importance of this aspect depends on the prominence of Neptune or Pluto in the horoscope. If either planet is placed in the first house, rules the Ascendant, or displaces the ruler of the chart, the Sun, or the Moon, then this aspect suggests intense spiritual evolvement is possible.

Neptune Sextile or Trine Nodes. Your uncanny instincts about social trends put you in the professional driver's seat. Your spiritual pursuits allow you to evolve and overcome the limitations of the South Node.

Neptune Sextile or Trine Ascendant. This aspect favors marriages and partnerships. You're compassionate, sympathetic, and idealistic and have a mysterious allure that attracts the good will of others. You feel psychically attuned and connected to your mate.

Neptune Sextile or Trine Midheaven and IC. If you're in the arts, then your chance for public recognition is greatly enhanced by this aspect. You use your intuition in your profession to alert you to opportunities. You share a psychic connection with your parents, a significant other, and close family members.

Neptune Sextile or Trine Part of Fortune. Intuition is a major factor in your life. Use it to recognize opportunities and to manifest what you desire.

Pluto Sextiles and Trines

If Pluto is strong or prominent in your chart, then these aspects are definitely good ones to have on your side.

Pluto Sextile or Trine Nodes. Your intuition is well-developed and one of your most valuable assets. It allows you to see past appearances to the truth of a situation. You have the ability to influence how others think on a broad scale. These aspects favor people in public life.

Pluto Sextile or Trine Ascendant. Your willpower and natural clairvoyance give you a decided edge on your competition. You're able to raise the level of consciousness in other people and are presented with many opportunities to increase your personal power.

If you have the aspect of nodes sextile or trine your ascendant, midheaven, or **IC**, your luck can seem to come out of nowhere in regard to ambitions, both professionally and in your domestic life. Usually, family is somehow involved with your career.

Pluto Sextile or Trine Midheaven and IC. Your career opportunities are many and varied. Through them you gain professional prominence and power. Your intuition helps you to direct your career and overcome any obstacles or challenges in your domestic life.

Chapter 12

Oppositions: 180 Degrees

Oppositions are as easy to spot in a chart as conjunctions are. They lie directly across from each other. Planets in the first house, for example, are in opposition to planets in the seventh house. Oppositions involve conflict and tension. They often represent our own personal attributes that we project onto others. Read this chapter to find out all about the oppositions in a chart and what they mean for you.

Sun Oppositions

Do you remember the example of the Siamese twins from Chapter 8? Twin A wants to go left, and Twin B wants to go right. This is the nature of an opposition: tension. To overcome it, you have to reach a compromise. With Sun oppositions, the tensions manifest as a conflict of wills. Note that no opposition exists between the Sun and Mercury and the Sun and Venus.

Sun Opposed Moon. Your emotions are pitted against your ego. The stress may show up in your relationships with the opposite sex. It can also affect your health, especially in a woman's horoscope. You're forced to be more objective about everything in your life, which often results in a sense that you constantly have to choose between your affairs and those of someone else. By understanding the nature of the aspect, you go a long way toward overcoming it.

Sun Opposed Mars. When people disagree with you, take a dozen deep breaths and remove yourself temporarily from the situation. This will ultimately get more results than your usual hostile reactions. Even though you're physically strong, never use physical force to make your point; that only creates an enemy.

Sun Opposed Jupiter. Your inflated ego and grandiose schemes don't exactly endear you to others. You waste energy on excess of all kinds and if you don't cut back, it may affect your health. Stop pontificating. Learn to listen sincerely to other people, and you can mitigate the influence of this opposition.

Sun Opposed Saturn. Your conflicts usually boil down to one salient factor: you chafe and rebel against the restrictions imposed on you by others. These restrictions may come from heavy responsibilities you take on for a spouse, parent, or child. This aspect asks that you attempt to take all things in stride. Cultivate optimism. Lighten up.

Some astrologers say that, with Sun opposed Saturn, the privilege of having children is sometimes denied (as part of a planetary "bump" or lesson learned), or they may just get lucky and have babies born later in their lives. Also, marriage generally happens later in life with this aspect.

Sun Opposed Uranus. The bottom line is that you can't have everything your way all the time. Your insistence on this, coupled with your extreme independence, makes it difficult for you to get along with other people. The very freedom you insist upon for yourself is not something that you allow others. Until you clear up this dichotomy in your life, expect a lot of tension with friends and partners.

Sun Opposed Neptune. Meeting the challenge of this aspect requires strength of will and great focus. You're easily deceived by other people and confused about your religious beliefs and personal relationships. Strive for objectivity.

Sun Opposed Pluto. Your overbearing nature can get on other people's nerves. You need to step back, relax, and stop trying to control everything around you. Many people are intimidated by the forcefulness of your personality, so you tend to lose support you might have otherwise.

Sun Opposed North Node, Conjunct South Node. Vanquish your selfishness and learn to cooperate with other people. Look to the houses occupied by the Sun and the Nodes to determine which areas will be affected.

Sun Opposed Ascendant. This aspect means the Sun is also conjunct the seventh house cusp. This focuses energy on marriages and partnerships. These intimate relationships fulfill and ground you. They provide you with the self-confidence to assume leadership roles.

Sun Opposed Midheaven, Conjunct IC. Your professional achievements are largely dependent on the harmony of your domestic life. You need a fulfilling home life to be able to function well in the larger world.

Moon Oppositions

This aspect creates tension and conflict in your emotional nature. You may have trouble relating to others on an emotional level and are always very aware that you need to develop in the areas influenced by the Moon opposition.

Moon Opposed Mercury. You talk too much about nothing, have trouble finding the proper words to express your opinions and thoughts, and have difficulty relating to people emotionally. As a result, you're indecisive and frustrated. Trines or sextiles to this opposition mitigate its influence.

Moon Opposed Venus. You sometimes erect emotional walls to protect yourself. This creates distance between you and the people you love and causes unnecessary problems. Your emotional vulnerability may go back to your early childhood.

ALERT!

Since Venus relates to feminine power, Moon opposed Venus may indicate feelings of not getting the love you want from your mother or a mother-like figure. Extravagance may also be directly related to these early instances of hurt childhood feelings.

Moon Opposed Mars. You're wired too tightly emotionally. This causes impulsiveness and makes you impatient, restless, and volatile. There can be some dislike for women in general. In men, this can manifest as abusiveness toward women; in women, it may show up as an overbearing attitude toward other women.

Moon Opposed Jupiter. You're much too emotional. You waste a lot of energy fretting about small things in your life. You're very rigid about your religious and spiritual beliefs, defend them emotionally, and tend to get involved in emotional causes. Step back from your emotions.

Moon Opposed Saturn. You withdraw emotionally to protect yourself from other people. You're the proverbial turtle, ducking back into its shell. This creates problems with other people, who may see you as somewhat inhibited, even cold. Your professional ambitions drive you.

Moon Opposed Uranus. The emotional connection with this aspect often originates in an insecure childhood. You shy away from restrictive emotional ties of any sort, move frequently, and your relationships with others begin and end abruptly. Parents with this aspect tend to be irresponsible, easily bored with child-raising duties.

Moon Opposed Neptune. You're a psychic sponge who absorbs the emotions and attitudes of the people around you. Be careful not to hang out with people who exude negativity. You tend to project your own emotional confusion onto other people, which makes it difficult in your relationships to determine who is feeling what.

E ALERT!

With Moon opposed Neptune, one has to be careful to talk things through and analyze the past. You're prone to negative energy—in fact, your body shows it. Any health problems you have now may just stem from early childhood experiences and belief patterns. Work these things out.

Moon Opposed Pluto. Your conflicts with others revolve around joint finances and inheritances. You also keep trying to re-invent the people around you. Step back and honestly assess where you are in your life and where you would like to be five years from now. Then implement a plan to get there. A creative outlet for your emotional energy would be most beneficial.

Moon Opposed North Node, Conjunct South Node. The belief patterns that hold you back originated in early childhood and are deeply immersed in your psychological makeup. If you work at breaking these patterns, do so gently. The house the North Node occupies will tell you which area of your life you should work with in overcoming these patterns.

Moon Opposed Ascendant. You have excellent insight into the needs and wants of the public, which benefits you professionally. Most of the time, you prefer the company of others to solitude; you find emotional fulfillment through others. Be aware that this tendency can make you dependent on your spouse or on other people you're close to.

Moon Opposed Midheaven, Conjunct IC. You're close to your parents and have warm memories of your early childhood. The death of a parent can result in deep shock. You don't like being away from your family and may not take jobs that cause you to be away from them for any length of time. This could inhibit your career opportunities if you allow it to.

Mercury Oppositions

This aspect creates enormous tension in your communication with others. Heated disagreements often occur, usually because of intellectual beliefs you hold.

Mercury Opposed Mars. You're intolerant of people's ideas that differ from your own. You argue about everything, and when you can't win an argument, you resort to shouting. Your behavior is often crude and hostile, even when you don't mean it to be. This can be frustrating for you as well as for those around you.

Those with their Mercury opposed their Mars need to cultivate patience and less aggression—the need to dominate and be right. Advice if this is your aspect: Get rid of the chip on your shoulder and detach from your emotions when dealing with others. Work on your ability to listen and understand before you speak.

Mercury Opposed Jupiter. You tend to blame others for your own failures. But the truth is that your grand plans and ideas lack practicality, and you usually promise more than you can deliver. Religious and spiritual ideas interest you, and you may pursue them educationally at the expense of everything else in your life. You need to cultivate responsibility for yourself and your own actions.

Mercury Opposed Saturn. You're bright, you have ability, and you're an excellent listener. But you fret too much over inconsequential details and throw up blocks that impede the natural flow of ideas. Your overall nature leans toward pessimism and a somber demeanor. Lighten up on yourself and be more patient.

Mercury Opposed Uranus. In all probability, you're a genius. But your ideas may be too eccentric to be practical. Your complete indifference to other people's opinions often results in bad timing: You say or do things that offend others. Good aspects to either planet mitigate the influence of the opposition. You should nurture an interest in other people and try to bring your genius down to earth.

Mercury Opposed Neptune. You're very sensitive to other people's feelings, but sometimes you can't seem to help what you do or say to them. You hate being pinned down in any way, so instead of saying yes or no to something, you simply refuse to commit. This produces chaos in the areas of your life influenced by the opposition.

E
ALERT!

Because those with their Mercury opposed their Neptune are so intuitive, they can often guess the right way to easily manipulate those around them—purposely or even subconsciously. Someone with this aspect would be better off being direct with others and attempting to focus his considerable psychic ability on improving himself.

Mercury Opposed Pluto. This aspect can be found among spies, diplomats, researchers, and people involved in secretive pursuits. It may also be found among novelists who write books that deal with these themes. You're very good at organizing secretive or sensitive information and have an innate understanding of opposing views. Your language, however, sometimes borders on the obscene, which offends others.

Mercury Opposed North Node, Conjunct South Node. You need to keep learning and not settle with the knowledge that you already have. There's a tendency toward mental laziness with this aspect. Through education and intellectual growth, you overcome the limitations of the South Node.

Mercury Opposed Ascendant. Since this aspect means that Mercury is conjunct the seventh house cusp, it indicates a solid mental rapport with significant others. You may attract a younger lover or spouse.

Mercury Opposed Midheaven, Conjunct IC. Your home is loaded with books and other intellectual materials. You have a good rapport with your family, even though they may not always support your professional ambitions.

Venus Oppositions

This aspect usually suggests conflict in the romantic and social arena. This can mean challenges in marriages and partnerships, artistic expression, and financial matters.

Venus Opposed Mars. This isn't a particularly happy aspect for marriage. For a woman with Venus more dominant in the horoscope, it implies that you may leave yourself open for abusive relationships. If Mars is dominant, you may be sexually aggressive and act without consideration for anyone else's feelings. Your jealousy and generally contentious personality create problems in your relationships.

Venus Opposed Jupiter. Your insincerity toward others shows up as grandiose gestures toward strangers and people you barely know. As a result, most of your relationships are superficial. You're an extravagant spender and probably live well beyond your means. You need to cultivate balance.

Venus Opposed Saturn. It's difficult for you to reach out to others emotionally. You may be shy and withdrawn with the opposite sex. When you do marry, your partner may be emotionally cold and possibly older than you. Your finances suffer setbacks. To overcome this challenge, you need to get in touch with your emotions.

Venus Opposed Uranus. You're attracted to eccentric people who provide excitement and romance. Your relationships begin and end abruptly. Emotionally, your need for personal freedom is constantly at odds with your need for companionship and stimulation. This aspect can suggest homosexuality. You need to find balance in your relationships and in yourself.

Venus Opposed Neptune. Your idealized notions about love, romance, and money prevent you from seeing things as they are. This aspect doesn't favor a harmonious marriage because your blind spots gradually undermine the relationship. Your expectations are unrealistic. This aspect may also indicate homosexual tendencies.

Venus Opposed Pluto. You need to be more aware of the motives for your actions. Are you trying to remake your significant other rather than working on yourself or your own beliefs? Why do you feel such a hunger for power over other people? What parts of yourself are you projecting onto others?

Here's some important counsel for those with Venus opposed Pluto: Shed your dictatorial attitudes, control your passions, and stay clear of anyone involved in illegal activities. Ultimately, this will take you farther in life and keep you out of too much trouble.

Venus Opposed North Node, Conjunct South Node. The problem in overcoming this aspect is that you get pleasure out of your habitual patterns regarding relationships and finances. Unless you seriously scrutinize these patterns and attempt to change them, it will be very difficult to overcome the restrictions of the South Node.

Venus Opposed Ascendant. Since this aspect means that Venus is conjunct the seventh-house cusp, it indicates happiness and success in marriage and partnerships. You derive much pleasure and happiness through your personal relationships, which allows you to relate well in society.

Venus Opposed Midheaven, Conjunct IC. Your deepest pleasure comes through your home life. Look for aspects to the tenth house that may create harmony or conflict with ambition goals because of your attachment to home and family.

Mars Oppositions

This aspect infuses a horoscope with aggression, energy, and anger. Your reaction to sensitive issues is likely to be rash, impulsive, and hostile. You've got a short fuse. If other adverse aspects to Mars are present, you may experience physical danger.

Mars Opposed Jupiter. Forget gambling and financial speculation if this aspect is in your chart. To engage in either is to invite financial disaster. Scrutinize your own motives in the way you treat other people. Are you being friendly or gracious just to get something out of them? Your restlessness and thirst for adventure send you off on trips to foreign countries. These trips are exciting, but they don't mitigate your restlessness.

Mars Opposed Saturn. These two planets are really at odds. Mars wants to rush ahead impulsively; Saturn wants to plan. You're frustrated and angry much of the time and resent others whose lives seem to be clicking along smoothly. Try to go out of your way to help others. This cooperative spirit will trigger more positive responses from other people toward you.

Mars Opposed Uranus. Your life is literally screaming for balance. You either work to the point of exhaustion or are consumed by laziness. Your explosions of temper are followed by remorse. You make sweeping changes in your life without taking the possible consequences into account. Step back, chill out, and seek balance.

Mars Opposed Neptune. This one reads like a manual of things to avoid in your life. You're better off avoiding alcohol, drugs, sexual excesses, and clandestine activities of any sort. Make great efforts not to lie, cheat, or act in an underhanded way with anyone. Above all, examine your own motives.

Mars Opposed Pluto. Your personal desires are at war with your higher or spiritual self. In the charts of self-aware people, this aspect tests what you're made of: Do you bow to your personal desires or do you follow a higher path?

What's a good example of Mars opposed Pluto?
The conflict of personal desire with spiritual self here is a lot like the struggle between Darth Vader and Luke Skywalker, especially once Luke knows that Darth Vader is his father. Luke must decide to kill or to connect with Darth Vader. In this way, he's caught in an internal battle with himself.

Mars Opposed North Node, Conjunct South Node. If you learn to control your flagrant disregard for social conventions and traditions, you'll break the restrictions and limitations that hold you back.

Mars Opposed Ascendant. This aspect means that Mars conjuncts the seventh-house cusp. A lot of energy goes into your close partnerships. Your confidence attracts dynamic partners whose ambitions match your own. Friction that arises may have to do with who calls the shots.

Mars Opposed Midheaven, Conjunct IC. Your home life may be riddled with arguments and disagreements. Your responsibilities toward your family may interfere with your career ambitions. Balance is key. Cultivate it.

Jupiter Oppositions

This aspect creates conflict in terms of expansion, religious and spiritual issues, higher education, the law, and any of the other affairs ruled by Jupiter.

Jupiter Opposed Saturn. Professional success may be gradual with this aspect, but your perseverance and dedication make it happen. You may feel somewhat conflicted about your religious and spiritual beliefs. However, you benefit by working with your beliefs in a constructive, positive way. The negative parts of this aspect are greatly mitigated by trines, sextiles, and conjunctions to Saturn.

Always remember that your core beliefs determine your reality; the patterns in your horoscope merely reflect what is possible. If you cultivate and maintain optimism, even when faced with enormous challenges in this aspect, you will stay well ahead of the game.

Jupiter Opposed Uranus. This aspect usually manifests in one of two ways. In a chart that lacks direction and focus, it may lead to involvement with revolutionary groups who do little more than make trouble and break rules. There can be involvement in religious cults and get-rich-quick scams. You may be prone to a purposeless wanderlust and flights of imagination that have no grounding in reality.

ALERT!

In a strong horoscope, Jupiter opposed Uranus can lead to great humanitarian efforts that instigate progressive change that affects large numbers of people. With this kind of characteristic in your birth chart, don't ever let yourself be tempted to follow a less evolved path.

Jupiter Opposed Neptune. Spiritual conflicts sometimes come up with this aspect. Illusory thinking and utopian ideals fail to find practical outlets unless there are positive aspects to Saturn. You may be too trusting of smooth talkers with devious plans. To overcome this aspect, ground yourself through physical and spiritual practices like yoga, meditation, or some sort of exercise program. Also cultivate pragmatism and look beyond the masks that other people present to the world.

Jupiter Opposed Pluto. Your religious and spiritual convictions are an intrinsic part of your life. Unfortunately, you try to convert everyone to your way of thinking about these issues and create considerable animosity. In extreme cases, this aspect indicates a complete disregard for laws and conventions.

Jupiter Opposed North Node, Conjunct South Node. You get pleasure out of your excesses, even though they're actually impeding your development. You would be better off breaking your habits, whatever they are. Work to develop yourself through the house placement of the North Node.

Jupiter Opposed Ascendant. Since this means that Jupiter is conjunct the seventh-house cusp, it indicates good fortune generally in marriage and partnerships. Your significant other supports your ambitions, and you benefit through the cooperation of others.

Jupiter Opposed Midheaven, Conjunct IC. Your family's generosity embraces all areas of your life. They fully support your professional and personal endeavors. Your spiritual beliefs are strongly influenced by your parents.

Saturn Oppositions

With this aspect, look for conflicts concerning tradition, authority, discipline, structure, and anything that Saturn stands for.

Saturn Opposed Uranus. These two planets are locked in combat. They represent totally opposite traits. Discipline and structure are pitted against freedom and reform. Even though you demand total freedom from others, you tend to be dictatorial toward other people.

Saturn Opposed Neptune. Your sense of reality may be seriously flawed. You need to step back from your life and take a long, hard look at what you're doing and where you're going. Are you being deceitful or dishonest? Instead of using subterfuge to deal with people, attempt to cultivate directness. The results may astonish you.

Saturn Opposed Pluto. If you're up to the task of personal evolution, this aspect helps you do it, but only through hard work and discipline. It's a good idea to study this aspect in light of the rest of the chart. If criminal tendencies appear elsewhere, this aspect can confirm it.

Saturn Opposed North Node, Conjunct South Node. To evolve, you need to break with tradition and convention. Try the new; seek out the unconventional.

Saturn Opposed Ascendant. Since Saturn is conjunct the seventh-house cusp, this aspect indicates a solid marriage and partnerships. You may marry later in life or to someone older than you. You definitely shoulder your part of the overall responsibility.

Saturn Opposed Midheaven, Conjunct IC. Your childhood was probably far too strict and your early life, too rigid. You feel a heavy duty to your parents and/or family, and this feeling inhibits your career ambitions.

If you know that your Saturn opposes Part of Fortune, heed this advice. To achieve what you want, you need to cultivate discipline and patience and be willing to work very hard. On the surface, it hardly looks like a pot of gold. But if you follow Saturn work ethics, your success will be beyond anything you dared imagine.

Uranus Oppositions

This is a tough aspect. It tends to bring about traumatic experiences that cause shattering disruptions and irresolute change. Once the pieces fall, you have to rebuild. The success or failure of your transition is entirely up to you. If you rise to the challenge, you succeed. If you don't, you fail.

Uranus Opposed Neptune. On a broad, societal scale, this aspect causes major disasters, upheaval, and turmoil. On a personal level, if either planet rules or is prominent in your chart, it creates deception and delusion related to the houses Uranus and Neptune occupy.

Uranus Opposed Pluto. In a generational sense, this aspect causes sweeping and destructive change in society: mobs, riots, the collective madness of people out of control. If Uranus or Pluto prevail in your chart, this aspect indicates sweeping and often violent changes in your life.

Uranus Opposed North Node, Conjunct South Node. You should temper your eccentric attitudes and try to go with the prevailing social flow. Even if it seems to block your personal freedom, it will do more for your freedom in the long run.

Uranus Opposed Ascendant. This aspect means that Uranus is conjunct the seventh-house cusp, so hold onto your hat! Your partnerships, romantic and otherwise, tend to happen suddenly. The partners you attract are exciting and unusual. Even if the relationships don't last long, it's a great adventure.

If you have Uranus opposed Ascendant, remember one important thing: When you're ready for stability in a relationship, try not to worry so much about your personal freedom. You may discover that love— real love—can also be incredibly liberating.

Uranus Opposed Midheaven, Conjunct IC. This aspect means frequent moves and a disruptive home life. You need to be your own boss and call your own shots. Your hunger for personal freedom seems to interfere with everything else in your life.

Neptune Oppositions

Even when Neptune is badly aspected, it's not all bad. Its better attributes—psychic ability, imagination, artistic talent—remain. The problem with the oppositions is that they create conflict between ideals and the reality.

Neptune Opposed Pluto. This one reads like a Shakespearean play. It comes down to the archetypal struggle between good and evil, destruction and regeneration. It last occurred in the early 1800s and will come around again in the twenty-first century.

FACT

At its worst, Neptune opposed Pluto suggests an era of psychic and spiritual depravity, when sexual perversion and debauchery are the norm. On the other hand, within the rubble of changed old belief systems, a spiritual alignment can take place that revolutionizes the way we perceive reality—for good.

Neptune Opposed North Node, Conjunct South Node. Your habits are so ingrained that you may not even recognize them as habits. But unless you break them, you fail to evolve to your potential.

Neptune Opposed Ascendant. This aspect means Neptune is conjunct the seventh-house cusp and the news is far from good. Relationships are your blind spot, but you can be just as deceptive as the people you get involved with. Your intuitive ability is so finely tuned it can literally give you the inside track on whatever you focus on.

Neptune Opposed Midheaven, Conjunct IC. Your illusions about your career can work to your advantage once you recognize them. You may have an unstable home life where psychic abilities are the norm rather than the exception. Good. Take it for its worth, then head out into the world on your own and satisfy your spiritual hunger.

Pluto Oppositions

Think of the marriage vow: for better or for worse. That's the nature of all aspects to Pluto, but this is particularly true in the case of oppositions.

Pluto Opposed North Node, Conjunct South Node. This aspect is all about the Western view of karma. Old debts need to be repaid before you can progress or evolve through the area indicated by the house placement of the North Node. On some level, you'll recognize the debts when they enter your life, and circumstances will force you to deal with them one way or another.

Pluto Opposed Ascendant. As an opposition here, Pluto conjuncts the seventh-house cusp. Relationships and partnerships may not be entirely pleasant for you. Get rid of your need to dominate, keep your spiritual self uplifted, and the influence will be diminished considerably.

Pluto Opposed Midheaven, Conjunct IC. There are easier ways to evolve as a spiritual being. But one thing is certain with this aspect: Much of your inner life will wrestle with the issue of spiritual evolvement. You may have to overcome an early childhood that was the equivalent of living under Hitler. You may get sidetracked. One way or another, the events and conditions in your life bring you back to the bottom line: Get it right this time around or you'll be back to try again.

Chapter 13

E Love Compatibility: Fire

Love compatibility is a tricky thing. On the one hand, there are so many obvious matches, but some supposed mismatches work, too. It's difficult to know everything from a couple's set of Sun signs. However, Sun signs will give you a basic idea of whether or not you'll get along as a couple. In this chapter, find out more about Fire signs and their idea of love. Check out the "Matches" section of each sign for some big hints.

Aries in Love

Aries man has a penchant for doing things his way. He's as sharp as a tack and people respect him, even though they think he's bossy and domineering. He'll decide how he wants it done, and he's a perfectionist about it. If he likes you, he'll listen to your take on it, and perhaps tailor it a bit. But if he doesn't like you, watch out! There is no better debater than Aries. He must win every argument—even when he's wrong.

ALERT!

Never get too jealous with Aries man or Aries woman. They need to know that they can do whatever they want to do. If you're too jealous, they'll run out and start a fling, just to prove that they're in charge.

Aries woman, on the other hand, handles people with more charm and finesse. She's a lot less aggressive than Aries man—on the outside—though her thought process is very similar. Where he drives forward, she'll pull back and wait for the masses to come to her—and they always do. When it comes to love, she's just as fickle and stubborn as Aries man.

Seduction Tips with Aries

You won't have a problem seducing Aries if he likes you. Better yet, resist a little and let him work for it. You'll have Aries intrigued and more excited about the encounter. Aries, it is said, is basic. That's not really true: Aries is a wordsmith and sometimes better at talking about the deed and thrilling you with words than he is at actually performing the action. He's bigger on promises and idealistic futures than on living up to his seemingly fluent words of love and the future.

ESSENTIAL

With Aries, take everything with a grain of salt, and you'll be ahead of the game. Remember that they're the children of the zodiac, too, and that they'll always want more what they cannot truly have. With Aries, you have to change the rules frequently, or they'll get bored.

Aries, unfortunately, can woo you into bed with well-placed words. Whether or not he can accomplish the tasks at hand depends on each Aries. Well, let's just say that Aries is confident—too confident in bed. And he's sensitive, too. He might tell you about his own weaknesses, but he'll absolutely freak out if you start listing your own.

Aries can be a bit selfish in bed, too. Sure, he's creative, exciting, and extremely inventive. He thinks he's sensitive but he's not necessarily—unless his Venus is in Taurus, Cancer, or Pisces. If his Venus is in Aquarius or Aries, beware! He can woo you to the ends of the earth, but he can also be so detached. You'll believe you know him, and then he'll change right before your eyes.

Tips

Aries can be incredibly loving and sweet, and she almost always gets what she wants in love. Her only regret is that someone she loves may not be "good enough" for her, as she perceives it. Most times, once she falls out of love, it's gone forever.

Go slow with Aries and make her work for it. Never put her on a pedestal. Praise her only when she deserves it. Make her listen to you but understand that she'll only see her side of it. Accept this. Don't ever try to control her, or she'll run the other way. Give her freedom but also set boundaries.

ALERT!

If Aries pulls away, let him. Don't go chasing after him, or he'll run even faster. When he's ready, he'll come back. He wants to make sure you're independent enough for him. Be strong and don't be too needy.

Matches with Aries

Here's the kicker: If you want a faithful Aries, try to stay away from those who have their Venus (their love sign) in Aries, Sagittarius, or even Aquarius. They tend to wander. If you're an Earth sign, pick an Aries with lots of Air in his chart—he'll be drawn to you. If you're a Water sign, you'll probably do well with Aries if he has a lot of Fire.

And if you want an Aries who lives for love, find an Aries with his Venus in Cancer or Pisces. Aries, because it's a Fire sign, is often attracted to other Fire signs—Sagittarius or Leo. But generally, unless aspects in the chart indicate otherwise, romance with another Fire sign can be explosive. Aries gets along well with Air signs—Gemini, Libra, Aquarius—or a sign that's sextile (60 degrees) or trine (120 degrees) from Aries. Sometimes, an Earth sign helps ground all that Aries energy. In chart comparisons, a Venus or Moon in Aries in the other person's chart would indicate compatibility.

Watch out! Romance with an Aries is an experience you won't quickly forget. Man or woman, these people are all passion and fire. They often form impulsive, rash attachments, and they don't hold back emotionally. But they're fickle, too!

Leo in Love

Leos are passionate. They can also be impulsive and irrational, but it's all part of the charm. They're fickle, and they like to test their partners before they put their hearts into anything. They're difficult, too, particularly when their egos need to be stroked. If you treat a Leo with anything but the ultimate respect, he may not say anything, but he'll remember it—and count it against you in the game of love.

Leo fights for the underdog, but be sure to stick up for yourself with him. On the other hand, arguing for the sake of arguing will make a Leo insane. Leos are intense and will argue, but their sunny, calm natures are truly made for being content and feeling safe and comfortable with a partner.

Though Leo gives the appearance of being confident and secure, this is often an act. Leo's innermost desire is to be accepted for who he is, and his biggest worry is that he'll soon discover he's just normal or boring. It's very important for a Leo to feel special.

For the most part, Leos need to feel needed and need to know they are loved before they commit entirely. Once they're committed, everything is bigger than life and brighter than the Sun. They're known to be loyal, but this is only true after they've found themselves. If they haven't, and they're not yet emotionally evolved or secure, they can be as two-faced as Gemini can be.

Many astrologers say Leos are arrogant, but this is not true. Actually, they're such perfectionists that they're worried their insecurities will show unless they "perform." They show off sometimes and try to be larger than life to compensate for their flaws.

FACT

Like all Fire signs, Leo needs to respect you in order to fall in love. This means that you need to be ambitious in career, straightforward in your dealings with people, and truthful with them. Anything else will be the end of the relationship.

Seduction Tips with Leo

Courtship is often a series of dramatic gestures: five dozen roses that arrive at your office, an erotic call at 3:00 A.M., or a chopper ride over Manhattan. It's the truth—Leo is a big spender—or, at least, he has big ideas about luxury in life. However, one thing that is sure to turn off a Leo forever is pettiness. If you're petty in any way—asking for money for something big or small (that should be water under the bridge) or being vindictive with a friend or family member—Leo will be annoyed and leave you in the dust.

Obviously, it's the same situation if you're frugal. Leo simply can't tolerate paying for things he doesn't deem worthy. True, he understands the difference between paying for a $300 hotel and a $500 hotel; but if you'd prefer to stay in a mud hut with no air conditioning or heat, you'd better find another Sun Sign to do it with.

Leo needs to believe that it's his idea to give a relationship a chance. If you push too hard, you'll scare him off. He likes to win—always likes a prize. *You* need to be the prize he wins. Leo won't mind putting up a fight for you. There needs to be a fine line, though. If you make Leo work too hard, he'll just walk away. This, for example, isn't true of Aries, another Fire sign.

ALERT!

If you're involved with a Leo, make sure you know his intentions with you. Ask him. He'll tell you. Leo is not a very good liar. If you ask him in person, chances are that you'll get the truth from him. (Or you'll at least read it in his facial expressions—pay attention!)

Again, deep down, Leo wants everything but isn't quite sure he's really worthy. Though this is actually a healthier way to be than brash Aries, for example, or silently righteous Sagittarius, it still won't work in your favor. Therefore, Leo must feel special, yet not fawned upon (until he's in love, and then it's fine). Finding a perfect balance is essential in order to gain Leo's trust and affection.

Matches with Leo

Another Fire sign is good for a Leo simply because their energy levels are similar. Any sign that is sextile (Gemini, for instance) or trine (Aries) would be fine, too—though Leo has little patience for Aries who aren't spiritually evolved. True, he may win her for a while, but then what? He can be too headstrong. Aries is a lot like Sagittarius with Leo—lots of fire, but not the same temperament. Sagittarius can be a bit too wise and quiet (or even too superficial or stubborn) for Leo; Aries can be too demanding and controlling.

The polarity between Leo and Aquarius, its polar opposite sign, may elevate a Leo's consciousness to where it succeeds best—to the wider world beyond himself, if the Leo has some Air signs in his chart. Capricorn can be an interesting match and Scorpio seems like a go until Leo realizes that she may not like the way he may raise their children. But they're surely a good match in bed.

Sagittarius in Love

In the movie *Two for the Road* with Audrey Hepburn and Albert Finney, the romance between the two fell under a Sagittarian influence. The exotic place, their individual searches for truth, and the truths they ultimately found in each other are Sagittarian themes. No matter who a Sagittarian loves, a part of him or her is always slightly aware of the larger picture.

FACT

The surest way to get rid of a Sagittarius is to disrespect his words. You must listen to everything he says—Sagittarius is very big on authority. He *is* wise (a lot wiser than Aries, who sometimes talks without thinking). Heed Sagittarius's "lectures" and he'll appreciate you for it.

Sagittarius is pretty clear in what he wants. He knows if he's in love—truly—or not. It's simply not a question. "Making" a Sagittarius fall in love is difficult. You can play a little hard to get in the beginning, and this will help, but, ultimately, Sagittarius is instinctive and wise—and knows what he needs.

He's so blunt and tactless with his words that they can sometimes cut to the core. But believe everything that comes out of Sagittarius's mouth. If he tells you he's in love, he is. If he tells you he's not, he's not. Sagittarius is not a very diplomatic soul. In his mind, honesty and straightforwardness is everything, and he likes someone who will listen carefully to everything he has to say.

It's well known that Sagittarians love their freedom. But here's a lesser known piece of information: Sagittarius loves language—everything about it. She loves exotic cultures and people, too. Bring up etymology with your Sagittarius, and she'll be eating out of the palm of your hand.

Strangely enough, Sagittarius sometimes gives the impression that he's lost in another world. He seems quiet—or into himself. This isn't entirely true. It always seems that Sagittarius is deeper than he really is. In truth, he's probably thinking about work or some kind of problem in quantum physics—he's not thinking about your relationship.

Sagittarius wants everything to go smoothly. In his mind, if things are not moving forward, he's not going to waste his precious time devoting it to you. Just don't badger him for his thoughts. Let Sagittarius come to you to ask you how you're feeling. He needs to be left alone to experience his space and freedom, and then he'll come search you out.

Seduction Tips with Sagittarius

If you keep Sagittarius guessing, you'll keep him. Be direct with your words, and quieter with your emotions. Sagittarius likes to be steered in love in a very subtle way. He's very physical and sometimes expresses his feelings through actions, rather than through words. Never be needy with a Sagittarius. He'll be out the door faster than you can blink.

Sagittarius is also one sign that will absolutely do what you tell him not to do. Don't even try it. Instead, try using reverse psychology. Say, "Oh, you're right . . . you're *so* right . . . but maybe just this once, could we try it *this* way—just for me?" In other words, if you use love as an incentive, Sagittarius might just go for it.

Here's another tip with Sagittarius: Don't ask for too much in the beginning. He'll give you his heart—and everything else—if you don't ask for a lot right away. He needs to be "there" in the moment with you. And he needs to be truly in love to give of himself. Sagittarius is very capable of separating sex and love. If he's sleeping with you, it doesn't necessarily mean he's in love. Again, you need to ask him what's going on. Don't do it in a needy way. Ask him in a direct way—he'll tell you. Just remember to believe what he says. Sagittarius doesn't mince words.

He's more sensitive than he seems, and he'll care for anyone he gets involved with (unlike Aries, who can go to bed and wipe the slate clean the next day, if he chooses). As passionate Fire signs go, Sagittarius is a good guy—and he's even better when he's in love. Just make sure not to lie to him. Sagittarius won't appreciate that at all. If he doesn't trust you, he'll be nice to you, but he'll run the other way looking for a better mate.

Matches with Sagittarius

Other Air signs are compatible with Sagittarius. The Sagittarius-Gemini polarity confers a natural affinity between the two signs. But other Fire signs might work well, too. It just depends. Sagittarius, above all other Fire signs, is the most emotionally secure. Sagittarius is not the most stable (Leo is), but he thinks he is. He doesn't tolerate as much as Leo, but he's not as ridiculously immature as Aries can sometimes be.

He comes off as a natural, quiet leader. And he is. Actually, the best match for Sagittarius is a Water sign—particularly Pisces. These two go together so well because Pisces is strong and sensual enough for Sagittarius, but is also a master in the art of silent persuasion. Sagittarius needs someone who is loving, sweet, and tender, will let him do what he feels like doing, and isn't nitpicky about the little things. Again, a Water sign might just do him good because he likes being "shown the way;" yet, all the while, he's the one who can act "in charge" of things.

FACT

When Sagittarius falls in love with "the one," she's set for life. Sagittarius can be the least faithful sign of the zodiac, but she can also be the most faithful. If she finds what she's looking for, Sagittarius will settle down and not look any further.

In essence, you can get a Sagittarius to fall in love with you if you are sweet, yet strong. He hates being argued with; so, if he does something stupid, approach him in that moment and just tell him what he's done wrong. He won't put up with silent passive-aggressive tactics. These drive him crazy (though once in a while these will keep him on his toes). He doesn't go for the shy, sensitive type, though. He needs to feel that his mate can do fine without him. Only then will he stay.

Chapter 14

E

Love Compatibility: Air

Overall, Air sign compatibility is tough to discern. They're so quick and mentally agile, and they like to stir things up. They're all havoc-seekers on some level. Libra does it quietly; Gemini is a drama queen and a gossip; and Aquarius is hard to pin down. But all Air signs will give a relationship that extra uncertainty factor. Read through this chapter and get a glimpse into the secret worlds of Libra, Gemini, and Aquarius.

Gemini in Love

The problem with Gemini is that he doesn't really know what he wants. He thinks he knows, but then it changes. Gemini needs to work for love—then he'll give his all. Also, he needs a partner who makes him laugh—but not about himself. Geminis can be touchy and sensitive when the humor comes at their expense.

Geminis love first with their minds. Even a relationship that begins primarily because of a sexual attraction won't last if there's no mental connection. Quite often, Geminis seek friendship first with the opposite sex and, once a mental rapport is established, the friendship deepens into love. But this happens when they're really ready for something serious. Otherwise, they can have affairs like no other sign in the zodiac. True, they can be quite fickle in their affections, sometimes carrying on simultaneous relationships. But once their hearts are won, they love deeply.

E ALERT!

Once Gemini is over you, it's really over. Don't ever take a "break" with Gemini—it won't ever come back around to the way it was. Gemini has this power to cut it off clean and never look back once he's decided it's through.

Geminis have a "need to try everything once" attitude. They're like children who need to stick their hands in the cookie jar. True, there are some Geminis who won't sleep with a person if they're not in love, but chances are, they'll try it all with the one they're with at the moment.

Geminis can also be drama queens (and kings). They like to entertain people, make others laugh, and give good, grown-up advice (that they only wish they could follow themselves). No one can tell a story like a Gemini. She'll use her eyes and her body to create a moment. And she'll get as emotionally worked up the first time she tells a tale as she does the seventh time. Don't ever take the stories at face value, though. Gemini has a habit of exaggerating, even when she doesn't mean to.

Again, Geminis give great advice, though they're just not very good at taking the advice, themselves. So, they're a little lost. And they change their minds frequently, so it's sometimes difficult for them to get to the heart of the matter. All of that aside, Geminis do love with every bit of their hearts. They're pretty quick to put their hearts on the table when they feel it—sometimes too quickly. They can be diplomatic when they need to—but not when it comes to romance, love, and you.

Gemini, in love, always likes to leave a few options open. Before you get comfy and cozy with a Gemini, make sure he's smitten! Boredom, to a Gemini, is death. He needs the challenge of tempting and wooing you. Let him court you fully before you succumb!

Seduction Tips with Gemini

Gemini is the biggest flirt in the zodiac. If you can't deal with this, just forget Gemini. He'll flirt in front of you, and has charm like no one else (except maybe Libra), but this is all part of the game. Sure, he can be faithful—you have to win his heart first. Unfortunately, this isn't an easy task. Gemini will always go for the "coolest" person in the room, unless he's looking to settle down for real. Then, he may go for the perfect person who grounds him.

In fact, you may get a little dizzy watching a Gemini work the room. The "sexy" thing works for Gemini, and he plays it up to the hilt. He likes having a throng of fans and gets distracted easily. Therefore, one of the only ways you're going to get Gemini to chase after you is to start up a great conversation—then leave and look like you're having a blast. This may be a game, but it works. When Gemini finally realizes you've bailed, he'll come looking for you.

Also, if you have a head for business or simply a good job, this will impress Gemini to the umpteenth degree. He wants to respect his partner and know that his partner has big ambitions. Gemini is not a wallflower. He wants to be out and about and to brag about what a great person he's got at his side.

Gemini needs to feel like he's got the prize that other people covet. In other words, it's not just okay that he thinks you're great, he needs to know that his friends think you're amazing, too. So, don't hang on him at parties. Show that you're independent but that you're on his side.

Never go against Gemini in front of his friends. He'll be instantly offended and look elsewhere for romantic company (who will be "faithful," in his eyes). True, Gemini has a bit of a paranoid, insecure thing. You may not see it right away, but it's there. You don't have to show him your love and devotion immediately, just make sure you agree with him in front of people he deems important.

Gemini really does need a little drama to know that you're interested, but he doesn't like being alone for long. He can get caught up with his work, but work will never be the most important thing in his life—not deep down. Love is the real focus. In fact, he'll stay with someone he thinks is the best thing he can find. And if you stay on top, for him, he'll be with you—always.

FACT

There's a fine line between making Gemini jealous and making him insane. If you make him jealous in an innocent way—but he still trusts you—it's fine. If you truly make him jealous, there's no one more vindictive and crazy than he will be. You won't like this side of him at all. It's not pretty.

Geminis also know that sarcasm and humor with an edge is the best remedy for everything. Make a Gemini laugh—at himself and at others, in general—and he'll instantly think you're smart. With Gemini, it's not always about book-smart, it's about street-smarts and ironic, sarcastic comebacks that are funny, not biting or nasty. They can be sensitive, in general, but they love to gossip and to make fun of others.

Matches with Gemini

Geminis are social enough to get along with and be attracted to just about anyone on a superficial basis. They feel most at home with other Air signs, particularly Aquarians, whose minds are as quick as theirs. They also get along with Sagittarius, their polar opposites in the zodiac, who share some of the same attributes. Again, though, these are broad generalizations. For compatibility purposes, it's important to compare the individual charts.

When Gemini is truly ready to settle down, an Earth sign may be a good option for a partner. A Virgo will be a bit too critical for the thin-skinned Gemini, but a Taurus, with his feisty sensual side, may be just what the doctor ordered. Capricorn can go either way, but most Capricorns won't put up with Gemini's otherwise flighty antics or superficial skimming of political ideas that hold great truths for Capricorns.

Again, an Air sign like Libra may be ideal for Gemini if they can find a balance of minds. If anyone can find that rare balance, it's Libra. The only problem is that Libra despises confrontation and Gemini tends to go that way. Water signs are probably too side-stepping for feisty Gemini—unless they have a lot of Earth or Air in their charts. Scorpio and Gemini are a good match in bed, but Scorpio sometimes weighs Gemini down when he wants to go out and play. Leo can be a fun dating partner for Gemini—with a lot of laughter—but Leo may get annoyed when Gemini doesn't praise the ground she walks on. If Gemini does, it's a match made in heaven.

Libra in Love

Libras are drawn to beauty, whatever its form. The only thing they enjoy as much as beauty is harmony. Even when a relationship has gone sour, a Libra hesitates to be the one who ends it. Libras can't stand hurting anyone's feelings; emotional rawness is one of those ugly realities that they don't like to see. As a result, they may remain in a relationship longer than they should just because disharmony is so distasteful. Libras seek harmony because, in their hearts, they know that enlightenment lies at the calm dead center of the storm.

In fact, Libra is just that—the eye of the storm. He'll start something and then walk away to watch things unfold at a distance, where it's safe. Libra is the ultimate "watcher" of human behavior. He studies it—studies you—and determines what he knows and what he believes. He'll have his friends study you and see if you're faithful and "worthy." Ultimately, he'll make up his own mind. But if a Libra doesn't trust you, you're history.

Libra has a wonderful social circle and many people who believe in him. But watch closely. Libra keeps his true self hidden. There's often only one person he truly trusts—usually a family member. If he opens up to you completely on a consistent basis, you've got a real mate for life.

Libra has a very fixed idea in his head of what he's looking for. If you don't fit that perfect mold, he's not going to waste his time on you. Find out what Libra wants. If you don't, you may seduce him for one night, but he won't get serious with you.

Librans are masters in the disguise of their own fate. In fact, they can be very stubborn when deciding what the roads of life all lead to. It's sometimes difficult for them to make a tough decision, but when they do, no one can talk them out of it. Librans believe in signs, red flags, and even superstitions. They'll consider omens and apply them to their own lives.

Also, Librans want to be calm and comfortable in a relationship. Many Libra men choose younger women just to have this feeling of ultimate control. Sometimes they also pick women a lot older than they are so that the woman does all of the deciding. You'll also find that Librans are mostly faithful when they find the one they want to spend time with. True, they may have strange arrangements set up, but when they love, they love deeply.

Seduction Tips with Libra

With Libra, you must first determine if he's learned to cope with emotional feelings. Many Librans can be immature—they like to push sentimentalities away in an attempt to rationalize them. They're Air signs, after all. But they can also be overwhelmingly idealistic and sensitive. So, it takes a Libra a bit longer to get to know himself (and show himself). All the while, it may be difficult for a partner to deal with this constant back-and-forth of letting himself go and reining himself in.

Librans have a tough time figuring out what they really want. On one hand, they want a partner who's carefree and easy to deal with. On the other side, they want someone who's a true confidante and partner for life. Let them battle it out on their own. If they haven't yet determined what they want, stay away.

Remember, too, that Libra likes to feel in control. In this way, you may have to be demure in the beginning. Let Libra chase you. Don't let his friends know that you're interested. Libra will get the hint just by looking you in the eyes. His eyes are the key to his soul.

Libras are very sensitive, so try not to make the first move. Because of the internal battle all Libras must face, they like to have a little bit of dominance in the situation. And they tend to judge a mate unfairly if she's too aggressive. Once again, let Libra man steer the conversation and the relationship. Pull back, at first, and let him court you. He'll do it in a grand way, and you'll be glad you did.

Matches with Libra

Librans can get along with just about anyone. They are most compatible with other Air signs, Aquarius and Gemini. Though seriously outgoing, Geminis can sometimes scare them—they understand the way Librans think. Scorpios get to the heart of the matter with Libra; they have the intensity and emotional depth that Librans crave. In fact, Librans might even get attached to Scorpios in a volatile and unhealthy way, if they're not careful. Though Scorpios can be a good match for Libras, they should watch out for signs of control. If Librans feel they're being manipulated in any way, they'll be out the door in a flash.

When you pick someone of the same Sun sign as you, it will magnify all of your good traits—and your bad ones, too. It's like looking in the mirror. Do you like what you see? Or does it bring up issues for you? Always choose a partner who brings out your best side.

Librans also gravitate toward people who reflect their refined tastes and aesthetic leanings, like Leo. Also, an Earth sign may provide a certain grounding that a Libran needs. Taurus is a wonderful, sensual match with Libra. Or a Water sign, like Cancer, may offer a fluidity of emotion that a Libran may lack. But, with Cancer, it may be an uphill battle. Cancers can be too moody, sometimes, and too self-involved for harmony-seeking Librans.

Since opposites attract, Aries can sometimes be a good fit for Librans—though Aries needs to have spiritually "found herself" before this can work. On another note, a Libra with a Libra can be a good match—but watch out! Two of the same signs together can be wonderful or a big mess.

Aquarius in Love

Aquarians need the same space and freedom in a relationship that they crave in every other area of their lives. Even when they commit, the need doesn't evaporate. They must follow the dictates of their individuality above all else. This stubbornness can work against them if they aren't careful. Aquarians usually are attracted to people who are unusual or eccentric in some way. Their most intimate relationships are marked by uniqueness.

Aquarians can be very instinctive but usually for other people, not for themselves. They also try to root for the underdog, but sometimes pick the wrong underdog or victim to defend. Their upbeat, positive outlook on life can be tempered by idealistic notions they try hard to suppress. The biggest goal in life, for them, is to remain calm and cool. This is very important for Aquarius because, when they let loose, they can be big fireballs. And, if they get too wound up, the aggression they exude can be harsh for other people to cope with. Instinctively, they know this and try to temper it, often unsuccessfully.

ALERT!

Aquarians are survivors—know this. So, if you want to be with one, know that they're hard-headed with their decisions. Under that cool exterior is a person who must, eventually, follow their heart and mind. And this can be difficult, too, because the two forces don't always agree! But sticking around with an Aquarius will pay off. They'll trust you and slowly get attached.

Aquarians know that they're strong individuals and that they can turn the tides to their favor. Luck follows them everywhere—even if they're not aware of it. There's something of a destined feeling to the relationships of Aquarians. They may even sense where they're headed before the fact. An Aquarius is not a big mystery, though. If you want an answer about love, just ask. Aquarians will tell you if your relationship is headed somewhere or not. If they're not sure, chances are that the answer is no, but they can be swayed over time.

Aquarius also must see a bit of the world before settling down. He plays a little game with himself. He may even get married a couple of times before realizing that he just wasn't ready for what he thought he was. An ideal partner for Aquarius will show his own mental agility, his independence, and his emotional strength of will. This will get an Aquarius to follow you to the ends of the earth, but only if he's ready for something real to enter his life.

Seduction Tips with Aquarius

Aquarius loves to shock! He tests people to see how smart and cool they'll be when they realize they've been had. If someone overreacts or is too sensitive to this test, Aquarius will lose interest. It's all part of being fascinating, interesting, and fun for Aquarius. He has to know you'll play the mental games he loves to play—and that you're strong enough to handle them. Therefore, don't get angry when Aquarius tests you. Laugh about it—and do it back. Aquarius will appreciate this!

Unlike some other signs, Aquarius is impressed with bold, aggressive moves. You can grab an Aquarius when you want and he certainly won't shy away. Just make sure you have the mental connection first, or you'll be wasting your time. Aquarians are capable of having sex or a fling without getting emotionally connected at all. They won't judge you if you sleep with them right away, usually, but if you get overly romantic or clingy when Aquarius isn't quite as into it as you are, Aquarius will definitely back away from the situation.

If Aquarius is not getting what he wants out of the relationship, in any way, he's more likely to cheat than any other sign. Aquarians, like Sagittarius, will only be faithful to The One—and, even then, it's still difficult for an Aquarius to be completely and utterly devoted.

If an Aquarius has a short fling, or encounter, it doesn't mean their hearts will be in it. Aquarians can definitely turn their emotions on and off, but only when they're not in love. When they're in love, it's another story altogether. What will keep an Aquarius going is challenge. Like Aries, Aquarius always needs a challenge on some level in all of their relationships—or they won't take you seriously. Remember, Aquarius is a survivor and knows that nothing worth having comes too easily.

Matches with Aquarius

Due to the lack of prejudice in this sign, Aquarians usually get along with just about everyone. They're particularly attracted to people with whom they share an intellectual camaraderie—someone who makes them laugh and makes them feel good about themselves. In this way, Gemini can be a fabulous match for Aquarius, as long as they don't butt heads. This relationship can work only if the two find balance between neediness and independence. Also, Gemini can be extremely jealous and possessive with mates, which Aquarius abhors.

ESSENTIAL

Aries is usually a good match for Aquarius. Together, they have lively, fascinating conversations, plenty of spunk, and mental camaraderie. Unfortunately, the flakiness factor of Aries can be evident to Aquarius, and he's not sure if he can trust her. However, he likes the challenge.

Many Aquarians wind up with Virgos. Virgos have the kind of stubbornness and organized stability that Aquarians secretly crave. But this may also be an ego thing. Remember, Aquarius loves a challenge and Virgo keeps them squirming with their moral lectures and hard-headed ways. But, mentally and in bed, these two can do very well together.

A Libra or another Aquarius can be a good match—especially if one is more outgoing and gregarious than the other and lets his partner shine. This is a good example of two of the same (air) signs doing well together.

Aquarians are usually secure enough to see bad and good traits in a partner that are similar to their own, and still be able to deal with it and move ahead with the relationship.

A sign that's sextile or trine to Aquarius will also work. And Aquarius's polar opposite, Leo, can be an interesting mate for Aquarius. If Aquarius doesn't get too self-involved and gives Leo her fair due, this can work. But Leo is usually running after Aquarius, and Aquarius can get tired of that—fast. If Leo pulls away a little, this rapport can function well. All in all, Aquarius is a great partner if you've truly won his heart. If not, you'll just be a stop along the way for lively Aquarius, who craves adventure and experience.

Chapter 15

Love Compatibility: Water

Water signs in love are the craftiest and most manipulative of all the signs. But they get away with it because they're very special. However, try wronging a Water sign like Pisces, Cancer, or Scorpio, and you'll be sorry. They have a way of pushing your buttons, getting to the heart of the matter, and forcing you to fall all over yourself to accommodate them. They're "feeling" signs, like Fire, but they have patient endurance that the Fire signs lack, allowing them to win in the end. In this chapter, find out more about Water signs in love.

Cancer in Love

Cancers can be evasive when it comes to romance. They flirt coyly, yet all the while they're feeling their way through the maze of their own emotions. It's true. Astrologers will tell you that Cancers feel deeply; but what they don't tell you is that Cancers are also very good at putting their feelings "on hold." In other words, if they're not already in love with you, they can pull back and see the relationship for what it is at a distance.

On the other hand, if they're in love, it's not so easy for them to let go. They tend to go the cheating route to push away a partner rather than fess up and just say how they feel. In fact, beware of Cancers dodging questions and important issues. They find it difficult to open up and talk about their true, personal feelings. If they do, with you, you've got an edge over all the others. Once again the whole "side-stepping" part of Cancer is absolutely true. True to their crab sign, they mimic the crustacean with surprising accuracy.

Some Cancers dislike the courtship of romance altogether and prefer to get right down to the important questions: Are we compatible? Do we love each other? The problem is, they tend to go through this by themselves or with a very close friend—not with you. You'll only see the wheels turning. In this case, you must be direct and ask what's going on.

They enjoy entertaining at home because it's where they feel most comfortable, surrounded by all that's familiar to them. They feel comfortable around water, too. From the fluidity and calmness of water springs their vivid, fantastical imaginations. Cancers are "idea" people—and can truly explain any strange, unusual, or outrageous concept to you.

Just remember: to live with and love a Cancer, you have to accept the intensity of their emotions. It's a war they have within themselves, and they'll want to embroil you in it. Unfortunately, they're too busy taking care of you and others to know (and show) what's eating at them. You'll have to get to the heart of the matter yourself.

Seduction Tips with Cancer

There's one thing that many astrologers don't tell you: Cancers are like Geminis in that they love to laugh. They're usually funny, themselves—though in either a biting or subtly ironic way. But here's the thing. Geminis like making people laugh even more than they appreciate others who make them laugh. Cancer is the opposite. One way to truly win a Cancer is to show him you two have the same sense of intelligent, dark humor. In fact, if you don't make a Cancer laugh, chances are that he'll have a hard time falling in love with you.

Here's another thing: Cancer men tend to go for only three types of women: the victim, the wild (Fire sign) card, or the good girl—in that order. In other words, when they're younger, they'll fall for someone who needs to lean on their shoulders. However, when they realize that a partner won't reciprocate, they'll get sick of it and walk away.

Later on in life, they'll go for all kinds of women—especially the "wild card," whom they can't control. However, this is not a good match for them and they'll see it clearly, eventually. But they like a little drama, even if they despise confrontation. Cancer men, many times, will date women who are older than them—or much younger. Or both.

ALERT!

Cancers like to poke and prod. They like to make fun—and will do it just to get your goat. Don't let them get the best of you. Play along! If you act too touchy if they joke with you, they'll think you're too rigid.

Perhaps the worst thing you can do with a Cancer is to take everything too literally. If you don't understand the idea of "concept" and the subtleties of grand schemes, forget Cancer. Cancer is good at seeing the big picture. They stall at the idea of future and forever-after, but they'll know, deep down, when they get there. Cancers don't have to be faithful at all, but once they make the wedding type of commitment, they're settled for good.

Matches with Cancer

On the surface, Pisces, as the other dreamy Water sign, would seem to be the most compatible with a Cancer. But Pisces's all-over-the-map sense of style with Cancer's sidestepping could be frustrating for both. Plus, the duality of Pisces would, most likely, drive a Cancer person crazy. One of the best combinations here is Water sign, Scorpio. Cancer manages Scorpio with bravado and knows how to get the ever-changing Scorpio hooked. A little mystery goes a long way with Scorpio, and, in the case of this match, Cancer cannot help but induce a little intrigue with her onslaught of bottled-up emotions that just lie beneath the surface. Scorpio might just bring it out of Cancer.

Earth signs—Taurus, Virgo, and Capricorn—are particularly good for Cancers with Taurus and Virgo because they are sextile to Cancer. Fire signs with Cancer, on the other hand, tend to bring out the worst in Cancer— unless it's, perhaps, a very evolved Fire sign. In rare cases, Leos do well with Cancers (especially if the Leo is the man).

Scorpio in Love

You don't know the meaning of the word intensity unless you've been involved with a Scorpio. No other sign brings such raw power to life. The rawness probably isn't something you understand or even like very much, but there's no question that it's intricately woven through the fabric of your relationship.

ESSENTIAL

If you're in for the long haul, then accept your Scorpio the way he or she is. If you're not in for the long haul, why try to work it out? In any case, a Scorpio will, indeed, have a profound effect on your life. Scorpio is all about transformation and changing the way others around him see the world.

The odd part is that you're never quite sure how the intensity is going to manifest: jealousy, fury, endless questions, or soft and intriguing, but effective passion. Sometimes, the intensity doesn't have anything to do with the relationship, but with the personal dramas in the Scorpio's life. Many times, you may even hear from work colleagues that he's a "perfectionist, and difficult to work with." The word "crazy" may even get into the picture.

Scorpios have a magnetism that is legendary. It doesn't even matter if he's good-looking—it's always there. Consider this: Scorpio is always the sexiest person in the room. Astrologers say that Scorpio is also known for his bedroom prowess: this isn't myth. Unfortunately, other problems can weigh Scorpio down so he's got to be clear of mind and calm in order to woo you in his cool, mysterious way.

Speaking of mysterious: there's something with Scorpio that you may just not be able to put your finger on. If he's completely direct with you, that's good. Chances are, though, he's got a number of secrets he keeps hidden from the world. It may be something that's happened in his past, or a fetish he doesn't want to let you in on, or even another woman he sees occasionally. Beware.

FACT

You'll always be able to tell when Scorpio is fibbing. You can feel it. The energy around him changes. If you keep insisting that he tell you the truth, he may even get angry. If he does—it's a good sign that there's something he's not telling you. The only way to get it out of him is to get him in a good mood, pretend you don't really care, and then get him to confess.

Scorpio's senses are strong, especially those of sight, touch, and taste. If he touches you, you'll feel it down to your toes. He has keen sight, meaning instincts. And taste: if he cooks, he's wonderful. If not, he appreciates everything about food. However, there's one sense he lacks: hearing. It seems as if he doesn't hear anything you say. It's not that he doesn't really remember. Instead, he has a mental block on the things he doesn't want to hear, or he's very likely to pretend he doesn't know what you're talking about. The truth is, Scorpios have excellent memories. Don't let him get away with this.

Seduction Tips with Scorpio

Scorpio man needs to woo his woman. Do not chase after him. He may do it subtly, at first, but eventually he'll invite you for a weekend away somewhere. Scorpio has a knack for finding a romantic way to court (and win) a partner. Scorpio is also relentless in his pursuit and usually gets what he wants.

He likes very sexy, yet tasteful. He'll negatively judge a potential mate if the sexy part extends to flirting with his friends—don't do it. Scorpio might keep his rage hidden for a while, but it won't work in your favor to make him over-the-top jealous. He'll just think you're not the good girl he thought. Scorpios will have flings with too-sexy women, but they will never marry them.

Be aware that many Scorpios are hidden workaholics. They're very good, in the beginning, at hiding this fact. This is why: they need to complete a task before they can go on to the next. Therefore, the thing that will be most important for a Scorpio is to "get you," and then, predictably, he can go back to his normal routine of working crazy hours, complaining about it, and never resolving the problem.

Many Scorpios have obsessive tendencies—whether or not you see them in the beginning. Truth is, at first it may just seem like you're the obsession. He'll be so bent on getting you that you'll wonder if you've just stepped into a romance novel. Be aware that this may change later. Scorpio can't leave the duties of his job for long—he defines himself by it.

Know, too, that if he's having many problems at work, your relationship will suffer. He needs to resolve work issues before he can think of getting intimate again. He absolutely cannot separate these two parts of his life—try as he does. In this respect, you must understand and be supportive. There's no way around it.

In the case of Scorpio, before you even think of letting romance get the best of you, you must determine something to make sure you're getting involved with someone who can handle a real relationship: the pitying factor. Many Scorpios are perfectionists, with work and with themselves, so ask yourself: Is this person happy with his life? In other words, does he constantly say "poor me"? The thing is, if a Scorpio is not happy, deep down, he will go into periods of self-doubt and pity—and will bring you down with him. Some Scorpios are emotionally mature and can handle the world around them. Find out first, though.

ALERT!

Keep in mind that Scorpio will stay in a romantic situation that's not working for longer than he should. If he starts pulling away a little, or is less jealous or possessive than he was before, you're probably losing him. The worst thing that you can do at this point is to chase after him. Be busy, pull away, and let him come after you. Scorpio is a lonely, private soul—but he absolutely hates being alone, too.

The best time to approach a Scorpio about something important is after lovemaking. His guard is let down almost completely. Be aware of Scorpio's temper. He bottles things up inside and then it all comes out at once—in a huff. Don't try to convince Scorpio he is wrong at this point. Let him calm down first. If not, he'll never see your side of it.

Matches with Scorpio

Scorpio is usually compatible with Taurus, because the signs are polar opposites and balance each other. The Water of Scorpio and the Earth of Taurus mix well. However, both signs are fixed, which means that in a disagreement neither will give in to the other. Scorpios can be compatible with other Scorpios as long as each person understands the other's intensity and passions. Pisces and Cancer, the other two Water signs, may be too weak for Scorpio's intensity, unless a comparison of natal charts indicates otherwise.

Fire signs may blend well with Scorpio, depending on their charts. If a Scorpio is emotionally solid, a Leo may be a good match. Scorpio loves Leo's sunny nature, and is drawn to it. If Scorpio doesn't pull Leo down with him, this can work okay. Sagittarius, especially if Scorpio is near the cusp of Sagittarius, can be the same—but ditto with the "bringing her down with the house." If the two can respect each other and find a good balance, this can work. Aries and Scorpio, however, will find that the emotional gap is probably too much of a chasm to cross.

Pisces in Love

Through the heart, sensitive Pisces experiences his subjective reality as real, solid, perhaps even more tangible than the external world. For some Pisces, romance can be the point of transcendence—the source where he penetrates to the larger mysteries that have concerned him most of his life. To be romantically involved with a Pisces is to be introduced to many levels of consciousness and awareness. If you're not up to it, then get out now because your Pisces isn't going to change.

There is nothing weak about Pisces, as many astrologers claim. Instead, Pisces watches from a distance and determines the best point of attack.

Pisces, also, many times seems the quiet type, who's sweet and kind. But know this: when Pisces is in a relationship, and feels comfortable, there is no one who can manipulate you and your feelings like Pisces can (except, maybe, Cancer). The way a Pisces does this is to play cold and walk away until you follow. Pisces knows that this always works in human nature and has this move down to a science.

He's strong because he'll get you to come to him without any effort on his part. Pisces are ten times craftier than they appear. They're incredibly good at hiding this side of themselves. They're so adept at playing along with you, and being "on your side," that you won't even know what hit you when they use something—something you've told them—against you, in the future.

ALERT!

Know this: Pisces will test you. All Pisces know how to test and how to get the answer they're looking for at the moment. If you're smart enough, you'll recognize this and pass the test. If not, Pisces will turn away without warning and find someone worthier of his affections.

They say Pisces is idealistic. This is true. But they also say that Pisces is a dreamer, and there is a misconception about this. Yes, Pisces is a dreamer: but he's a dreamer with a vision. Most Pisces know what they want and go after it with a kind of slow, methodical gait. Eventually, most of them get what they want, even if it takes time. But Pisces instinctively know how best to get the most out of their astonishingly calm composure and patience.

Pisces includes a little bit of every sign and can usually pull out this grab bag of talents at will. He can be a little mysterious like Scorpio, play the noble like Leo, insert the commanding attitude like Sagittarius, be the charmer like Gemini, and act the part of smooth-talker like Aries. The only role that Pisces has difficulty playing is Aquarius, whose sign sits right next to Pisces.

In fact, Pisces has a hard time hiding disdain for those he truly doesn't like while Aquarius is perfectly capable of fraternizing with the enemy, if need be. And Aquarius does not turn up his nose at anyone, while Pisces does so often. Pisces has a regal Air about him like Leo. While Leo is more of the caring, noble set, Pisces has a proud, capable, and studious air about him, which, try as he may, he cannot shake.

Pisces is intelligent and sympathetic. Don't ever confuse sympathetic with empathetic, though. Pisces will not feel your particular brand of sadness, though he seems to. Instead, he's likely to bring you out of the despair by "understanding" your plight and giving you good advice for it. But the sadness he shows you will never reach his heart.

However, there is no one like Pisces to give you good advice. Aries may be good at it, but he orders you around while doing so. His words are more command and "truth" than suggestion. Gemini is good at it, but usually comes up with the overly aggressive way. Instead, Pisces will put the idea into your head and let you come up with the solution. This is, indeed, most effective and one of Pisces' best traits.

Seduction Tips with Pisces

Pisces, in love, would do anything for his mate. If he's not truly in love, though, he can look at the relationship with astonishing coldness (even if he finds it difficult to break away). Pisces, like Cancer, has a tough time deciding what he truly wants. There's something always in the back of a Pisces mind that says "I could probably do better." And, because of Pisces' idealism, he'll always wonder what kind of mate he'd have in a perfect world. Also, in all likelihood, he could make you a list of how he imagines this "perfection."

FACT

Pisces also has a thing for power. If you're someone he can look up to and admire, you'll win Pisces' heart for sure. Unlike the Air signs, Libra, Gemini, and Aquarius, Pisces will be more won over with accomplishment and quiet romantic gestures than pure physical beauty.

Also, since Pisces likes the cool and understated, your manners, gestures, and even dress should be tasteful and elegant, not showy or ostentatious, ever. Again, the way someone puts herself together will be more important to Pisces than makeup or any other superficial marks or anything but natural, regal beauty. Pisces also appreciate directness and fire—gumption and energy. They love intensity and romance, in a grounded and refined way.

Matches with Pisces

Other Water signs seem the obvious choice here. But Scorpio might overpower Pisces, and Cancer might be too clingy. The signs sextile to Pisces are Capricorn and Taurus. While Capricorn might be too limited and grounded for the Piscean imagination, Taurus probably fits right in. Gemini, also, because it's a mutable sign like Pisces, can be compatible.

The real shocker here is that Sagittarius may just be the best combination for Pisces. Though they're such opposites, they complement each other quite well. Pisces is able to soothe the Sagittarius savage beast—and they fit like two pieces of a puzzle. Pisces also lets Sagittarius do what he wants, yet always keeps the upper hand with a cool, polished, quietly strong demeanor. And this is what Sagittarius likes best. As for the other Fire signs, there doesn't seem to be much chance, but it truly depends on the other factors in the two separate charts.

Chapter 16

Love Compatibility: Earth

In love, Earth signs can fall hard. But they'll struggle and protest along the way. They're ten times more sensitive than people think they are—only because they don't necessarily wear their hearts on their sleeves. For Earth signs, most things are black and white, and love is no exception. Earth signs are known to be stubborn, but when they love, they love truly and deeply. This chapter has all you need to know about Taurus, Virgo, and Capricorn in matters of the heart.

Taurus in Love

In romance with a Taurus, a lot goes on beneath the surface. Taureans are subtle and quiet about what they feel. Once they fall, though, they fall hard. In fact, their inherent fixed natures simply won't allow them to give up. Perhaps this sounds like it could be good for you and bad for them. Maybe. But Taurus people get in way over their heads and then find that there's no turning back.

However, a Taurus will never really fall in love unless he thinks he can trust you. Trust definitely goes a long way with Taurus. Deep down, Taurus knows that he's sensitive and that he takes himself a little too seriously. His sense of responsibility weighs heavily on his shoulders and he'll always fulfill any task he believes he must.

But, remember: he'll also feel like it's up to him to judge the world. If he's critical, take it as a warning. He definitely has an idea in his head of how things should be, and he'll try to mold you into how he sees you or how he'd like to see you. Pay close attention to his naggings because, though it may seem otherwise, he means every word he says.

Sometimes, you're never quite sure if a Taurus is in love with you or in love with the idea of you. Ego comes into play with a Taurus and sometimes his "win, win" attitude will outweigh his real need for you. If you're not sure, trust your gut. Deep down, you'll know the difference.

As a Venus-ruled sign, Taureans are true sensualists and romantic lovers. Their romantic attachments ground and stabilize them. Love is like air to them: they need it to breathe. Again, they'll want to trust and rely on you. This is essential. In fact, it's very easy to see if Taurus trusts you, at least to some degree. Taurus can't touch and make love unless he feels he can. Taurus and Virgo may be the only men in the zodiac who are mainly like this. They might entertain a fling or two in their lifetime, but that's not what they're about.

Instead, they're looking for meaning and true love—someone who'll put up with their obstinate nature and even revel in it. Most Taurus men are quite macho. Like the bull, they're quite direct and will usually take a problem on—head on (quite the opposite of the way Cancer would handle it).

Give them a good love challenge and they won't shy away. Taurus is built for competition. The problem is, he may never really stop to consider if you two are actually good for one another.

FACT

Taurus women (and sometimes men) have a habit of falling for Fire signs. In the beginning, the Fire sign will conquer her. But once she starts getting comfortable, he begins flirting with others and testing her. If she lightens up, she just may be able to keep him.

Seduction Tips with Taurus

Never make a Taurus too jealous. He'll punish you for it and get revenge. Sure, he'll do it quietly and methodically, but it will come back to you. Meanwhile, Taurus men like the slow art of seduction. Don't go to bed with a Taurus too quickly. He'll never respect you for it.

Taurus wants to make love, not just have sex, and it's a slow, seductive tango. Taurus definitely doesn't rush. If you're not into languid, sensual lovemaking, a Taurus may not be for you. Even if Taurus likes to talk "dirty," he still wants to know that the feelings there are real. Then he'll be able to loosen up and be himself in bed.

ALERT!

Unlike most other signs, Taurus should not be dealt with on a physical level when the two of you fight. In other words, you'll probably need to talk things out before you make love again. Remember, Taurus is sensitive and puts his heart into lovemaking.

Again, with Taurus, deal with issues as they come up. Don't go to bed angry. Work out your problems. Taurus is good at dealing with the issues at hand. Instead, if he pushes them deeper and deeper, you will never get them out of him again. When you bring it up, he'll look at you like he has no idea what you're talking about—even if he's steaming inside. Instead, he'll talk about it years from now when you least expect it.

In fact, Taurus is capable of holding a grudge for decades. It's very difficult for him to let go of the past. He remembers everything and never forgets anything. Try to be direct and honest with Taurus all the time. And don't let Taurus get on a self-pity track. It's his self-defense and armor. If a partner from his past has wronged him, he'll look for every conceivable reason that you'll do the same to him.

Find out where he's sensitive and make sure you stay far away from that route. In other words, if an ex cheated on him, go out of your way to show him that you're more than trustworthy. If an ex was using him for money (or, more likely, he was simply convinced that she was), make sure he knows that you're just the opposite.

When he's relaxed with you, you can give him a massage or touch him in any way—he'll get the hint. He's sensitive with touch as well. Just don't rush things. Make sure he's in love before you go to bed with him. If you don't, he'll lose respect for you and think that you do the same with everyone.

Taurus loves all sensual things—including food! And he loves domestic prowess. Cook a wonderful dinner for Taurus man or Taurus woman and you'll get extra potential husband or wife Brownie points.

Also, a woman Taurus wants to know that she's truly loved before she'll hit the sack with a man. She can have flings but, as she gets older and gets to know herself better, she'll realize that this is not the best of all possible worlds. She'll want to wait and be romanced. And there's no one who knows how to seduce and romance like Taurus.

Matches with Taurus

Conventional astrological wisdom says that the lot of us is better off with those who share the same element we do or with those who feed our element (Earth with Water, for instance). This makes Taurus compatible with other Earth signs (Virgo and Capricorn) and with Water signs. Unfortunately, other Earth signs—unless they have some Air in their charts—can sometimes be too serious for Taurus, who needs a good laugh in order to let his guard down. And though Virgo is more critical of himself (and thin-skinned with others' criticisms), Taurus can sometimes take it the wrong way, too.

Quite often, Taureans are fatally attracted to Scorpios, their polar opposites. Although their elements, Earth and Water, should make them compatible, this tends to be a superficial connection. Instead, beneath the surface, they're probably at war with one other. But this just kicks up the chemistry. Taurus is also very attracted to Fire signs. This may work okay in a relationship with a Leo, but in the long run, Sagittarius and Aries may just be too big a bite to chew for more down-to-earth Taurus.

ALERT!

A huge problem with Taurus and Leo together is that Leo likes to spend! Taurus, while generous, is very concerned with having a nest egg. Therefore, he'll woo someone with expensive dinners in the beginning, but he'll come to resent anyone who makes him spend too much in the end.

Air signs mesh well with Earth signs, too, because they're both thinking signs, whereas Water and Fire signs are more spontaneous and apt to follow their hearts. Gemini will entertain Taurus, but Taurus won't necessarily trust her. Libra may be a good bet for Taurus, as both have an incredible affinity for an elegant, sumptuous, and refined life. Libra and Taurus manage to acquire it together by spurring each other on. Aquarius' lifestyle will drive conservative Taurus crazy, despite his attraction to her.

Virgo in Love

Virgos are inscrutable in affairs of the heart. They seem remote and quiet one minute, then open and talkative the next. This is due only to Virgo's battle within himself. He's sensitive but doesn't like to show it. Sometimes he'll need to show you how he feels; other times, he'll keep his feelings a secret. Unfortunately, he doesn't always let you see this true side of himself. He's too busy weighing all the options and trying to act the way he thinks he should, not how he truly feels.

Virgos always need to perfect everything: every moment, every deed, and every word. They're idealists, but in a practical way. They truly believe that everything should fall into place on its own (even if it shows no sign of happening) and tend to stay in relationships much longer than they should simply because they don't want to give up and walk away. To them, you are the investment of their precious time. They also hold on to the past, like Cancers, and, unfortunately, apply past experiences to present ones. In a perfect world, this would make sense (to them). Unfortunately, each situation is different, and Virgos must face this fact.

FACT

The world is a complicated place, and most of us have skeletons in our closets. But for Virgo, there are too many skeletons. He wants perfection (mostly from himself). He'll generally keep his imperfections in the dark, though he'll be the first to point out some of his more superficial flaws. Pay attention to what Virgo tells you, as it's usually all true.

It is said that Virgos generally don't entertain romantic illusions. There is truth to this, but it's not the whole story. Virgos are incredibly romantic when they truly feel it. They have a wonderful appreciation of love—and know how to woo the "right" way. They *seem* more practical than idealistic, but deep down, Virgos suffer for love and feel their emotions intensely.

Virgos try to make everything fit into their idea of a perfect world. For example, they're very serious about the words they and others use. If you tell a Virgo something, he expects you to follow through on your promise. He's put his heart and soul into finding a solution for you. If you don't at least try it his way, he'll seriously discredit you.

QUESTION?

It's said that Virgos are critical. Is this true?
Yes—Virgos are critical, and they can't help it. Don't take it personally, though. A Virgo is never harder on the people he loves than he is on himself. Virgo needs to analyze, sort through, and mentally take stock once in a while in order to feel grounded and stable.

Here's the bottom line: If you ask Virgo for advice, you'd better take it or at least make him think you're doing something practical about your situation. Like Sagittarius, Virgo will always tell you what to do and expect you to do it. If you get advice from Virgo and ignore it, he'll be less likely to help you in the future.

Seduction Tips with Virgo

Unfortunately, Virgos have a penchant for getting involved with emotionally abusive partners early on. Or it can go the other way: they have a relationship with someone they're able to boss around, but never quite get to the place where they respect a mate enough to stay with him or her in the long run.

Virgo, like Taurus, needs to feel some kind of purity and sweetness in order to make love—even if he's not in love. He definitely prefers being in love than not, and sometimes won't even have sex unless he's feeling love. One thing's for sure: Virgo must feel special, or it's just not happening. He can have adventurous affairs, but, as he gets to know himself, he'll simply want more and will despise the thought of getting close without the presence of deeper feelings.

ESSENTIAL

You have to do some grunt work to get on a Virgo's good side. If you show a Virgo that you're easy to get along with and can take his criticism with a healthy show of acceptance, he'll feel more comfortable with you and will eventually let his guard down completely.

Virgos are conflicted within and, therefore, will come across as being nit-picky or too precise. The truth is, they've got thin skins. The best way to handle a Virgo lecturing and criticizing you is to tell her she's right about whatever she's picking at, at the moment. Then bring it up later to dispute, if you like. Virgos must have a sense that they're right. They know this about themselves. In fact, they'll be the first to admit that they're difficult and hardheaded.

Matches with Virgo

Virgos are mentally attracted to Geminis, but they find the twins a bit hard to take for the long run. The light, airy nature of Geminis, too, contrasts with Virgo's obstinate nature. Gemini likes interesting discussions (as does Virgo) and entertains Virgo well, but Virgo sometimes fights more than Gemini would like.

Instead, the "grounding" present in other Earth signs may seem appealing on the surface, but leave it to a Virgo to find fault with his fellow Earth signs. Scorpios and Cancers may be the best bets, with mystical Pisces a close second. Libra sometimes goes well with Gemini but it may seem like Virgo is always just 'round the bend with Libra—never quite getting all the love and devotion he wants. Libra makes it tough.

Fire signs can be great friends with Virgo, but the two might never truly understand the other's intentions, in general. It depends on the rest of their charts. If one is true Earth, and the other is true Fire, Virgo patronizes without knowing it, and sensitive Fire signs take offense without realizing that Virgo is just trying to help. In the end, anyone with a good heart and a sensitive but practical nature will get along well with Virgo, though. Like all astrological love matches, it all depends on the partners involved.

Capricorn in Love

At times, Capricorn needs a partner who is serious, while at other times he needs a lighthearted mate who will simply make him laugh. The latter will have an almost innocent quality—a purity—that Capricorn is drawn to. Which mate Capricorn ends up with, though, depends on where he is emotionally and mentally in life. This may be true for all of us to one extent or another, but it's especially true for Capricorn.

Ultimately, Capricorn's path is always serious business. No matter how hard you make him laugh about himself and the world, his path always leads back to the same riddle. Regardless of how hard he works, how far he climbs, or how emotionally or physically rich he becomes, it's never enough.

That said, Capricorns can be very independent. They don't like being told what to do or how to do it. They seem malleable enough, and can get along with anybody, though they don't necessarily enjoy the company of all.

A mate must be stimulating, engaging, knowledgeable, and, most importantly, grounded, in order for Capricorn to truly respect him. If Capricorn senses that his partner is off kilter, he'll run for the hills. He won't try to change her or help her as, say, Cancer would.

ALERT!

Capricorns respect those who are well informed. If you talk a good game and don't know your stuff, for example, forget Capricorn. He'll smell you out! Make sure to admit it if you don't know what you're talking about. Don't fake it. Capricorn will know anyway.

Meanwhile, if you're getting words of passion, love, and forever-after, pay attention. Capricorn doesn't spew out or toss around romantic words just to woo you and then leave you cold. He's got to be somewhat convinced in order to do it. True, he's a little better at having meaningless adventures than Virgo is, but eventually he'll want something that means family and future to him. And he takes that very seriously, indeed.

Seduction Tips with Capricorn

Capricorn wants a loyal, stable, solid, and devoted partner. If you have a huge group of friends (like Aquarius) and don't give Capricorn his due, you can forget it. Capricorn needs to know that you'll be there when he needs you or he'll never consider you for the long term.

ALERT!

Yes, Capricorn wants security with emotions, but financial security is sometimes even more important. Not all Capricorns are great at earning money, but they're good at keeping it or saving it all for a rainy day. If you're a spender, and your Capricorn mate is not, watch out!

Capricorns have a tough time walking away from a relationship, even one that's not that great. Therefore, you'll get little hints if Capricorn is not happy. They'll be subtle, though. If Capricorn, for instance, is spending a lot of time away from you or is talking more to others than to you, find out what's wrong before Capricorn pulls away completely. You'll always get some kind of tip-off.

Capricorns can seriously appreciate sexiness but will admire a conservative style of dress even more. If you combine sexy with conservative, you've got it made. Actually, if you're able to dress for the occasion, Capricorn will adore this quality in you. Capricorn gets better at doing it himself, later in life, but he'll definitely notice if you make an effort for him.

Matches with Capricorn

Virgos may be too literal and spirited for Capricorn. Plus, Virgo in bed can bring out Capricorn's traditional side, which bothers Capricorn, who secretly longs for someone who can open him up, emotionally and spiritually (both in bed and out). Taurus may be too fixed, but because they both have the Earth element in common, Capricorn and Taurus can get along well.

Of all the Water signs, the intensity of Scorpios may be overwhelming— though Capricorn will get a real kick out of Scorpio's tendency to be jealous. In bed, these two can be smolderingly hot. Instead, the ambivalence of Pisces will, most likely, drive Capricorn nuts.

ESSENTIAL

Capricorns may just get along with Cancer because they're both Cardinal signs (though this could be a possible mad rush to the finish line, too! The two can be competitive!). Cancer and Capricorn both have refined senses of humor. If Capricorn has patience with Cancer's moods (not likely), this can work.

Strangely enough, a Leo might be the best bet for Capricorn. If Leo has some Earth in her chart—or some balanced Air—they get along well. Certainly, the attraction is there. Capricorn mystifies Leo. Capricorn praises Leo the way she needs to be praised. They complement each other, and that's what it's all about.

Appendix A

Mercury and Venus Charts

1950					
MERCURY			**VENUS**		
month	day	sign	month	day	sign
JAN	1	AQU	JAN	1	AQU
JAN	15	CAP	APR	6	PIS
FEB	14	AQU	MAY	5	ARI
MAR	7	PIS	JUN	1	TAU
MAR	24	ARI	JUN	27	GEM
APR	8	TAU	JUL	22	CAN
JUN	14	GEM	AUG	16	LEO
JUL	2	CAN	SEP	10	VIR
AUG	2	VIR	OCT	28	SCO
AUG	27	LIB	NOV	21	SAG
SEP	10	VIR	DEC	14	CAP
OCT	9	LIB			
OCT	27	SCO			
NOV	15	SAG			
DEC	5	CAP			

1951					
MERCURY			**VENUS**		
month	day	sign	month	day	sign
JAN	1	CAP	JAN	1	CAP
FEB	9	AQU	JAN	7	AQU
FEB	28	PIS	JAN	31	PIS
MAR	16	ARI	FEB	24	ARI
APR	2	TAU	MAR	21	TAU
MAY	1	ARI	APR	15	GEM
MAY	15	TAU	MAY	11	CAN
JUN	9	GEM	JUN	7	LEO
JUN	24	CAN	JUL	8	VIR
JUL	8	LEO	NOV	9	LIB
OCT	2	LIB			
OCT	19	SCO			
NOV	8	SAG			
DEC	1	CAP			
DEC	12	SAG			

1952

MERCURY			VENUS		
month	day	sign	month	day	sign
JAN	1	SAG	JAN	1	SCO
FEB	13	CAP	JAN	2	SAG
FEB	3	AQU	JAN	27	CAP
MAR	7	ARI	MAR	16	PIS
MAY	14	TAU	APR	9	ARI
MAY	31	GEM	MAY	4	TAU
JUN	14	CAN	MAY	28	GEM
JUN	30	LEO	JUN	22	CAN
SEP	7	VIR	JUL	16	LEO
SEP	23	LIB	AUG	9	VIR
OCT	11	SCO	SEP	3	LIB
NOV	1	SAG	SEP	27	SCO
			OCT	22	SAG
			NOV	15	CAP
			DEC	10	AQU

1953

MERCURY			VENUS		
month	day	sign	month	day	sign
JAN	1	SAG	JAN	1	AQU
JAN	6	CAP	JAN	5	PIS
JAN	25	AQU	FEB	2	ARI
FEB	11	PIS	MAR	14	TAU
MAR	2	ARI	MAR	31	ARI
MAR	15	PIS	JUN	5	TAU
APR	17	ARI	JUL	7	GEM
MAY	8	TAU	AUG	4	CAN
MAY	23	GEM	AUG	30	LEO
JUN	6	CAN	SEP	24	VIR
JUN	26	LEO	OCT	18	LIB
JUL	28	CAN	NOV	11	SCO
AUG	11	LEO	DEC	5	SAG
AUG	30	VIR	DEC	29	CAP
SEP	15	LIB			
OCT	4	SCO			
OCT	31	SAG			
NOV	6	SCO			
DEC	10	SAG			
DEC	30	CAP			

1954					
MERCURY			**VENUS**		
month	day	sign	month	day	sign
JAN	1	CAP	JAN	2	CAP
JAN	18	AQU	JAN	22	AQU
FEB	4	PIS	FEB	15	PIS
APR	13	ARI	MAR	11	ARI
APR	30	TAU	APR	4	TAU
MAY	14	GEM	APR	28	GEM
MAY	30	CAN	MAY	23	CAN
AUG	7	LEO	JUN	17	LEO
AUG	22	VIR	JUL	13	VIR
SEP	8	LIB	AUG	9	LIB
SEP	29	SCO	SEP	6	SCO
NOV	4	LIB	OCT	23	SAG
NOV	11	SCO	OCT	27	SCO
DEC	4	SAG			
DEC	23	CAP			

1955					
MERCURY			**VENUS**		
month	day	sign	month	day	sign
JAN	1	CAP	JAN	1	SCO
JAN	10	AQU	JAN	6	SAG
MAR	17	PIS	FEB	6	CAP
APR	6	ARI	MAR	4	AQU
APR	22	TAU	MAR	30	PIS
MAY	6	GEM	APR	24	ARI
JUL	13	CAN	MAY	19	TAU
JUL	30	LEO	JUN	13	GEM
AUG	14	VIR	JUL	8	CAN
SEP	1	LIB	AUG	1	LEO
NOV	8	SCO	AUG	25	VIR
NOV	27	SAG	SEP	18	LIB
DEC	16	CAP	OCT	13	SCO
			NOV	6	SAG
			NOV	30	CAP
			DEC	24	AQU

1956

MERCURY			VENUS		
month	day	sign	month	day	sign
JAN	1	CAP	JAN	1	AQU
JAN	4	AQU	JAN	15	PIS
FEB	2	CAP	FEB	11	ARI
FEB	15	AQU	MAR	7	TAU
MAR	11	PIS	APR	4	GEM
MAR	28	ARI	MAY	8	CAN
APR	12	TAU	JUN	23	GEM
APR	29	GEM	AUG	4	CAN
JUL	6	CAN	SEP	8	LEO
JUL	21	LEO	OCT	6	VIR
AUG	26	LIB	NOV	25	SCO
SEP	29	VIR	DEC	19	SAG
OCT	11	LIB			
OCT	31	SCO			
NOV	18	SAG			
DEC	8	CAP			

1957

MERCURY			VENUS		
month	day	sign	month	day	sign
JAN	1	CAP	JAN	1	SAG
FEB	12	AQU	JAN	12	CAP
MAR	4	PIS	FEB	5	AQU
APR	4	TAU	MAR	25	ARI
JUN	12	GEM	APR	19	TAU
JUN	28	CAN	MAY	13	GEM
JUL	12	LEO	JUN	6	CAN
JUL	30	VIR	JUL	1	LEO
OCT	6	LIB	JUL	26	VIR
OCT	23	SCO	AUG	20	LIB
LOV	11	SAG	SEP	14	SCO
DEC	2	CAP	OCT	10	SAG
DEC	28	SAG	NOV	5	CAP
			DEC	6	AQU

1958

MERCURY			VENUS		
month	day	sign	month	day	sign
JAN	1	SAG	JAN	1	AQU
JAN	14	CAP	APR	6	PIS
FEV	6	AQU	MAY	5	ARI
FEB	24	PIS	JUN	1	TAU
MAR	12	ARI	JUN	26	GEM
APR	2	TAU	JUL	22	CAN
APR	10	ARI	AUG	16	LEO
MAY	17	TAU	SEP	9	VIR
JUN	5	GEM	OCT	Q3	LIV
JUN	20	CAN	OCT	27	SCO
JUL	4	LEO	NOV	20	SAG
JUL	26	VIR	DEC	4	CAP
AUG	23	LEO			
SEP	11	VIR			
SEP	28	LIB			
OCT	16	SCO			
NOV	5	SAG			

1959

MERCURY			VENUS		
month	day	sign	month	day	sign
JAN	1	SAG	JAN	1	CAP
JAN	10	CAP	JAN	7	AQU
JAN	30	AQU	JAN	31	PIS
FEB	17	PIS	FEB	24	ARI
MAR	5	ARI	MAR	20	TAU
MAY	12	TAU	APR	14	GEM
MAY	28	GEM	MAY	10	CAN
JUN	11	CAN	JUN	6	LEO
JUN	28	LEO	JUL	8	VIR
SEP	5	VIR	SEP	20	LEO
OCT	21	LIB	SEP	25	VIR
*OCT	9	SCO	NOV	9	LIB
OCT	31	SAG	DEC	7	SCO
NOV	25	SCO			
DEC	13	SAG			

1960					
MERCURY			**VENUS**		
month	day	sign	month	day	sign
JAN	1	SAG	JAN	1	SCO
JAN	4	CAP	JAN	2	SAG
JAN	23	AQU	JAN	27	CAP
FEB	9	PIS	FEB	20	AQU
APR	16	ARI	MAR	16	PIS
MAY	4	TAU	APR	9	ARI
MAY	19	GEM	MAY	3	TAU
JUN	2	CAN	MAY	28	GEM
JUL	1	LEO	JUN	21	CAN
JUL	6	CAN	JUL	16	LEO
	AUG	10	LEO	AUG	9 VIR
AUG	27	VIR	SEP	2	LIB
SEP	12	LIB	SEP	27	SCO
OCT	1	SCO	OCT	21	SAG
DEC	7	SAG	NOV	15	CAP
DEC	27	CAP	DEC	10	AQU

1961					
MERCURY			**VENUS**		
month	day	sign	month	day	sign
JAN	1	CAP	JAN	1	AQU
JAN	14	AQU	JAN	5	PIS
FEB	1	PIS	FEB	2	ARI
FEB	24	AQU	JUN	5	TAU
MAR	18	PIS	JUL	7	GEM
APR	10	ARI	AUG	3	CAN
APR	26	TAU	AUG	29	LEO
MAY	10	GEM	SEP	23	VIR
MAY	28	CAN	OCT	18	LIB
AUG	4	LEO	NOV	11	SCO
AUG	18	VIR	DEC	5	SAG
SEP	4	LIB	DEC	29	CAP
SEP	27	SCO			
OCT	22	LIB			
NOV	10	SCO			
DEC	20	CAP			

1962

MERCURY			VENUS		
month	day	sign	month	day	sign
JAN	1	CAP	JAN	1	CAP
JAN	7	AQU	JAN	21	AQU
MAR	15	PIS	FEB	14	PIS
APR	3	ARI	MAR	10	ARI
APR	18	TAU	APR	3	TAU
MAY	3	GEM	APR 28		GEM
JUL	11	CAN	MAY	23	CAN
JUL	26	LEO	JUN	17	LEO
AUG	10	VIR	JUL	12	VIR
AUG	29	LIB	AUG	8	LIB
NOV	5	SCO	SEP	7	SCO
NOV	23	SAG			
DEC	12	CAP			

1963

MERCURY			VENUS		
month	day	sign	month	day	sign
JAN	1	CAP	JAN	1	SCO
JAN	2	AQU	JAN	6	SAG
JAN	20	CAP	FEB	5	CAP
FEB	15	AQU	MAR	4	AQU
MAR	9	PIS	MAR	30	PIS
MAR	26	ARI	APR	24	ARI
APR	9	TAU	MAY	19	TAU
MAY	3	GEM	JUN	12	GEM
MAY	10	TAU	JUL	7	CAN
JUN	14	GEM	JUL	31	LEO
JUL	4	CAN	AUG	25	VIR
JUL	18	LEO	SEP	18	LIB
AUG	3	VIR	OCT	12	SCO
AUG	26	LIB	NOV	5	SAG
SEP	16	VIR	NOV	29	CAP
OCT	10	LIB	DEC	23	AQU
OCT	28	SCO			
NOV	16	SAG			
DEC	6	CAP			

1964					
MERCURY			**VENUS**		
month	day	sign	month	day	sign
JAN	1	CAP	JAN	1	AQU
FEB	10	AQU	JAN	17	PIS
FEB	29	PIS	FEB	10	ARI
MAR	16	ARI	MAR	7	TAU
APR	2	TAU	APR	4	GEM
JUN	9	GEM	MAY	9	CAN
JUN	24	CAN	JUN	17	GEM
JUL	9	LEO	AUG	5	CAN
JUL	27	VIR	SEP	8	LEO
OCT	3	LIB	OCT	5	VIR
OCT	20	SCO	OCT	31	LIB
NOV	8	SAG	NOV	25	SCO
NOV	30	CAP	DEC	19	SAG
DEC	16	SAG			

1965					
MERCURY			**VENUS**		
month	day	sign	month	day	sign
JAN	1	SAG	JAN	1	SAG
JAN	13	CAP	JAN	12	CAP
FEB	3	AQU	FEB	5	AQU
FEB	21	PIS	MAR	1	PIS
MAR	9	ARI	MAR	25	ARI
MAY	15	TAU	APR	18	TAU
JUN	2	GEM	MAY	12	GEM
JUN	16	CAN	JUN	6	CAN
JUL	1	LEO	JUN	30	LEO
JUL	31	VIR	JUL	25	VIR
AUG	3	LEO	AUG	19	LIB
SEP	8	VIR	SEP	13	SCO
SEP	25	LIB	OCT	9	SAG
OCT	12	SCO	NOV	5	CAP
NOV	2	SAG	DEC	7	AQU

1966

MERCURY			VENUS		
month	day	sign	month	day	sign
JAN	1	SAG	JAN	1	AQU
JAN	7	CAP	FEB	6	CAP
JAN	27	AQU	FEB	25	AQU
FEB	13	PIS	APR	6	PIS
MAR	3	ARI	MAY	5	ARI
MAR	22	PIS	MAY	31	TAU
APR	17	ARI	JUN	26	GEM
MAY	9	TAU	JUL	21	CAN
MAY	24	GEM	AUG	15	LEO
JUN	7	CAN	SEP	8	VIR
JUN	26	LEO	OCT	3	LIB
SEP	1	VIR	OCT	27	SCO
SEP	17	LIB	NOV	20	SAG
OCT	5	SCO	DEC	13	CAP
OCT	30	SAG			
NOV	13	SCO			
DEC	11	SAG			

1967

MERCURY			VENUS		
month	day	sign	month	day	sign
JAN	1	CAP	JAN	1	CAP
JAN	19	AQU	JAN	6	AQU
FEB	6	PIS	JAN	30	PIS
APR	14	ARI	FEB	23	ARI
MAY	1	TAU	MAR	20	TAU
MAY	16	GEM	APR	14	GEM
MAY	31	CAN	MAY	10	CAN
AUG	8	LEO	JUN	6	LEO
AUG	24	VIR	JUL	8	VIR
SEP	9	LIB	SEP	9	LEO
SEP	30	SCO	OCT	1	VIR
DEC	5	SAG	NOV	9	LIB
DEC	24	CAP	DEC	7	SCO

1968

MERCURY			VENUS		
month	day	sign	month	day	sign
JAN	1	CAP	JAN	2	SAG
JAN	12	AQU	JAN	26	CAP
FEB	1	PIS	FEB	20	AQU
FEB	11	AQU	MAR	15	PIS
MAR	17	PIS	APR	8	ARI
APR	8	ARI	MAY	3	TAU
MAY	6	GEM	JUN	21	CAN
MAY	29	CAN	JUL	15	LEO
JUN	13	FEM	AUG	8	VIR
JUL	13	CAN	SEP	2	LIB
JUL	31	LEO	SEP	26	SCO
AUG	15	VIR	OCT	21	SAG
SEP	1	LIB	NOV	14	CAP
SEP	28	SCO	DEC	9	AQU
OCT	7	LIB			
NOV	8	SCO			
NOV	27	SAG			
DEC	16	CAP			

1969

MERCURY			VENUS		
month	day	sign	month	day	sign
JAN	1	CAP	JAN	1	AQU
JAN	4	AQU	JAN	4	PIS
MAR	12	PIS	FEB	2	ARI
MAR	30	ARI	JUN	6	TAU
APR	14	TAU	JUL	6	GEM
APR	30	GEM	AUG	3	CAN
JUL	8	CAN	AUG	29	LEO
JUL	22	LEO	SEP	23	VIR
AUG	7	VIR	OCT	17	LIB
AUG	27	LIB	NOV	10	SCO
OCT	7	VIR	DEC	4	SAG
OCT	9	LIB	DEC	28	CAP
NOV	1	SCO			
NOV	20	SAG			
DEC	9	CAP			

1970

MERCURY			VENUS		
month	day	sign	month	day	sign
JAN	1	CAP	JAN	1	CAP
JAN	4	AQU	JAN	21	AQU
JAN	4	CAP	FEB	14	PIS
FEB	13	AQU	MAR	10	ARI
MAR	5	PIS	APR	3	TAU
MAR	22	ARI	APR	27	GEM
APR	6	TAU	MAY	22	CAN
JUN	13	GEM	JUN	16	LEO
JUN	30	CAN	JUL	12	VIR
JUL	14	LEO	AUG	8	LIB
JUL	31	VIR	SEP	7	SCO
OCT	7	LIB			
OCT	25	SCO			
NOV	13	SAG			
DEC	3	CAP			

1971

MERCURY			VENUS		
month	day	sign	month	day	sign
JAN	1	CAP	JAN	1	SCO
JAN	2	SAG	JAN	7	SAG
JAN	14	CAP	FEB	5	CAP
FEB	7	AQU	MAR	4	AQU
FEB	26	PIS	MAR	29	PIS
MAR	14	ARI	APR	23	ARI
APR	1	TAU	MAY	18	TAU
APR	18	ARI	JUN	12	GEM
MAY	17	TAU	JUL	6	CAN
JUN	7	GEM	JUL	31	LEO
JUN	21	CAN	AUG	24	VIR
JUL	6	LEO	SEP	17	LIB
JUL	26	VIR	OCT	11	SCO
AUG	29	LEO	NOV	5	SAG
SEP	11	VIR	NOV	29	CAP
SEP	30	LIB	DEC	23	AQU
OCT	17	SCO			
NOV	6	SAG			

1972

MERCURY			VENUS		
month	day	sign	month	day	sign
JAN	1	SAG	JAN	1	AQU
JAN	11	CAP	JAN	16	PIS
JAN	31	AQU	FEB	10	ARI
FEB	18	PIS	MAR	7	TAU
MAR	5	ARI	APR	3	GEM
MAY	12	TAU	MAY	10	CAN
MAY	29	GEM	JUN	11	FEM
JUN	12	CAN	AUG	6	CAN
JUN	28	LEO	SEP	7	LEO
SEP	5	VIR	OCT	5	VIR
SEP	21	LIB	OCT	30	LIB
OCT	9	SCO	NOV	24	SCO
OCT	30	SAG	DEC	18	SAG
NOV	29	SCO			
DEC	12	SAG			

1973

MERCURY			VENUS		
month	day	sign	month	day	sign
JAN	1	SAG	JAN	1	SAG
JAN	4	CAP	JAN	11	CAP
JAN	23	AQU	FEB	4	AQU
FEB	9	PIS	FEB	28	PIS
APR	16	ARI	MAR	24	ARI
MAY	6	TAU	APR	18	TAU
MAY	20	GEM	MAY	12	GEM
JUN	4	CAN	JUN	5	CAN
JUN	27	LEO	JUN	30	LEO
JUL	16	CAN	JUL	25	VIR
AUG	11	LEO	AUG	19	LIB
AUG	28	VIR	SEP	13	SCO
SEP	13	LIB	OCT	9	SAG
OCT	2	SCO	NOV	5	CAP
DEC	8	SAG	DEC	7	AQU
DEC	28	CAP			

1974

MERCURY			VENUS		
month	day	sign	month	day	sign
JAN	1	CAP	JAN	1	AQU
JAN	16	AQU	JAN	29	CAP
FEB	2	PIS	FEB	28	AQU
MAR	2	AQU	APR	6	PIS
MAR	17	PIS	MAY	4	ARI
APR	11	ARI	MAY	31	TAU
APR	28	TAU	JUN	25	GEM
MAY	12	GEM	JUL	21	CAN
MAY	29	CAN	AUG	14	LEO
AUG	5	LEO	SEP	8	VIR
AUG	20	VIR	OCT	2	LIB
SEP	6	LIB	OCT	26	SCO
SEP	28	SCO	NOV	19	SAG
OCT	26	LIB	DEC	13	CAP
NOV	11	SCO			
DEC	2	SAG			
DEC	21	CAP			

1975

MERCURY			VENUS		
month	day	sign	month	day	sign
JAN	1	CAP	JAN	1	CAP
JAN	8	AQU	JAN	6	AQU
MAR	16	PIS	JAN	30	PIS
APR	4	ARI	FEB	23	ARI
APR	19	TAU	MAR	19	TAU
MAY	4	GEM	APR	13	GEM
JUL	12	CAN	MAY	9	CAN
JUL	28	LEO	JUN	6	LEO
AUG	12	VIR	JUL	9	VIR
AUG	30	LIB	SEP	2	LEO
NOV	6	SCO	OCT	4	VIR
NOV	25	SAG	NOV	9	LIB
DEC	14	CAP	DEC	7	SCO

1976

MERCURY			VENUS		
month	day	sign	month	day	sign
JAN	1	CAP	JAN	1	SAG
JAN	2	AQU	JAN	26	CAP
JAN	25	CAP	FEB	19	AQU
FEB	15	AQU	MAR	15	PIS
MAR	9	PIS	APR	8	ARI
MAR	26	ARI	MAY	2	TAU
APR	10	TAU	MAY	27	GEM
APR	29	GEM	JUN	20	CAN
MAY	19	TAU	JUL	14	LEO
JUN	13	GEM	AUG	8	VIR
JUL	4	CAN	SEP	1	LIB
JUL	18	LEO	SEP	26	SCO
AUG	3	VIR	OCT	20	SAG
AUG	25	LIB	NOV	14	CAP
SEP	21	VIR	DEC	9	AQU
OCT	10	LIB			
OCT	29	SCO			
NOV	16	SAG			
DEC	6	CAP			

1977

MERCURY			VENUS		
month	day	sign	month	day	sign
JAN	1	CAP	JAN	1	AQU
FEB	10	AQU	JAN	4	PIS
MAR	2	PIS	FEB	2	ARI
MAR	18	ARI	JUN	6	TAU
APR	3	TAU	JUL	6	GEM
JUN	10	GEM	AUG	2	CAN
JUN	26	CAN	AUG	28	LEO
JUL	10	LEO	SEP	22	VIR
JUL	28	VIR	OCT	17	LIB
OCT	4	LIB	NOV	10	SCO
OCT	21	SCO	DEC	4	SAG
NOV	9	SAG	DEC	27	CAP
DEC	1	CAP			
DEC	21	SAG			

1978

MERCURY			VENUS		
month	day	sign	month	day	sign
JAN	1	SAG	JAN	1	CAP
JAN	13	CAP	JAN	20	AQU
FEB	4	AQU	FEB	13	PIS
FEB	22	PIS	MAR	9	ARI
MAR	10	ARI	APR	2	TAU
MAY	17	TRAU	APR	27	GEM
JUN	3	GEM	MAY	22	CAN
JUN	17	CAN	JUN	16	LEO
JUL	2	LEO	JUL	12	VIR
JUL	27	VIR	AUG	8	LIB
AUG	13	LEO	JUL	12	VIR
SEP	9	VIR			
SEP	26	LIB			
OCT	14	SCO			
NOV	3	SAG			

1979

MERCURY			VENUS		
month	day	sign	month	day	sign
JAN	1	SAG	JAN	1	SCO
JAN	8	CAP	JAN	7	SAG
JAN	28	AQU	FEB	5	CAP
FEB	14	PIS	MAR	3	AQU
MAR	3	ARI	MAR	29	PIS
MAR	28	PIS	APR	23	ARI
APR	17	ARI	MAY	18	TAU
MAY	10	TAU	JUN	11	GEM
MAY	26	GEM	JUL	6	CAN
JUN	9	CAN	JUL	30	LEO
JUN	27	LEO	AUG	24	VIR
SEP	2	VIR	SEP	17	LIB
SEP	18	LIB	OCT	11	SCO
OCT	7	SCO	NOV	4	SAG
OCT	30	SAG	NOV	28	CAP
NOV	18	SCO	DEC	22	AQU
DEC	12	SAG			

1980					
MERCURY			**VENUS**		
month	day	sign	month	day	sign
JAN	1	SAG	JAN	1	AQU
JAN	2	CAP	JAN	16	PIS
JAN	21	AQU	FEB	9	ARI
FEB	7	PIS	MAR	6	TAU
APR	14	ARI	APR	3	GEM
MAY	2	TAU	MAY	12	CAN
MAY	16	GEM	JUN	5	GEM
MAY	31	CAN	AUG	6	CAN
AUG	9	LEO	SEP	7	LEO
AUG	24	VIR	OCT	4	LIB
SEP	10	LIB	OCT	30	LIB
SEP	30	SCO	NOV	24	LIB
DEC	5	SAG	DEC	18	SAG
DEC	25	CAP			

1981					
MERCURY			**VENUS**		
month	day	sign	month	day	sign
JAN	1	CAP	JAN	1	SAG
JAN	12	AQU	JAN	11	CAP
JAN	31	PIS	FEB	4	AQU
FEB	16	AQU	FEB	28	PIS
MAR	18	PIS	MAR	24	ARI
APR	8	ARI	APR	17	TAU
APR	24	TAU	MAY	11	GEM
MAY	8	GEM	JUN	5	CAN
MAY	28	CAN	JUN	29	LEO
JUN	22	GEM	JUL	24	VIR
JUL	12	CAN	AUG	18	LIB
AUG	1	LEO	SEP	12	SCO
AUG	16	VIR	OCT	9	SAG
SEP	2	LIB	NOV	5	CAP
SEP	27	SCO	DEC	8	AQU
OCT	14	LIB			
NOV	9	SCO			
NOV	28	SAG			
DEC	17	CAP			

1982

MERCURY			VENUS		
month	day	sign	month	day	sign
JAN	1	CAP	JAN	1	AQU
JAN	5	AQU	JAN	23	CAP
MAR	13	PIS	MAR	2	AQU
MAR	31	ARI	APR	6	PIS
APR	15	TAU	MAY	4	ARI
MAY	1	FEM	MAY	30	TAU
JUL	9	CAN	JUN	25	GEM
JUL	24	LEO	JUL	20	CAN
AUG	8	CIR	AUG	14	LEO
AUG	28	LIB	SEP	7	VIR
NOV	3	SCO	OCT	2	LIB
NOV	21	SAG	OCT	26	SCO
DEC	10	CAP	NOV	18	SAG
			DEC	12	CAP

1983

MERCURY			VENUS		
month	day	sign	month	day	sign
JAN	1	AQU	JAN	1	CAP
JAN	12	CAP	JAN	5	AQU
FEB	14	AQU	JAN	29	PIS
MAR	7	PIS	FEB	22	ARI
MAR	23	ARI	MAR	19	TAU
APR	7	TAU	APR	13	GEM
JUN	14	GEM	MAY	9	CAN
JUL	1	CAN	JUN	6	LEO
JUL	15	LEO	JUL	10	VIR
AUG	1	VIR	AUG	27	LEO
AUG	29	LIB	OCT	5	VIR
SEP	6	VIR	NOV	9	LIB
OCT	8	LIB	DEC	6	SCO
OCT	26	SCO			
NOV	14	SAG			
DEC	4	CAP			

1984

MERCURY			VENUS		
month	day	sign	month	day	sign
JAN	1	CAP	JAN	1	SAG
FEB	9	AQU	JAN	25	CAP
FEB	27	PIS	FEB	19	AQU
MAR	14	ARI	MAR	14	PIS
MAR	31	TAU	APR	7	ARI
APR	25	ARI	MAY	2	TAU
MAY	15	TAU	MAY	26	GEM
JUN	7	GEM	JUN	20	CAN
JUN	22	CAN	JUL	14	LEO
JUL	6	LEO	AUG	7	VIR
JUL	26	VIR	SEP	1	LIB
SEP	30	LIB	SEP	25	SCO
OCT	17	SCO	OCT	20	SAG
NOV	6	SAG	NOV	13	CAP
DEC	1	CAP	DEC	9	AQU
DEC	7	SAG			

1985

MERCURY			VENUS		
month	day	sign	month	day	sign
JAN	1	SAG	JAN	1	AQU
JAN	11	CAP	JAN	4	PIS
FEB	1	AQU	FEB	2	ARI
FEB	18	PIS	JUN	6	TAU
MAR	7	ARI	JUL	6	GEM
MAY	14	TAU	AUG	2	CAN
MAY	30	GEM	AUG	28	LEO
JUN	13	CAN	SEP	22	VIR
JUN	29	LEO	OCT	16	LIB
SEP	6	VIR	NOV	9	SCO
SEP	22	LIB	DEC	3	SAG
OCT	10	SCO	DEC	27	CAP
OCT	31	SAG			
DEC	4	SCO			
DEC	12	SAG			

1986

MERCURY			VENUS		
month	day	sign	month	day	sign
JAN	1	SAG	JAN	1	CAP
JAN	5	CAP	JAN	20	AQU
JAN	25	AQU	FEB	13	PIS
FEB	11	PIS	MAR	9	ARI
MAR	3	ARI	APR	2	TAU
MAR	11	PIS	APR	26	GEM
APR	17	ARI	MAY	21	CAN
MAY	7	TAU	JUN	15	LEO
MAY	22	GEM	JUL	11	VIR
JUN	5	CAN	AUG	7	LIB
JUN	26	LEO	SEP	7	SCO
JUL	23	CAN			
AUG	11	LEO			
AUG	30	VIR			
SEP	15	LIB			
OCT	4	SCO			
DEC	10	SAG			
DEC	29	CAP			

1987

MERCURY			VENUS		
month	day	sign	month	day	sign
JAN	1	CAP	JAN	1	SCO
JAN	17	AQU	JAN	7	SAG
FEB	4	PIS	FEB	5	CAP
MAR	11	AQU	MAR	3	AQU
MAR	13	PIS	MAR	28	PIS
APR	12	ARI	APR	22	ARI
APR	29	TAU	MAY	17	TAU
MAY	13	GEM	JUN	11	GEM
MAY	30	CAN	JUL	5	CAN
AUG	6	LEO	JUL	30	LEO
AUG	21	VIR	AUG	23	VIR
SEP	7	LIB	SEP	16	LIB
SEP	28	SCO	OCT	10	SCO
NOV	1	LIB	NOV	3	SAG
NOV	11	SCO	NOV	28	CAP
DEC	3	SAG	DEC	22	AQU
DEC	22	CAP			

1988

MERCURY			VENUS		
month	day	sign	month	day	sign
JAN	1	CAP	JAN	1	AQU
JAN	10	AQU	JAN	15	PIS
MAR	16	PIS	FEB	9	ARI
APR	4	ARI	MAR	6	TAU
APR	20	TAU	APR	3	GEM
MAY	4	GEM	MAY	17	CAN
JUL	12	CAN	MAY	27	GEM
JUL	28	LEO	AUG	6	CAN
AUG	12	VIR	SEP	7	LEO
AUG	30	LIB	OCT	4	VIR
NOV	6	SCO	OCT	29	LIB
NOV	25	SAG	NOV	23	SCO
DEC	14	CAP	DEC	17	SAG

1989

MERCURY			VENUS		
month	day	sign	month	day	sign
JAN	1	CAP	JAN	1	SAG
JAN	2	AQU	JAN	10	CAP
JAN	29	CAP	FEB	3	AQU
FEB	14	AQU	FEB	27	PIS
MAR	10	PIS	MAR	23	ARI
MAR	28	ARI	APR	16	TAU
APR	11	TAU	MAY	11	GEM
APR	29	GEM	JUN	4	CAN
MAY	28	TAU	JUN	29	LEO
JUN	12	GEM	JUL	24	VIR
JUL	6	CAN	AUG	18	LIB
JUL	20	LEO	SEP	12	SCO
AUG	5	VIR	OCT	8	SAG
AUG	26	LIB	NOV	5	CAP
SEP	26	VIR	DEC	10	AQU
OCT	11	LIB			
OCT	30	SCO			
NOV	18	SAG			
DEC	7	CAP			

1990

MERCURY			VENUS		
month	day	sign	month	day	sign
JAN	1	CAP	JAN	1	AQU
FEB	12	AQU	JAN	16	CAP
MAR	3	PIS	MAR	3	AQU
MAR	20	ARI	APR	6	PIS
APR	4	TAU	MAY	4	ARI
JUN	12	GEM	MAY	30	TAU
JUN	27	CAN	JUN	25	GEM
JUL	11	LEO	JUL	30	CAN
JUL	29	VIR	AUG	13	LEO
OCT	5	LIB	SEP	7	VIR
OCT	23	SCO	OCT	1	LIB
NOV	11	SAG	OCT	25	SAG
DEC	2	CAP	NOV	18	SAG
DEC	25	SAG	DEC	12	CAP

Appendix B

Mars Charts

1950 MARS		
month	**day**	**sign**
JAN		LIB
FEB		LIB
MAR	28	VIR
APR		VIR
MAY		VIR
JUN	11	LIB
JUL		LIB
AUG	10	SCO
SEP	25	SAG
OCT		SAG
NOV	6	CAP
DEC	15	AQU

1951 MARS		
month	**day**	**sign**
JAN	22	PIS
FEB		PIS
MAR	1	ARI
APR	10	TAU
MAY	21	GEM
JUN		GEM
JUL	3	CAN
AUG	18	LEO
SEP		LEO
OCT	4	VIR
NOV	24	LIB
DEC		LIB

1952 MARS		
month	**day**	**sign**
JAN	19	SCO
FEB		SCO
MAR		SCO
APR		SCO
MAY		SCO
JUN		SCO
JUL		SCO
AUG	27	SAG
SEP		SAG
OCT	11	CAP
NOV	21	AQU
DEC	30	PIS

1953 MARS		
month	day	sign
JAN		PIS
FEB	7	ARI
MAR	20	TAU
APR		TAU
MAY	1	GEM
JUN	13	CAN
JUL	29	LEO
AUG		LEO
SEP	14	VIR
OCT		VIR
NOV	1	LIB
DEC	20	SCO

1954 MARS		
month	day	sign
JAN		SCO
FEB	9	SAG
MAR		SAG
APR	12	CAP
MAY		CAP
JUN		CAP
JUL	3	SAG
AUG	24	CAP
SEP		CAP
OCT	21	AQU
NOV		AQU
DEC	4	PIS

1955 MARS		
month	day	sign
JAN	14	ARI
FEB	26	TAU
MAR		TAU
APR	10	GEM
MAY	25	CAN
JUN		CAN
JUL	11	LEO
AUG	27	VIR
SEP		VIR
OCT	13	LIB
NOV	28	SCO
DEC		SCO

1956 MARS		
month	day	sign
JAN	13	SAG
FEB	28	CAP
MAR		CAP
APR	14	AQU
MAY		AQU
JUN	3	PIS
JUL		PIS
AUG		PIS
SEP		PIS
OCT		PIS
NOV		PIS
DEC	6	ARI

1957 MARS		
month	day	sign
JAN	28	TAU
FEB		TAU
MAR	17	GEM
APR		GEM
MAY	4	CAN
JUN	21	LEO
JUL		LEO
AUG	8	VIR
SEP	23	LIB
OCT		LIB
NOV	8	SCO
DEC	22	SAG

1958 MARS		
month	day	sign
JAN		SAG
FEB	3	CAP
MAR	17	AQU
APR	26	PIS
MAY		PIS
JUN	7	ARI
JUL	21	TAU
AUG		TAU
SEP	21	GEM
OCT	28	TAU
NOV		TAU
DEC		TAU

1959 MARS		
month	day	sign
JAN		TAU
FEB	10	GEM
MAR		GEM
APR	10	CAN
MAY	31	LEO
JUN		LEO
JUL	20	VIR
AUG		VIR
SEP	5	LIB
OCT	21	SCO
NOV		SCO
DEC	3	SAG

1960 MARS		
month	day	sign
JAN	14	CAP
FEB	22	AQU
MAR		AQU
APR	2	PIS
MAY	11	ARI
JUN	20	TAU
JUL		TAU
AUG	1	GEM
SEP	20	CAN
OCT		CAN
NOV		CAN
DEC		CAN

1961 MARS		
month	day	sign
JAN		CAN
FEB	4	GEM
	7	CAN
MAR		CAN
APR		CAN
MAY	5	LEO
JUN	28	VIR
JUL		VIR
AUG	16	LIB
SEP		LIB
OCT	1	SCO
NOV	13	SAG
DEC	24	CAP

1962 MARS		
month	day	sign
JAN		CAP
FEB	1	AQU
MAR	12	PIS
APR	19	ARI
MAY	28	TAU
JUN		TAU
JUL	8	GEM
AUG	22	CAN
SEP		CAN
OCT	11	LEO
NOV		LEO
DEC		LEO

1963 MARS		
month	day	sign
JAN		LEO
FEB		LEO
MAR		LEO
APR		LEO
MAY		LEO
JUN	3	VIR
JUL	26	LIB
AUG		LIB
SEP	12	SCO
OCT	25	SAG
NOV		SAG
DEC	5	CAP

1964 MARS		
month	day	sign
JAN	13	AQU
FEB	20	PIS
MAR	29	ARI
APR		ARI
MAY	7	TAU
JUN	17	GEM
JUL	30	CAN
AUG		CAN
SEP	15	LEO
OCT		LEO
NOV	5	VIR
DEC		VIR

1965 MARS		
month	day	sign
JAN		VIR
FEB		VIR
MAR		VIR
APR		VIR
MAY		VIR
JUN	28	LIB
JUL		LIB
AUG	20	SCO
SEP		SCO
OCT	4	SAG
NOV	14	CAP
DEC	23	AQU

1966 MARS		
month	day	sign
JAN	30	PIS
FEB		PIS
MAR	9	ARI
APR	17	TAU
MAY	28	GEM
JUN		GEM
JUL	10	CAN
AUG	25	LEO
SEP		LEO
OCT	12	VIR
NOV		VIR
DEC	3	LIB

1967 MARS		
month	day	sign
JAN		LIB
FEB	12	SCO
MAR	31	LIB
APR		LIB
MAY		LIB
JUN		LIB
JUL	19	SCO
AUG		SCO
SEP	9	SAG
OCT	22	CAP
NOV		CAP
DEC	1	AQU

1968 MARS		
month	day	sign
JAN	9	PIS
FEB	16	ARI
MAR	27	TAU
APR		TAU
MAY	8	GEM
JUN	21	CAN
JUL		CAN
AUG	5	LEO
SEP	21	VIR
OCT		VIR
NOV	9	LIB
DEC	29	SCO

1969 MARS		
month	day	sign
JAN		SCO
FEB	25	SAG
MAR		SAG
APR		SAG
MAY		SAG
JUN		SAG
JUL		SAG
AUG		SAG
SEP	21	CAP
OCT		CAP
NOV	4	AQU
DEC	15	PIS

1970 MARS		
month	day	sign
JAN	24	ARI
FEB		ARI
MAR	6	TAU
APR	18	GEM
MAY		GEM
JUN	2	CAN
JUL	18	LEO
AUG		LEO
SEP	2	VIR
OCT	20	LIB
NOV		LIB
DEC	6	SCO

1971 MARS		
month	day	sign
JAN	22	SAG
FEB		SAG
MAR	12	CAP
APR		CAP
MAY	3	AQU
JUN		AQU
JUL		AQU
AUG		AQU
SEP		AQU
OCT		AQU
NOV	6	PIS
DEC	26	ARI

1972 MARS		
month	day	sign
JAN		ARI
FEB	10	TAU
MAR	26	GEM
APR		GEM
MAY	12	CAN
JUN	28	LEO
JUL		LEO
AUG	14	VIR
SEP	30	LIB
OCT		LIB
NOV	15	SCO
DEC	30	SAG

1973 MARS		
month	day	sign
JAN		SAG
FEB	12	CAP
MAR	26	AQU
APR		AQU
MAY	7	PIS
JUN	20	ARI
JUL		ARI
AUG	12	TAU
SEP		TAU
OCT	29	ARI
NOV		ARI
DEC	24	TAU

1974 MARS		
month	day	sign
JAN		TAU
FEB	27	GEM
MAR		GEM
APR	20	CAN
MAY		CAN
JUN	8	LEO
JUL	27	VIR
AUG		VIR
SEP	12	LIB
OCT	28	SCO
NOV		SCO
DEC	10	SAG

1975 MARS		
month	day	sign
JAN	21	CAP
FEB		CAP
MAR	3	AQU
APR	11	PIS
MAY	21	ARI
JUN	30	TAU
JUL		TAU
AUG	14	GEM
SEP		GEM
OCT	17	CAN
NOV	25	GEM
DEC		GEM

1976 MARS		
month	day	sign
JAN		GEM
FEB		GEM
MAR	18	CAN
APR		CAN
MAY	16	LEO
JUN		LEO
JUL	6	VIR
AUG	24	LIB
SEP		LIB
OCT	8	SCO
NOV	20	SAG
DEC	31	CAP

1977 MARS		
month	day	sign
JAN		CAP
FEB	9	AQU
MAR	19	PIS
APR	27	ARI
MAY		ARI
JUN	5	TAU
JUL	17	GEM
AUG	31	CAN
SEP		CAN
OCT	26	LEO
NOV		LEO
DEC		LEO

1978 MARS		
month	day	sign
JAN	25	CAN
FEB		CAN
MAR		CAN
APR	10	LEO
MAY		LEO
JUN	13	VIR
JUL		VIR
AUG	4	LIB
SEP	19	SCO
OCT		SCO
NOV	1	SAG
DEC	12	CAP

1979 MARS		
month	day	sign
JAN	20	AQU
FEB	27	PIS
MAR		PIS
APR	6	ARI
MAY	15	TAU
JUN	25	GEM
JUL		GEM
AUG	8	CAN
SEP	24	LEO
OCT		LEO
NOV	19	VIR
DEC		VIR

1980 MARS		
month	day	sign
JAN		VIR
FEB		VIR
MAR	11	LEO
APR		LEO
MAY	3	VIR
JUN		VIR
JUL	10	LIB
AUG	29	SCO
SEP		SCO
OCT	12	SAG
NOV	21	CAP
DEC	30	AQU

1981 MARS		
month	day	sign
JAN		AQU
FEB	6	PIS
MAR	16	ARI
APR	25	TAU
MAY		TAU
JUN	5	GEM
JUL	18	CAN
AUG		CAN
SEP	1	LEO
OCT	20	VIR
NOV		VIR
DEC	15	LIB

1982 MARS		
month	day	sign
JAN		LIB
FEB		LIB
MAR		LIB
APR		LIB
MAY		LIB
JUN		LIB
JUL		LIB
AUG	3	SCO
SEP	19	SAG
OCT	31	CAP
NOV		CAP
DEC	10	AQU

1983
MARS

month	day	sign
JAN	17	PIS
FEB	24	ARI
MAR		ARI
APR	5	TAU
MAY	16	GEM
JUN	29	CAN
JUL		CAN
AUG	13	LEO
SEP	29	VIR
OCT		VIR
NOV	18	LIB
DEC		LIB

1984
MARS

month	day	sign
JAN	10	SCO
FEB		SCO
MAR		SCO
APR		SCO
MAY		SCO
JUN		SCO
JUL		SCO
AUG	17	SAG
SEP		SAG
OCT	5	CAP
NOV	15	AQU
DEC	25	PIS

1985
MARS

month	day	sign
JAN		PIS
FEB	2	ARI
MAR	15	TAU
APR	26	GEM
MAY		GEM
JUN	9	CAN
JUL	24	LEO
AUG		LEO
SEP	9	VIR
OCT	27	LIB
NOV		LIB
DEC	14	SCO

1986
MARS

month	day	sign
JAN		SCO
FEB	2	SAG
MAR	27	CAP
APR		CAP
MAY		CAP
JUN		CAP
JUL		CAP
AUG		CAP
SEP		CAP
OCT	8	AQU
NOV	25	PIS
DEC		PIS

1987
MARS

month	day	sign
JAN	8	ARI
FEB	20	TAU
MAR		TAU
APR	5	GEM
MAY	20	CAN
JUN		CAN
JUL	6	LEO
AUG	22	VIR
SEP		VIR
OCT	8	LIB
NOV	23	SCO
DEC		SCO

1988
MARS

month	day	sign
JAN	8	SAG
FEB	22	CAP
MAR		CAP
APR	6	AQU
MAY	22	PIS
JUN		PIS
JUL	13	ARI
AUG		ARI
SEP		ARI
OCT	23	PIS
NOV	1	ARI
DEC		ARI

1989 MARS		
month	day	sign
JAN	19	TAU
FEB		TAU
MAR	11	GEM
APR	28	CAN
MAY		CAN
JUN	16	LEO
JUL		LEO
AUG	3	VIR
SEP	19	LIB
OCT		LIB
NOV	4	SCO
DEC	17	SAG

1990 MARS		
month	day	sign
JAN	29	CAP
FEB		CAP
MAR	11	AQU
APR	20	PIS
MAY	31	ARI
JUN		ARI
JUL	12	TAU
AUG	31	GEM
SEP		GEM
OCT		GEM
NOV		GEM
DEC	14	TAU

1991 MARS		
month	day	sign
JAN	20	GEM
FEB		GEM
MAR		GEM
APR	2	CAN
MAY	26	LEO
JUN		LEO
JUL	15	VIR
AUG		VIR
SEP	1	LIB
OCT	16	SCO
NOV	28	SAG
DEC		SAG

1992 MARS		
month	day	sign
JAN	9	CAP
FEB	17	AQU
MAR	27	PIS
APR		PIS
MAY	5	ARI
JUN	14	TAU
JUL	26	GEM
AUG		GEM
SEP	12	CAN
OCT		CAN
NOV		CAN
DEC		CAN

1993 MARS		
month	day	sign
JAN		CAN
FEB		CAN
MAR		CAN
APR	27	LEO
MAY		LEO
JUN	23	VIR
JUL		VIR
AUG	11	LIB
SEP	26	SCO
OCT		SCO
NOV	9	SAG
DEC	19	CAP

1994 MARS		
month	day	sign
JAN	27	AQU
FEB		AQU
MAR	7	PIS
APR	14	ARI
MAY	23	TAU
JUN		TAU
JUL	3	GEM
AUG	16	CAN
SEP		CAN
OCT	4	LEO
NOV		LEO
DEC	12	VIR

1995 MARS		
month	day	sign
JAN	22	LEO
FEB		LEO
MAR		LEO
APR		LEO
MAY	25	VIR
JUN		VIR
JUL	21	LIB
AUG		LIB
SEP	7	SCO
OCT	20	SAG
NOV	30	CAP
DEC		CAP

1996 MARS		
month	day	sign
JAN	8	AQU
FEB	15	PIS
MAR	24	ARI
APR		ARI
MAY	2	TAU
JUN	12	GEM
JUL	25	CAN
AUG		CAN
SEP	9	LEO
OCT	30	VIR
NOV		VIR
DEC		VIR

1997 MARS		
month	day	sign
JAN	3	LIB
FEB		LIB
MAR	8	VIR
APR		VIR
MAY		VIR
JUN	19	LIB
JUL		LIB
AUG	14	SCO
SEP	28	SAG
OCT		SAG
NOV	9	CAP
DEC	18	AQU

1998 MARS		
month	day	sign
JAN	25	PIS
FEB		PIS
MAR	4	ARI
APR	12	TAU
MAY	23	GEM
JUN		GEM
JUL	6	CAN
AUG	20	LEO
SEP		LEO
OCT	7	VIR
NOV	27	LIB
DEC		LIB

1999 MARS		
month	day	sign
JAN	26	SCO
FEB		SCO
MAR		SCO
APR		SCO
MAY	5	LIB
JUN		LIB
JUL	4	SCO
AUG		SCO
SEP	2	SAG
OCT	16	CAP
NOV	26	AQU
DEC		AQU

2000 MARS		
month	day	sign
JAN	3	PIS
FEB	11	ARI
MAR	22	TAU
APR		TAU
MAY	3	GEM
JUN	16	CAN
JUL	31	LEO
AUG		LEO
SEP	16	VIR
OCT		VIR
NOV	3	LIB
DEC	23	SCO

2001 MARS		
month	day	sign
JAN		SCO
FEB	14	SAG
MAR		SAG
APR		SAG
MAY		SAG
JUN		SAG
JUL		SAG
AUG		SAG
SEP	8	CAP
OCT	27	AQU
NOV		AQU
DEC	8	PIS

2002 MARS		
month	day	sign
JAN	18	ARI
FEB		ARI
MAR	1	TAU
APR	13	GEM
MAY	28	CAN
JUN		CAN
JUL	13	LEO
AUG	29	VIR
SEP		VIR
OCT	15	LIB
NOV		LIB
DEC	1	SCO

2003 MARS		
month	day	sign
JAN	16	SAG
FEB		SAG
MAR	4	CAP
APR	21	AQU
MAY		AQU
JUN	16	PIS
JUL		PIS
AUG		PIS
SEP		PIS
OCT		PIS
NOV		PIS
DEC	16	ARI

2004 MARS		
month	day	sign
JAN		ARI
FEB	3	TAU
MAR	21	GEM
APR		GEM
MAY	7	CAN
JUN	23	LEO
JUL		LEO
AUG	10	VIR
SEP	26	LIB
OCT		LIB
NOV	11	SCO
DEC	25	SAG

2005 MARS		
month	day	sign
JAN		SAG
FEB	6	CAP
MAR	20	AQU
APR	30	PIS
MAY		PIS
JUN	11	ARI
JUL	28	TAU
AUG		TAU
SEP		TAU
OCT		TAU
NOV		TAU
DEC		TAU

2006 MARS		
month	day	sign
JAN		TAU
FEB	17	GEM
MAR		GEM
APR	13	CAN
MAY		CAN
JUN	3	LEO
JUL	22	VIR
AUG		VIR
SEP	7	LIB
OCT	23	SCO
NOV		SCO
DEC	5	SAG

2007 MARS		
month	day	sign
JAN	16	CAP
FEB	25	AQU
MAR		AQU
APR	6	PIS
MAY	15	ARI
JUN	24	TAU
JUL		TAU
AUG	7	GEM
SEP	28	CAN
OCT		CAN
NOV		CAN
DEC	31	GEM

2008 MARS		
month	day	sign
JAN		GEM
FEB		GEM
MAR	4	CAN
APR		CAN
MAY	9	LEO
JUN		LEO
JUL	1	VIR
AUG	19	LIB
SEP		LIB
OCT	3	SCO
NOV	16	SAG
DEC	27	CAP

2009 MARS		
month	day	sign
JAN		CAP
FEB	4	AQU
MAR	14	PIS
APR	22	ARI
MAY	31	TAU
JUN		TAU
JUL	11	GEM
AUG	25	CAN
SEP		CAN
OCT	16	LEO
NOV		LEO
DEC		LEO

2010 MARS		
month	day	sign
JAN		LEO
FEB		LEO
MAR		LEO
APR		LEO
MAY		LEO
JUN	7	VIR
JUL	29	LIB
AUG		LIB
SEP	14	SCO
OCT	28	SAG
NOV		SAG
DEC	7	CAP

Appendix C

Uranus Charts

year	dates	sign
1950–1954		CAN
1955	JAN 1–AUG 23	CAN
	AUG 24–DEC 31	LEO
1956	JAN 1–JAN 26	LEO
	JAN 27–JUN 8	CAN
	JUN 9–DEC 31	LEO
1957–1960		LEO
1961	JAN 1–OCT 31	LEO
	NOV 1–DEC 31	VIR
1962	JAN 1–JAN 9	VIR
	JAN 10–AUG 8	LEO
	AUG 9–DEC 31	VIR
1963–1967		VIR
1968	JAN 1–SEP 27	VIR
	SEP 28–DEC 31	LIB
1969	JAN 1–MAY 19	LIB
	MAY 20–JUN 23	VIR
	JUN 24–DEC 31	LIB
1970–1973		LIB
1974	JAN 1–NOV 20	LIB
	NOV 21–DEC 31	SCO
1975	JAN 1–APR 30	SCO
	MAY 1–SEP 7	LIB
	SEP 8–DEC 31	SCO
1976–1980		SCO

year	dates	sign
1981	JAN 1–FEB 16	SCO
	FEB 17–MAR 19	SAG
	MAR 20–NOV 15	SCO
	NOV 16–DEC 31	SAG
1982–1987		SAG
1988	JAN 1–FEB 13	SAG
	FEB 14–MAY 25	CAP
	MAY 26–DEC 1	SAG
	DEC 2–DEC 31	CAP
1989–1994		CAP
1995	JAN 1–MAR 31	CAP
	APR 1–JUN 7	AQU
	JUN 8–DEC 31	CAP
1996	JAN 1–JAN 11	CAP
	JAN 12–DEC 31	AQU
1997–2002		AQU
2003	JAN 1–MAR 9	AQU
	MAR 10–SEP 13	PIS
	SEP 14–DEC 29	AQU
	DEC 30–DEC 31	PIS
2004–2009		PIS
2010	JAN 1–MAY 26	PIS
	MAY 27–AUG 12	ARI
	AUG 13–DEC 31	PIS

Appendix D

Pluto Charts

year	dates	sign	year	dates	sign
1940–1955		LEO	1983	JAN 1–NOV 4	LIB
1956	JAN 1–OCT 19	LEO		NOV 5–DEC 31	SCO
	OCT 20–DEC 31	VIR	1984	JAN 1–MAY 17	SCO
1957	JAN 1–JAN 13	VIR		MAY 18–AUG 27	LIB
	JAN 14–AUG 17	LEO		AUG 28–DEC 31	SCO
	AUG 18–DEC 31	VIR	1985–1994		SCO
1958	JAN 1–APR 10	VIR	1995	JAN 1–JAN 16	SCO
	APR 11–JUN 9	LEO		JAN 17–APR 19	SAG
	JUN 10–DEC 31	VIR		APR 20–NOV 9	SCO
1959–1970		VIR		NOV 10–DEC 31	SAG
1971	JAN 1–OCT 4	VIR	1996–2007		SAG
	OCT 5–DEC 31	LIB	2008	JAN 1–JAN 24	SAG
1972	JAN 1–APR 16	LIB		JAN 25–JUN 12	CAP
	APR 17–JUL 29	VIR		JUN 13–NOV 25	SAG
	JUL 30–DEC 31	LIB		NOV 26–DEC 31	CAP
1973–1982		LIB	2009–2022		CAP

Appendix E

Neptune Charts

year	dates	sign
1944–1954		LIB
1955	JAN 1–DEC 23	LIB
	DEC 24–DEC 31	SCO
1956	JAN 1–MAR 10	SCO
	MAR 11–OCT 18	LIB
	OCT 19–DEC 31	SCO
1957	JAN 1–JUN 14	SCO
	JUN 15–AUG 5	LIB
	AUG 6–DEC 31	SCO
1958–1969		SCO
1970	JAN 1–JAN 3	SCO
	JAN 4–MAY 1	SAG
	MAY 2–NOV 5	SCO
	NOV 6–DEC 31	SAG
1971–1983		SAG
1984	JAN 1–JAN 17	SAG
	JAN 18–JUN 21	CAP
	JUN 22–NOV 20	SAG
	NOV 21–DEC 31	CAP
1985–1997		CAP
1998	JAN 1–JAN 27	CAP
	JAN 28–AUG 21	AQU
	AUG 22–NOV 26	CAP
	NOV 27–DEC 31	AQU
1999–2010		AQU

Appendix F

Saturn Charts

year	dates	sign	year	dates	sign
1950	JAN 1–NOV 19	VIR	1967	JAN 1–MAR 2	PIS
	NOV 20–DEC 31	LIB		MAR 3–DEC 31	ARI
1951	JAN 1–MAR 6	LIB	1968		ARI
	MAR 7–AUG 12	VIR	1969	JAN 1–APR 28	ARI
	AUG 13–DEC 31	LIB		APR 29–DEC 31	TAU
1952		LIB	1970		TAU
1953	JAN 1–OCT 21	LIB	1971	JAN 1–JUN 17	TAU
	OCT 22–DEC 31	SCO		JUN 18–DEC 31	GEM
1954–1955		SCO	1972	JAN 1–JAN 8	GEM
1956	JAN 1–JAN 11	SCO		JAN 9–FEB 20	TAU
	JAN 12–MAY 12	SAG		FEB 21–DEC 31	GEM
	MAY 13–OCT 9	SCO	1973	JAN 1–JUL 31	GEM
	OCT 10–DEC 31	SAG		AUG 1–DEC 31	CAN
1957–1958		SAG	1974	JAN 1–JAN 6	CAN
1959	JAN 1–JAN 4	SAG		JAN 7–APR 17	GEM
	JAN 5–DEC 31	CAP		APR 18–DEC 31	CAN
1960–1961		CAP	1975	JAN 1–SEP 15	CAN
1962	JAN 1–JAN 2	CAP		SEP 16–DEC 31	LEO
	JAN 3–DEC 31	AQU	1976	JAN 1–JAN 13	LEO
1963		AQU		JAN 14–JUN 4	CAN
1964	JAN 1–MAR 22	AQU		JUN 5–DEC 31	LEO
	MAR 23–SEP 15	PIS	1977	JAN 1–NOV 15	LEO
	SEP 16–DEC 15	AQU		NOV 16–DEC 31	VIR
	DEC 16–DEC 31	PIS	1978	JAN 1–JAN 3	VIR
1965–1966		PIS		JAN 4–JUL 25	LEO
				JUL 26–DEC 31	VIR

year	dates	sign	year	dates	sign
1979		VIR	1997		ARI
1980	JAN 1–SEP 20	VIR	1998	JAN 1–JUN 8	ARI
	SEP 21–DEC 31	LIB		JUN 9–OCT 24	TAU
1981		LIB		OCT 25–DEC 31	ARI
1982	JAN 1–NOV 28	LIB	1999	JAN 1–FEB 27	ARI
	NOV 29–DEC 31	SCO		FEB 28–DEC 31	TAU
1983	JAN 1–MAY 5	SCO	2000	JAN 1–AUG 8	TAU
	MAY 6–AUG 23	LIB		AUG 9–OCT 14	GEM
	AUG 24–DEC 31	SCO		OCT 15–DEC 31	TAU
1984		SCO	2001	JAN 1–APR 19	TAU
1985	JAN 1–NOV 15	SCO		APR 20–DEC 31	GEM
	NOV 16–DEC 31	SAG	2002		GEM
1986–1987		SAG	2003	JAN 1–JUN 2	GEM
1988	JAN 1–FEB 12	SAG		JUN 3–DEC 31	CAN
	FEB 13–JUN 9	CAP	2004		CAN
	JUN 10–NOV 11	SAG	2005	JAN 1–JUL 15	CAN
	NOV 12–DEC 31	CAP		JUL 16–DEC 31	LEO
1989–1990		CAP	2006		LEO
1991	JAN 1–FEB 5	CAP	2007	JAN 1–SEP 1	LEO
	FEB 6–DEC 31	AQU		SEP 2–DEC 31	VIR
1992		AQU	2008		VIR
1993	JAN 1–MAY 19	AQU	2009	JAN 1–OCT 28	VIR
	MAY 20–JUN 29	PIS		OCT 29–DEC 31	LIB
	JUN 30–DEC 31	AQU	2010	JAN 1–APR 6	LIB
1994	JAN 1–JAN 27	AQU		APR 7–JUL 20	VIR
	JAN 28–DEC 31	PIS		JUL 21–DEC 31	LIB
1995		PIS			
1996	JAN 1–APR 6	PIS			
	APR 7–DEC 31	ARI			

Appendix G

Jupiter Charts

year	dates	sign	year	dates	sign
1950	JAN 1–APR 14	AQU	1959	JAN 1–FEB 9	SCO
	APR 15–SEP 13	PIS		FEB 10–APR 23	SAG
	SEP 14–NOV 30	AQU		APR 24–OCT 4	SCO
	DEC 1–DEC 31	PIS		OCT 5–DEC 31	SAG
1951	JAN 1–APR 20	PIS	1960	JAN 1–FEB 28	SAG
	APR 21–DEC 31	AIR		MAR 1–JUN 8	CAP
1952	JAN 1–APR 27	ARI		JUN 9–OCT 24	SAG
	APR 28–DEC 31	TAU		OCT 25–DEC 31	CAP
1953	JAN 1–MAY 8	TAU	1961	JAN 1–MAR 14	CAP
	MAY 9–DEC 31	GEM		MAR 15–AUG 11	AQU
1954	JAN 1–MAY 22	GEM		AUG 12–NOV 2	CAP
	MAY 23–DEC 31	CAN		NOV 3–DEC 31	AQU
1955	JAN 1–JUN 11	CAN	1962	JAN 1–MAR 24	AQU
	JUN 12–NOV 15	LEO		MAR 25–DEC 31	PIS
	NOV 16–DEC 31	VIR	1963	JAN 1–APR 2	PIS
1956	JAN 1–JAN 16	VIR		APR 3–DEC 31	ARI
	JAN 17–JUL 6	LEO	1964	JAN 1–APR 11	ARI
	JUL 7–DEC 11	VIR		APR 12–DEC 31	TAU
	DEC 12–DEC 31	LIB	1965	JAN 1–APR 21	TAU
1957	JAN 1–FEB 18	LIB		APR 22–SEP 19	GEM
	FEB 19–AUG 5	VIR		SEP 20–NOV 15	CAN
	AUG 6–DEC 31	LIB		NOV 16–DEC 31	GEM
1958	JAN 1–JAN 12	LIB	1966	JAN 1–MAY 4	GEM
	JAN 13–MAR 19	SCO		MAY 5–SEP 26	CAN
	MAR 20–SEP 6	LIB		SEP 27–DEC 31	LEO
	SEP 7–DEC 31	SCO			

year	dates	sign	year	dates	sign
1967	JAN 1–JAN 14	LEO	1976	JAN 1–MAR 25	ARI
	JAN 15–MAY 22	CAN		MAR 26–AUG 22	TAU
	MAY 23–OCT 18	LEO		AUG 23–OCT 15	GEM
	OCT 19–DEC 31	VIR		OCT 16–DEC 31	TAU
1968	JAN 1–FEB 25	VIR	1977	JAN 1–APR 2	TAU
	FEB 26–JUN 14	LEO		APR 3–AUG 19	GEM
	JUN 15–NOV 14	VIR		AUG 20–DEC 29	CAN
	NOV 15–DEC 31	LIB		DEC 30–DEC 31	GEM
1969	JAN 1–MAR 29	LIB	1978	JAN 1–APR 10	GEM
	MAR 30–JUL 14	VIR		APR 11–SEP 4	CAN
	JUL 15–DEC 15	LIB		SEP 5–DEC 31	LEO
	DEC 16–DEC 31	SCO	1979	JAN 1–FEB 27	LEO
1970	JAN 1–APR 29	SCO		FEB 28–APR 19	CAN
	APR 30–AUG 14	LIB		APR 20–SEP 28	LEO
	AUG 15–DEC 31	SCO		SEP 29–DEC 31	VIR
1971	JAN 1–JAN 13	SCO	1980	JAN 1–OCT 26	VIR
	JAN 14–JUN 3	SAG		OCT 27–DEC 31	LEO
	JUN 4–SEP 10	SCO	1981	JAN 1–NOV 25	LIB
	SEP 11–DEC 31	SAG		NOV 26–DEC 31	SCO
1972	JAN 1–FEB 5	SAG	1982	JAN 1–DEC 24	SCO
	FEB 6–JUL 23	CAP		DEC 25–DEC 31	SAG
	JUL 24–SEP 24	SAG	1983		SAG
	SEP 25–DEC 31	CAP	1984	JAN 1–JAN 18	SAG
1973	JAN 1–FEB 22	CAP		JAN 19–DEC 31	CAP
	FEB 23–DEC 31	AQU	1985	JAN 1–FEB 5	CAP
1974	JAN 1–MAR 7	AQU		FEB 6–DEC 31	AQU
	MAR 8–DEC 31	PIS	1986	JAN 1–FEB 19	AQU
1975	JAN 1–MAR 17	PIS		FEB 20–DEC 31	PIS
	MAR 18–DEC 31	ARI	1987	JAN 1–MAR 1	PIS
				MAR 2–DEC 31	ARI

year	dates	sign	year	dates	sign
1988	JAN 1–MAR 7	ARI	2000	JAN 1–FEB 13	ARI
	MAR 8–JUL 20	TAU		FEB 14–JUN 29	TAU
	JUL 21–NOV 29	GEM		JUN 30–DEC 31	GEM
	NOV 30–DEC 31	TAU	2001	JAN 1–JUL 11	GEM
1989	JAN 1–MAR 9	TAU		JUL 12–DEC 31	CAN
	MAR 10–JUL 29	GEM	2002	JAN 1–JUL 31	CAN
	JUL 30–DEC 31	CAN		AUG 1–DEC 31	LEO
1990	JAN 1–AUG 17	CAN	2003	JAN 1–AUG 26	LEO
	AUG 18–DEC 31	LEO		AUG 27–DEC 31	VIR
1991	JAN 1–SEP 11	LEO	2004	JAN 1–SEP 23	VIR
	SEP 12–DEC 31	VIR		SEP 24–DEC 31	LIB
1992	JAN 1–OCT 9	VIR	2005	JAN 1–OCT 24	LIB
	OCT 10–DEC 31	LIB		OCT 25–DEC 31	SCO
1993	JAN 1–NOV 9	LIB	2006	JAN 1–NOV 22	SCO
	NOV 10–DEC 31	SCO		NOV 23–DEC 31	SAG
1994	JAN 1–DEC 8	SCO	2007	JAN 1–DEC 17	SAG
	DEC 9–DEC 31	SAG		DEC 18–DEC 31	CAP
1995		SAG	2008		CAP
1996	JAN 1–JAN 2	SAG	2009	JAN 1–JAN 4	CAP
	JAN 3–DEC 31	CAP		JAN 5–DEC 31	AQU
1997	JAN 1–JAN 20	CAP	2010	JAN 1–JAN 16	AQU
	JAN 21–DEC 31	AQU		JAN 17–JUN 5	PIS
1998	JAN 1–FEB 3	AQU		JUN 6–SEP 7	ARI
	FEB 4–DEC 31	PIS		SEP 8–DEC 31	PIS
1999	JAN 1–FEB 11	PIS			
	FEB 12–JUN 27	ARI			
	JUN 28–OCT 22	TAU			
	OCT 23–DEC 31	ARI			

Moon Charts

						1950					
JAN	**FEB**	**MAR**	**APR**	**MAY**	**JUN**	**JUL**	**AUG**	**SEP**	**OCT**	**NOV**	**DEC**
3 CAN	1 LEO	1 LEO	1 LIB	1 SCO	1 CAP	1 AQU	2 ARI	3 GEM	3 CAN	2 LEO	1 VIR
5 LEO	3 VIR	3 VIR	3 SCO	3 SAG	3 AQU	3 PIS	4 TAU	5 CAN	5 LEO	4 VIR	3 LIB
7 VIR	6 LIB	5 LIB	5 SAG	5 CAP	5 PIS	5 ARI	7 GEM	8 LEO	7 VIR	6 LIB	6 SCO
9 LIB	8 SCO	7 SCO	7 CAP	7 AQU	8 ARI	8 TAU	9 CAN	10 VIR	10 LIB	8 SCO	8 SAG
11 SCO	10 SAG	9 SAG	10 AQU	9 PIS	10 TAU	10 GEM	11 LEO	12 LIB	12 SCO	10 SAG	10 CAP
14 SAG	12 CAP	11 CAP	12 PIS	12 ARI	13 GEM	13 CAN	14 VIR	14 SCO	14 SAG	12 CAP	12 AQU
16 CAP	14 AQU	13 AQU	14 ARI	14 TAU	15 CAN	15 LEO	16 LIB	16 SAG	16 CAP	14 AQU	14 PIS
18 AQU	16 PIS	16 PIS	17 TAU	17 GEM	18 LEO	17 VIR	18 SCO	18 CAP	18 AQU	16 PIS	16 ARI
20 PIS	19 ARI	18 ARI	19 GEM	19 CAN	20 VIR	20 LIB	20 SAG	21 AQU	20 PIS	19 ARI	19 TAU
22 ARI	21 TAU	21 TAU	22 CAN	22 LEO	22 LIB	22 SCO	22 CAP	23 PIS	23 ARI	21 TAU	21 GEM
25 TAU	24 GEM	23 GEM	24 LEO	24 VIR	25 SCO	24 SAG	24 AQU	25 ARI	25 TAU	24 GEM	24 CAN
28 GEM	26 CAN	26 CAN	27 VIR	26 LIB	27 SAG	26 CAP	27 PIS	28 TAU	28 GEM	26 CAN	26 LEO
30 CAN		28 LEO	29 LIB	28 SCO	29 CAP	28 AQU	29 ARI	30 GEM	30 CAN	29 LEO	28 VIR
		30 VIR		30 SAG		30 PIS	31 TAU				31 LIB

1951

JAN	FEB	MAR	APR	MAY	JUN	JUL	AUG	SEP	OCT	NOV	DEC
2 SCO	2 CAP	2 CAP	2 PIS	2 ARI	3 GEM	3 CAN	1 LEO	3 LIB	2 SCO	1 SAG	2 AQU
4 SAG	4 AQU	4 AQU	5 ARI	4 TAU	5 CAN	5 LEO	4 VIR	5 SCO	4 SAG	3 CAP	4 PIS
6 CAP	7 PIS	6 PIS	7 TAU	7 GEM	8 LEO	8 VIR	6 LIB	7 SAG	6 CAP	5 AQU	6 ARI
8 AQU	9 ARI	8 ARI	9 GEM	9 CAN	10 VIR	10 LIB	9 SCO	9 CAP	8 AQU	7 PIS	9 TAU
10 PIS	11 TAU	11 TAU	12 CAN	12 LEO	13 LIB	12 SCO	11 SAG	11 AQU	11 PIS	9 ARI	11 GEM
12 ARI	14 GEM	13 GEM	14 LEO	14 VIR	15 SCO	14 SAG	13 CAP	13 PIS	13 ARI	11 TAU	13 CAN
15 TAU	16 CAN	16 CAN	17 VIR	16 LIB	17 SAG	16 CAP	15 AQU	15 ARI	15 TAU	14 GEM	16 LEO
17 GEM	19 LEO	18 LEO	19 LIB	19 SCO	19 CAP	18 AQU	17 PIS	18 TAU	17 GEM	16 CAN	19 VIR
20 CAN	21 VIR	20 VIR	21 SCO	21 SAG	21 AQU	20 PIS	19 ARI	20 GEM	20 CAN	19 LEO	21 LIB
22 LEO	23 LIB	23 LIB	23 SAG	23 CAP	23 PIS	23 ARI	21 TAU	23 CAN	22 LEO	21 VIR	23 SCO
25 VIR	25 SCO	25 SCO	25 CAP	25 AQU	25 ARI	25 TAU	24 GEM	25 LEO	25 VIR	24 LIB	25 SAG
27 LIB	28 SAG	27 SAG	27 AQU	27 PIS	28 TAU	27 GEM	26 CAN	28 VIR	27 LIB	26 SCO	27 CAP
29 SCO		29 CAP	29 PIS	29 ARI	30 GEM	30 CAN	29 LEO	30 LIB	29 SCO	28 SAG	29 AQU
31 SAG		31 AQU		31 TAU			31 VIR			30 CAP	31 PIS

1952

JAN	FEB	MAR	APR	MAY	JUN	JUL	AUG	SEP	OCT	NOV	DEC
3 ARI	1 TAU	2 GEM	1 CAN	3 VIR	2 LIB	2 SCO	2 CAP	1 AQU	2 ARI	1 TAU	2 CAN
5 TAU	3 GEM	4 CAN	3 LEO	5 LIB	4 SCO	4 SAG	4 AQU	3 PIS	4 TAU	3 GEM	5 LEO
7 GEM	6 CAN	7 LEO	6 VIR	8 SCO	6 SAG	6 CAP	6 PIS	5 ARI	6 GEM	5 CAN	7 VIR
10 CAN	9 LEO	9 VIR	8 LIB	10 SAG	8 CAP	8 AQU	8 ARI	7 TAU	9 CAN	7 LEO	10 LIB
12 LEO	11 VIR	12 LIB	10 SCO	12 CAP	10 AQU	10 PIS	10 TAU	9 GEM	11 LEO	10 VIR	12 SCO
15 VIR	14 LIB	14 SCO	13 SAG	14 AQU	12 PIS	12 ARI	13 GEM	11 CAN	14 VIR	13 LIB	15 SAG
17 LIB	16 SCO	16 SAG	15 CAP	16 PIS	15 ARI	14 TAU	15 CAN	14 LEO	16 LIB	15 SCO	17 CAP
20 SCO	18 SAG	19 CAP	17 AQU	18 ARI	17 TAU	16 GEM	18 LEO	16 VIR	19 SCO	17 SAG	19 AQU
22 SAG	20 CAP	21 AQU	19 PIS	21 TAU	19 GEM	19 CAN	20 VIR	19 LIB	21 SAG	19 CAP	21 PIS
24 CAP	22 AQU	23 PIS	21 ARI	23 GEM	22 CAN	21 LEO	23 LIB	21 SCO	23 CAP	21 AQU	23 ARI
26 AQU	24 PIS	25 ARI	23 TAU	25 CAN	24 LEO	24 VIR	25 SCO	24 SAG	25 AQU	24 PIS	25 TAU
28 PIS	26 ARI	27 TAU	26 GEM	28 LEO	27 VIR	26 LIB	27 SAG	26 CAP	27 PIS	26 ARI	27 GEM
30 ARI	29 TAU	29 GEM	28 CAN	30 VIR	29 LIB	29 SCO	30 CAP	28 AQU	29 ARI	28 TAU	30 CAN
		30 LEO				31 SAG		30 PIS		30 GEM	

1953

	JAN		FEB		MAR		APR		MAY		JUN		JUL		AUG		SEP		OCT		NOV		DEC
1	LEO	3	LIB	2	LIB	1	SCO	2	CAP	1	AQU	2	ARI	1	TAU	1	CAN	1	LEO	2	LIB	2	SCO
4	VIR	5	SCO	4	SCO	3	SAG	5	AQU	3	PIS	5	TAU	3	GEM	4	LEO	4	VIR	5	SCO	5	SAG
6	LIB	7	SAG	7	SAG	5	CAP	7	PIS	5	ARI	7	GEM	5	CAN	6	VIR	6	LIB	7	SAG	7	CAP
9	SCO	10	CAP	9	CAP	7	AQU	9	ARI	7	TAU	9	CAN	8	LEO	9	LIB	9	SCO	10	CAP	9	AQU
11	SAG	12	AQU	11	AQU	10	PIS	11	TAU	9	GEM	11	LEO	10	VIR	11	SCO	11	SAG	12	AQU	11	PIS
13	CAP	14	PIS	13	PIS	12	ARI	13	GEM	12	CAN	14	VIR	13	LIB	14	SAG	13	CAP	14	PIS	14	ARI
15	AQU	16	ARI	15	ARI	14	TAU	15	CAN	14	LEO	16	LIB	15	SCO	16	CAP	16	AQU	16	ARI	16	TAU
17	PIS	18	TAU	17	TAU	16	GEM	18	LEO	16	VIR	19	SCO	18	SAG	18	AQU	18	PIS	18	TAU	18	GEM
19	ARI	20	GEM	19	GEM	18	CAN	20	VIR	19	LIB	21	SAG	20	CAP	21	PIS	20	ARI	20	GEM	20	CAN
21	TAU	22	CAN	22	CAN	20	LEO	23	LIB	21	SCO	23	CAP	22	AQU	22	ARI	22	TAU	22	CAN	22	LEO
24	GEM	25	LEO	24	LEO	23	VIR	25	SCO	24	SAG	26	AQU	24	PIS	24	TAU	24	GEM	25	LEO	25	VIR
26	CAN	27	VIR	27	VIR	25	LIB	27	SAG	26	CAP	28	PIS	26	ARI	27	GEM	26	CAN	27	VIR	27	LIB
28	LEO			29	LIB	28	SCO	30	CAP	28	AQU	30	ARI	28	TAU	29	CAN	28	LEO	30	LIB	30	SCO
31	VIR					30	SAG			30	PIS			30	GEM			31	VIR				

1954

	JAN		FEB		MAR		APR		MAY		JUN		JUL		AUG		SEP		OCT		NOV		DEC
1	SAG	2	AQU	1	AQU	2	ARI	1	TAU	2	CAN	1	LEO	2	LIB	1	SCO	1	SAG	2	AQU	2	PIS
3	CAP	4	PIS	3	PIS	4	TAU	3	GEM	4	LEO	4	VIR	5	SCO	4	SAG	4	CAP	5	PIS	4	ARI
6	AQU	6	ARI	5	ARI	6	GEM	5	CAN	6	VIR	6	LIB	7	SAG	6	CAP	6	AQU	7	ARI	6	TAU
8	PIS	8	TAU	7	TAU	8	CAN	8	LEO	9	LIB	9	SCO	10	CAP	9	AQU	8	PIS	9	TAU	8	GEM
10	ARI	10	GEM	10	GEM	10	LEO	10	VIR	11	SCO	11	SAG	12	AQU	11	PIS	10	ARI	11	GEM	10	CAN
12	TAU	13	CAN	12	CAN	13	VIR	12	LIB	14	SAG	14	CAP	14	PIS	13	ARI	12	TAU	13	CAN	12	LEO
14	GEM	15	LEO	14	LEO	15	LIB	15	SCO	16	CAP	16	AQU	16	ARI	15	TAU	14	GEM	15	LEO	14	VIR
16	CAN	17	VIR	16	VIR	18	SCO	17	SAG	19	AQU	18	PIS	19	TAU	17	GEM	16	CAN	17	VIR	17	LIB
19	LEO	20	LIB	19	LIB	20	SAG	20	CAP	21	PIS	20	ARI	21	GEM	19	CAN	19	LEO	20	LIB	19	SCO
21	VIR	22	SCO	21	SCO	23	CAP	22	AQU	23	ARI	22	TAU	23	CAN	21	LEO	21	VIR	22	SCO	22	SAG
23	LIB	25	SAG	24	SAG	25	AQU	25	PIS	25	TAU	24	GEM	25	LEO	24	VIR	23	LIB	25	SAG	24	CAP
26	SCO	27	CAP	26	CAP	27	PIS	27	ARI	27	GEM	27	CAN	27	VIR	26	LIB	26	SCO	27	CAP	27	AQU
28	SAG			29	AQU	29	ARI	29	TAU	29	CAN	29	LEO	30	LIB	29	SCO	28	SAG	30	AQU	29	PIS
31	CAP			31	PIS			31	GEM			31	VIR					31	CAP			31	ARI

1955

JAN	FEB	MAR	APR	MAY	JUN	JUL	AUG	SEP	OCT	NOV	DEC
3 TAU	1 GEM	2 CAN	1 LEO	2 LIB	1 SCO	1 SAG	2 AQU	1 PIS	1 ARI	1 GEM	1 CAN
5 GEM	3 CAN	4 LEO	3 VIR	5 SCO	4 SAG	3 CAP	5 PIS	3 ARI	3 TAU	3 CAN	3 LEO
7 CAN	5 LEO	7 VIR	5 LIB	7 SAG	6 CAP	6 AQU	7 ARI	5 TAU	5 GEM	5 LEO	5 VIR
9 LEO	7 VIR	9 LIB	8 SCO	10 CAP	9 AQU	8 PIS	9 TAU	7 GEM	7 CAN	7 VIR	7 LIB
11 VIR	10 LIB	11 SCO	10 SAG	12 AQU	11 PIS	11 ARI	11 GEM	10 CAN	9 LEO	10 LIB	9 SCO
13 LIB	12 SCO	14 SAG	13 CAP	15 PIS	13 ARI	13 TAU	13 CAN	12 LEO	11 VIR	12 SCO	12 SAG
16 SCO	15 SAG	16 CAP	15 AQU	17 ARI	16 TAU	15 GEM	15 LEO	14 VIR	13 LIB	15 SAG	14 CAP
18 SAG	17 CAP	19 AQU	18 PIS	19 TAU	18 GEM	17 CAN	18 VIR	16 LIB	16 SCO	17 CAP	17 AQU
21 CAP	19 AQU	21 PIS	20 ARI	21 GEM	20 CAN	19 LEO	20 LIB	18 SCO	18 SAG	20 AQU	19 PIS
23 AQU	22 PIS	23 ARI	22 TAU	23 CAN	22 LEO	21 VIR	22 SCO	21 SAG	21 CAP	22 PIS	22 ARI
25 PIS	24 ARI	25 TAU	24 GEM	25 LEO	24 VIR	23 LIB	25 SAG	23 CAP	23 AQU	24 ARI	24 TAU
28 ARI	26 TAU	27 GEM	26 CAN	27 VIR	26 LIB	26 SCO	27 CAP	26 AQU	26 PIS	27 TAU	26 GEM
30 TAU	28 GEM	29 CAN	28 LEO	30 LIB	28 SCO	28 SAG	30 AQU	28 PIS	28 ARI	29 GEM	28 CAN
			30 VIR		31 CAP				30 TAU		30 LEO

1956

JAN	FEB	MAR	APR	MAY	JUN	JUL	AUG	SEP	OCT	NOV	DEC
1 VIR	2 SCO	3 SAG	1 CAP	1 AQU	3 ARI	2 TAU	1 GEM	1 LEO	1 VIR1	SCO 1	SAG
3 LIB	4 SAG	5 CAP	4 AQU	4 PIS	5 TAU	4 GEM	3 CAN	3 VIR	3 LIB	3 SAG	3 CAP
6 SCO	7 CAP	8 AQU	6 PIS	6 ARI	7 GEM	6 CAN	5 LEO	5 LIB	5 SCO	6 CAP	6 AQU
8 SAG	9 AQU	10 PIS	9 ARI	8 TAU	9 CAN	8 LEO	7 VIR	7 SCO	7 SAG	8 AQU	8 PIS
11 CAP	12 PIS	12 ARI	11 TAU	11 GEM	11 LEO	10 VIR	9 LIB	10 SAG	10 CAP	11 PIS	11 ARI
13 AQU	14 ARI	15 TAU	13 GEM	13 CAN	13 VIR	12 LIB	11 SCO	12 CAP	12 AQU	13 ARI	13 TAU
16 PIS	16 TAU	17 GEM	15 CAN	15 LEO	15 LIB	15 SCO	13 SAG	15 AQU	15 PIS	16 TAU	15 GEM
18 ARI	19 GEM	19 CAN	17 LEO	17 VIR	18 SCO	17 SAG	16 CAP	17 PIS	17 ARI	18 GEM	17 CAN
20 TAU	21 CAN	21 LEO	20 VIR	19 LIB	20 SAG	20 CAP	18 AQU	20 ARI	19 TAU	20 CAN	19 LEO
22 GEM	23 LEO	23 VIR	22 LIB	21 SCO	22 CAP	22 AQU	21 PIS	22 TAU	22 GEM	22 LEO	21 VIR
24 CAN	25 VIR	25 LIB	24 SCO	24 SAG	25 AQU	25 PIS	23 ARI	24 GEM	24 CAN	24 VIR	24 LIB
26 LEO	27 LIB	28 SCO	26 SAG	26 CAP	27 PIS	27 ARI	26 TAU	26 CAN	26 LEO	26 LIB	26 SCO
28 VIR	29 SCO	30 SAG	29 CAP	29 AQU	30 ARI	30 TAU	28 GEM	29 LEO	28 VIR	29 SCO	28 SAG
31 LIB				31 PIS			30 CAN		30 LIB		31 CAP

1957

JAN	FEB	MAR	APR	MAY	JUN	JUL	AUG	SEP	OCT	NOV	DEC
2 AQU	1 PIS	3 ARI	1 TAU	1 GEM	1 LEO	1 VIR	1 SCO	2 CAP	2 AQU	1 PIS	1 ARI
5 PIS	3 ARI	5 TAU	4 GEM	3 CAN	4 VIR	3 LIB	4 SAG	5 AQU	4 PIS	3 ARI	3 TAU
7 ARI	6 TAU	7 GEM	6 CAN	5 LEO	6 LIB	5 SCO	6 CAP	7 PIS	7 ARI	6 TAU	5 GEM
9 TAU	8 GEM	10 CAN	8 LEO	7 VIR	8 SCO	7 SAG	8 AQU	10 ARI	9 TAU	8 GEM	8 CAN
12 GEM	10 CAN	12 LEO	10 VIR	9 LIB	10 SAG	10 CAP	11 PIS	12 TAU	12 GEM	10 CAN	10 LEO
14 CAN	12 LEO	14 VIR	12 LIB	12 SCO	12 CAP	12 AQU	13 ARI	15 GEM	14 CAN	13 LEO	12 VIR
16 LEO	14 VIR	16 LIB	14 SCO	14 SAG	15 AQU	15 PIS	16 TAU	17 CAN	16 LEO	15 VIR	14 LIB
18 VIR	16 LIB	18 SCO	16 SAG	16 CAP	17 PIS	17 ARI	18 GEM	19 LEO	18 VIR	17 LIB	16 SCO
20 LIB	18 SCO	20 SAG	19 CAP	18 AQU	20 ARI	20 TAU	21 CAN	21 VIR	21 LIB	19 SCO	18 SAG
22 SCO	21 SAG	22 CAP	21 AQU	21 PIS	22 TAU	22 GEM	23 LEO	23 LIB	23 SCO	21 SAG	21 CAP
24 SAG	23 CAP	25 AQU	24 PIS	23 ARI	25 GEM	24 CAN	25 VIR	25 SCO	25 SAG	23 CAP	23 AQU
27 CAP	26 AQU	27 PIS	26 ARI	26 TAU	27 CAN	26 LEO	27 LIB	27 SAG	27 CAP	26 AQU	25 PIS
29 AQU	28 PIS	30 ARI	29 TAU	28 GEM	29 LEO	28 VIR	29 SCO	29 CAP	29 AQU	28 PIS	28 ARI
			30 CAN		30 LIB	31 SAG				30 TAU	

1958

JAN	FEB	MAR	APR	MAY	JUN	JUL	AUG	SEP	OCT	NOV	DEC
2 GEM	3 LEO	2 LEO	1 VIR	2 SCO	3 CAP	2 AQU	1 PIS	2 TAU	2 GEM	1 CAN	3 VIR
4 CAN	5 VIR	4 VIR	3 LIB	4 SAG	5 AQU	4 PIS	3 ARI	5 GEM	4 CAN	3 LEO	5 LIB
6 LEO	7 LIB	6 LIB	5 SCO	6 CAP	7 PIS	7 ARI	6 TAU	7 CAN	7 LEO	5 VIR	7 SCO
8 VIR	9 SCO	8 SCO	7 SAG	8 AQU	10 ARI	9 TAU	8 GEM	9 LEO	9 VIR	7 LIB	9 SAG
10 LIB	11 SAG	10 SAG	9 CAP	11 PIS	12 TAU	12 GEM	11 CAN	11 VIR	11 LIB	9 SCO	11 CAP
12 SCO	13 CAP	12 CAP	11 AQU	13 ARI	15 GEM	14 CAN	13 LEO	13 LIB	13 SCO	11 SAG	13 AQU
15 SAP	16 AQU	15 AQU	13 PIS	16 TAU	17 CAN	17 LEO	15 VIR	15 SCO	15 SAG	13 CAP	15 PIS
17 CAP	18 PIS	17 PIS	16 ARI	18 GEM	19 LEO	19 VIR	17 LIB	18 SAG	17 CAP	16 AQU	18 ARI
19 AQU	21 ARI	20 ARI	19 TAU	21 CAN	21 VIR	21 LIB	19 SCO	20 CAP	19 AQU	18 PIS	20 TAU
22 PIS	23 TAU	22 TAU	21 GEM	23 LEO	24 LIB	23 SCO	21 SAG	22 AQU	22 PIS	20 ARI	23 GEM
24 ARI	26 GEM	25 GEM	23 CAN	25 VIR	26 SCO	25 SAG	23 CAP	24 PIS	24 ARI	23 TAU	25 CAN
27 TAU	28 CAN	27 CAN	26 LEO	27 LIB	28 SAG	27 CAP	26 AQU	27 ARI	27 TAU	25 GEM	27 LEO
29 GEM		29 LEO	28 VIR	29 SCO	30 CAP	29 AQU	28 PIS	29 TAU	29 GEM	28 CAN	30 VIR
31 CAN			30 LIB	31 SAG			31 ARI			30 LEO	

1959

JAN	FEB	MAR	APR	MAY	JUN	JUL	AUG	SEP	OCT	NOV	DEC
1 LIB	1 SAG	1 SAG	1 AQU	1 PIS	2 TAU	2 GEM	1 CAN	2 VIR	1 LIB	2 SAG	1 CAP
3 SCO	4 CAP	3 CAP	4 PIS	3 ARI	5 GEM	4 CAN	3 LEO	4 LIB	3 SCO	4 CAP	3 AQU
5 SAG	6 AQU	5 AQU	6 ARI	6 TAU	7 CAN	7 LEO	5 VIR	6 SCO	5 SAG	6 AQU	5 PIS
7 CAP	8 PIS	7 PIS	8 TAU	8 GEM	9 LEO	9 VIR	8 LIB	8 SAG	7 CAP	8 PIS	8 ARI
9 AQU	10 ARI	10 ARI	11 GEM	11 CAN	12 VIR	11 LIB	10 SCO	10 CAP	10 AQU	10 ARI	10 TAU
12 PIS	13 TAU	12 TAU	14 CAN	13 LEO	14 LIB	13 SCO	12 SAG	12 AQU	12 PIS	13 TAU	13 GEM
14 ARI	15 GEM	15 GEM	16 LEO	16 VIR	16 SCO	16 SAG	14 CAP	15 PIS	14 ARI	15 GEM	15 CAN
17 TAU	18 CAN	17 CAN	18 VIR	18 LIB	18 SAG	18 CAP	16 AQU	17 ARI	17 TAU	18 CAN	18 LEO
19 GEM	20 LEO	20 LEO	20 LIB	20 SCO	20 CAP	20 AQU	18 PIS	19 TAU	19 GEM	20 LEO	20 VIR
21 CAN	22 VIR	22 VIR	22 SCO	22 SAG	22 AQU	22 PIS	20 ARI	22 GEM	22 CAN	23 VIR	22 LIB
24 LEO	24 LIB	24 LIB	24 SAG	24 CAP	24 PIS	24 ARI	23 TAU	24 CAN	24 LEO	25 LIB	25 SCO
26 VIR	27 SCO	26 SCO	26 CAP	26 AQU	27 ARI	27 TAU	25 GEM	27 LEO	26 VIR	27 SCO	27 SAG
28 LIB		28 SAG	28 AQU	28 PIS	29 TAU	29 GEM	28 CAN	29 VIR	29 LIB	29 SAG	29 CAP
30 SCO		30 CAP		30 ARI			30 LEO		31 SCO		31 AQU

1960

JAN	FEB	MAR	APR	MAY	JUN	JUL	AUG	SEP	OCT	NOV	DEC
2 PIS	3 TAU	1 TAU	2 CAN	2 LEO	1 VIR	1 LIB	1 SAG	2 AQU	1 PIS	2 TAU	2 GEM
4 ARI	5 GEM	4 GEM	5 LEO	5 VIR	3 LIB	3 SCO	3 CAP	4 PIS	3 ARI	4 GEM	4 CAN
6 TAU	8 CAN	6 CAN	7 VIR	7 LIB	6 SCO	5 SAG	5 AQU	6 ARI	6 TAU	7 CAN	7 LEO
9 GEM	10 LEO	9 LEO	10 LIB	9 SCO	8 SAG	7 CAP	7 PIS	8 TAU	8 GEM	9 LEO	9 VIR
11 CAN	13 VIR	11 VIR	12 SCO	11 SAG	10 CAP	9 AQU	10 ARI	11 GEM	10 CAN	12 VIR	12 LIB
14 LEO	15 LIB	13 LIB	14 SAG	13 CAP	12 AQU	11 PIS	12 TAU	13 CAN	13 LEO	14 LIB	14 SCO
16 VIR	17 SCO	15 SCO	16 CAP	15 AQU	14 PIS	13 ARI	14 GEM	16 LEO	15 VIR	16 SCO	16 SAG
19 LIB	19 SAG	17 SAG	18 AQU	17 PIS	16 ARI	15 TAU	17 CAN	18 VIR	18 LIB	19 SAG	18 CAP
21 SCO	21 CAP	20 CAP	20 PIS	20 ARI	18 TAU	18 GEM	19 LEO	20 LIB	20 SCO	21 CAP	20 AQU
23 SAG	23 AQU	22 AQU	22 ARI	22 TAU	21 GEM	20 CAN	22 VIR	23 SCO	22 SAG	23 AQU	22 PIS
25 CAP	26 PIS	24 PIS	25 TAU	24 GEM	23 CAN	23 LEO	24 LIB	25 SAG	24 CAP	25 PIS	24 ARI
27 AQU	28 ARI	26 ARI	27 GEM	27 CAN	26 LEO	25 VIR	26 SCO	27 CAP	26 AQU	27 ARI	26 TAU
29 PIS		28 TAU	30 CAN	29 LEO	28 VIR	28 LIB	29 SAG	29 AQU	28 PIS	29 TAU	29 GEM
31 ARI		31 GEM				30 SCO	31 CAP		31 ARI		31 CAN

1961

JAN	FEB	MAR	APR	MAY	JUN	JUL	AUG	SEP	OCT	NOV	DEC
3 LEO	2 VIR	1 VIR	2 SCO	2 SAG	2 AQU	1 PIS	2 TAU	1 GEM	3 LEO	2 VIR	1 LIB
5 VIR	4 LIB	3 LIB	4 SAG	4 CAP	4 PIS	4 ARI	4 GEM	3 CAN	5 VIR	4 LIB	4 SCO
8 LIB	6 SCO	6 SCO	6 CAP	6 AQU	6 ARI	6 TAU	7 CAN	5 LEO	8 LIB	6 SCO	6 SAG
10 SCO	9 SAG	8 SAG	9 AQU	8 PIS	8 TAU	8 GEM	9 LEO	8 VIR	10 SCO	9 SAG	8 CAP
12 SAG	11 CAP	10 CAP	11 PIS	10 ARI	11 GEM	10 CAN	12 VIR	10 LIB	13 SAG	11 CAP	10 AQU
14 CAP	13 AQU	12 AQU	13 ARI	12 TAU	13 CAN	13 LEO	14 LIB	13 SCO	15 CAP	13 AQU	13 PIS
16 AQU	15 PIS	14 PIS	15 TAU	14 GEM	16 LEO	15 VIR	17 SCO	15 SAG	17 AQU	15 PIS	15 ARI
18 PIS	17 ARI	16 ARI	17 GEM	17 CAN	18 VIR	18 LIB	19 SAG	18 CAP	19 PIS	17 ARI	17 TAU
20 ARI	19 TAU	18 TAU	19 CAN	19 LEO	21 LIB	20 SCO	21 CAP	20 AQU	21 ARI	20 TAU	19 GEM
23 TAU	21 GEM	21 GEM	22 LEO	22 VIR	23 SCO	23 SAG	23 AQU	22 PIS	23 TAU	22 GEM	21 CAN
25 GEM	24 CAN	23 CAN	25 VIR	24 LIB	25 SAG	25 CAP	25 PIS	24 ARI	25 GEM	24 CAN	24 LEO
28 CAN	26 LEO	26 LEO	27 LIB	27 SCO	27 CAP	27 AQU	27 ARI	26 TAU	28 CAN	26 LEO	26 VIR
30 LEO		28 VIR	29 SCO	29 SAG	29 AQU	29 PIS	29 TAU	28 GEM	30 LEO	29 VIR	29 LIB
		31 LIB		31 CAP		31 ARI		30 CAN			31 SCO

1962

JAN	FEB	MAR	APR	MAY	JUN	JUL	AUG	SEP	OCT	NOV	DEC
3 SAG	1 CAP	1 CAP	1 PIS	1 ARI	1 GEM	1 CAN	2 VIR	3 SCO	3 SAG	1 CAP	1 AQU
5 CAP	3 AQU	3 AQU	3 ARI	3 TAU	3 CAN	3 LEO	4 LIB	5 SAG	5 CAP	4 AQU	3 PIS
7 AQU	5 PIS	5 PIS	5 TAU	5 GEM	6 LEO	5 VIR	7 SCO	8 CAP	7 AQU	6 PIS	5 ARI
9 PIS	7 ARI	7 ARI	7 GEM	7 CAN	8 VIR	8 LIB	9 SAG	10 AQU	10 PIS	8 ARI	7 TAU
11 ARI	9 TAU	9 TAU	9 CAN	9 LEO	10 LIB	10 SCO	11 CAP	12 PIS	12 ARI	10 TAU	9 GEM
13 TAU	12 GEM	11 GEM	12 LEO	12 VIR	13 SCO	13 SAG	14 AQU	14 ARI	13 TAU	12 GEM	11 CAN
15 GEM	14 CAN	13 CAN	14 VIR	14 LIB	15 SAG	15 CAP	16 PIS	16 TAU	15 GEM	14 CAN	14 LEO
18 CAN	16 LEO	16 LEO	17 LIB	17 SCO	18 CAP	17 AQU	18 ARI	18 GEM	18 CAN	16 LEO	16 VIR
20 LEO	19 VIR	18 VIR	19 SCO	19 SAG	20 AQU	19 PIS	20 TAU	20 CAN	20 LEO	19 VIR	19 LIB
23 VIR	21 LIB	21 LIB	22 SAG	21 CAP	22 PIS	21 ARI	22 GEM	23 LEO	22 VIR	21 LIB	21 SCO
25 LIB	24 SCO	23 SCO	24 CAP	24 AQU	24 ARI	23 TAU	24 CAN	25 VIR	25 LIB	24 SCO	24 SAG
28 SCO	26 SAG	26 SAG	26 AQU	26 PIS	26 TAU	26 GEM	26 LEO	28 LIB	27 SCO	26 SAG	26 CAP
30 SAG		28 CAP	28 PIS	28 ARI	28 GEM	28 CAN	29 VIR	30 SCO	30 SAG	29 CAP	28 AQU
		30 AQU		30 TAU		30 LEO	31 LIB				30 PIS

1963

JAN	FEB	MAR	APR	MAY	JUN	JUL	AUG	SEP	OCT	NOV	DEC
1 ARI	2 GEM	1 GEM	2 LEO	2 VIR	3 SCO	3 SAG	1 CAP	2 PIS	2 ARI	2 GEM	2 CAN
4 TAU	4 CAN	3 CAN	4 VIR	4 LIB	5 SAG	5 CAP	4 AQU	4 ARI	4 TAU	4 CAN	4 LEO
6 GEM	6 LEO	6 LEO	7 LIB	7 SCO	8 CAP	7 AQU	6 PIS	7 TAU	6 GEM	6 LEO	6 VIR
8 CAN	9 VIR	8 VIR	9 SCO	9 SAG	10 AQU	10 PIS	8 ARI	9 GEM	8 CAN	9 VIR	8 LIB
10 LEO	11 LIB	11 LIB	12 SAG	12 CAP	12 PIS	12 ARI	10 TAU	11 CAN	10 LEO	11 LIB	11 SCO
12 VIR	14 SCO	13 SCO	14 CAP	14 AQU	15 ARI	14 TAU	12 GEM	13 LEO	12 VIR	14 SCO	13 SAG
15 LIB	16 SAG	16 SAG	17 AQU	16 PIS	17 TAU	16 GEM	14 CAN	15 VIR	15 LIB	16 SAG	16 CAP
17 SCO	19 CAP	18 CAP	19 PIS	18 ARI	19 GEM	18 CAN	17 LEO	18 LIB	17 SCO	19 CAP	18 AQU
20 SAG	21 AQU	20 AQU	21 ARI	20 TAU	21 CAN	20 LEO	19 VIR	20 SCO	20 SAG	21 AQU	21 PIS
22 CAP	23 PIS	23 PIS	23 TAU	22 GEM	23 LEO	23 VIR	21 LIB	23 SAG	22 CAP	24 PIS	23 ARI
25 AQU	25 ARI	25 ARI	25 GEM	24 CAN	25 VIR	25 LIB	24 SCO	25 CAP	25 AQU	26 ARI	25 TAU
27 PIS	27 TAU	26 TAU	27 CAN	27 LEO	28 LIB	27 SCO	26 SAG	28 AQU	27 PIS	28 TAU	27 GEM
29 ARI		29 GEM	29 LEO	29 VIR	30 SCO	30 SAG	29 CAP	30 PIS	29 ARI	30 GEM	29 CAN
31 TAU		31 CAN		31 LIB			31 AQU		31 TAU		31 LEO

1964

JAN	FEB	MAR	APR	MAY	JUN	JUL	AUG	SEP	OCT	NOV	DEC
2 VIR	1 LIB	2 SCO	1 SAG	1 CAP	2 PIS	1 ARI	2 GEM	2 LEO	2 VIR	3 SCO	2 SAG
5 LIB	4 SCO	4 SAG	3 CAP	3 AQU	4 ARI	4 TAU	4 CAN	5 VIR	4 LIB	5 SAG	5 CAP
7 SCO	6 SAG	7 CAP	6 AQU	5 PIS	6 TAU	6 GEM	6 LEO	7 LIB	6 SCO	8 CAP	7 AQU
10 SAG	9 CAP	9 AQU	8 PIS	8 ARI	8 GEM	8 CAN	8 VIR	9 SCO	9 SAG	10 AQU	10 PIS
12 CAP	11 AQU	12 PIS	10 ARI	10 TAU	10 CAN	10 LEO	10 LIB	11 SAG	11 CAP	13 PIS	12 ARI
15 AQU	13 PIS	14 ARI	12 TAU	12 GEM	12 LEO	12 VIR	13 SCO	14 CAP	14 AQU	15 ARI	15 TAU
17 PIS	16 ARI	16 TAU	14 GEM	14 CAN	14 VIR	14 LIB	15 SAG	16 AQU	16 PIS	17 TAU	17 GEM
19 ARI	18 TAU	18 GEM	16 CAN	16 LEO	17 LIB	16 SCO	18 CAP	19 PIS	19 ARI	19 GEM	19 CAN
21 TAU	20 GEM	20 CAN	19 LEO	18 VIR	19 SCO	19 SAG	20 AQU	21 ARI	21 TAU	21 CAN	21 LEO
24 GEM	22 CAN	22 LEO	21 VIR	20 LIB	22 SAG	21 CAP	23 PIS	23 TAU	23 GEM	23 LEO	23 VIR
26 CAN	24 LEO	25 VIR	23 LIB	23 SCO	24 CAP	24 AQU	25 ARI	25 GEM	25 CAN	25 VIR	25 LIB
28 LIB	26 VIR	27 LIB	26 SCO	25 SAG	27 AQU	26 PIS	27 TAU	28 CAN	27 LEO	28 LIB	27 SCO
30 VIR	28 LIB	29 SCO	28 SAG	28 CAP	29 PIS	29 ARI	29 GEM	30 LEO	29 VIR	30 SCO	30 SAG
				30 AQU		31 TAU	31 CAN		31 LIB		

1965

JAN	FEB	MAR	APR	MAY	JUN	JUL	AUG	SEP	OCT	NOV	DEC
1 CAP	2 PIS	2 PIS	3 TAU	2 GEM	1 CAN	2 VIR	3 SCO	1 SAG	1 CAP	2 PIS	2 ARI
4 AQU	5 ARI	4 ARI	5 GEM	4 CAN	3 LEO	4 LIB	5 SAG	4 CAP	4 AQU	5 ARI	5 TAU
6 PIS	7 TAU	6 TAU	7 CAN	6 LEO	5 VIR	6 SCO	7 CAP	6 AQU	6 PIS	7 TAU	7 GEM
9 ARI	9 GEM	9 GEM	9 LEO	8 VIR	7 LIB	9 SAG	10 AQU	9 PIS	9 ARI	9 GEM	9 CAN
11 TAU	11 CAN	11 CAN	11 VIR	11 LIB	9 SCO	11 CAP	13 PIS	11 ARI	11 TAU	12 CAN	11 LEO
13 GEM	13 LEO	13 LEO	13 LIB	13 SCO	12 SAG	14 AQU	15 ARI	14 TAU	13 GEM	14 LEO	13 VIR
15 CAN	16 VIR	15 VIR	16 SCO	15 SAG	14 CAP	16 PIS	17 TAU	16 GEM	15 CAN	16 VIR	15 LIB
17 LEO	18 LIB	17 LIB	18 SAG	18 CAP	16 AQU	19 ARI	20 GEM	18 CAN	17 LEO	18 LIB	17 SCO
19 VIR	20 SCO	19 SCO	20 CAP	20 AQU	19 PIS	21 TAU	22 CAN	20 LEO	20 VIR	20 SCO	20 SAG
21 LIB	22 SAG	22 SAG	23 AQU	23 PIS	21 ARI	23 GEM	24 LEO	22 VIR	22 LIB	22 SAG	22 CAP
23 SCO	25 CAP	24 CAP	25 PIS	25 ARI	24 TAU	25 CAN	26 VIR	24 LIB	24 SCO	25 CAP	25 AQU
26 SAG	27 AQU	27 AQU	28 ARI	27 TAU	26 GEM	27 LEO	28 LIB	26 SCO	26 SAG	27 AQU	27 PIS
28 CAP		29 PIS	30 TAU	30 GEM	28 CAN	29 VIR	30 SCO	29 SAG	28 CAP	30 PIS	30 ARI
31 AQU		31 ARI			30 LEO	31 LIB			31 AQU		

1966

JAN	FEB	MAR	APR	MAY	JUN	JUL	AUG	SEP	OCT	NOV	DEC
1 TAU	2 CAN	1 CAN	2 VIR	1 LIB	2 SAG	1 CAP	2 PIS	1 ARI	1 TAU	2 CAN	2 LEO
3 GEM	4 LEO	3 LEO	4 LIB	3 SCO	4 CAP	4 AQU	5 ARI	4 TAU	3 GEM	4 LEO	4 VIR
5 CAN	6 VIR	5 VIR	6 SCO	5 SAG	6 AQU	6 PIS	7 TAU	6 GEM	6 CAN	6 VIR	6 LIB
7 LEO	8 LIB	7 LIB	8 SAG	8 CAP	9 PIS	9 ARI	10 GEM	9 CAN	8 LEO	8 LIB	8 SCO
9 VIR	10 SCO	9 SCO	10 CAP	10 AQU	11 ARI	11 TAU	12 CAN	11 LEO	10 VIR	11 SCO	10 SAG
11 LIB	12 SAG	12 SAG	13 AQU	12 PIS	14 TAU	14 GEM	14 LEO	13 VIR	12 LIB	13 SAG	12 CAP
14 SCO	15 CAP	14 CAP	15 PIS	15 ARI	16 GEM	16 CAN	16 VIR	15 LIB	14 SCO	15 CAP	14 AQU
16 SAG	17 AQU	16 AQU	18 ARI	17 TAU	18 CAN	18 LEO	18 LIB	17 SCO	16 SAG	17 AQU	17 PIS
18 CAP	20 PIS	19 PIS	20 TAU	20 GEM	20 LEO	20 VIR	20 SCO	19 SAG	18 CAP	20 PIS	19 ARI
21 AQU	22 ARI	21 ARI	22 GEM	22 CAN	23 VIR	22 LIB	22 SAG	21 CAP	21 AQU	22 ARI	22 TAU
23 PIS	25 TAU	24 TAU	25 CAN	24 LEO	25 LIB	24 SCO	25 CAP	23 AQU	23 PIS	25 TAU	24 GEM
26 ARI	27 GEM	26 GEM	27 LEO	26 VIR	27 SCO	26 SAG	27 AQU	26 PIS	26 ARI	27 GEM	27 CAN
28 TAU		29 CAN	29 VIR	28 LIB	29 SAG	29 CAP	30 PIS	28 ARI	28 TAU	29 CAN	29 LEO
31 GEM		31 LEO		31 SCO		31 AQU			31 GEM		31 VIR

1967

JAN	FEB	MAR	APR	MAY	JUN	JUL	AUG	SEP	OCT	NOV	DEC
2 LIB	3 SAG	2 SAG	3 AQU	2 PIS	1 ARI	1 TAU	2 CAN	1 LEO	2 LIB	1 SCO	2 CAP
4 SCO	5 CAP	4 CAP	5 PIS	5 ARI	4 TAU	3 GEM	4 LEO	3 VIR	4 SCO	3 SAG	4 AQU
6 SAG	7 AQU	6 AQU	8 ARI	7 TAU	6 GEM	6 CAN	7 VIR	5 LIB	6 SAG	5 CAP	7 PIS
9 CAP	10 PIS	9 PIS	10 TAU	10 GEM	9 CAN	8 LEO	9 LIB	7 SCO	9 CAP	7 AQU	9 ARI
11 AQU	12 ARI	11 ARI	13 GEM	12 CAN	11 LEO	10 VIR	11 SCO	9 SAG	11 AQU	9 PIS	12 TAU
13 PIS	15 TAU	14 TAU	15 CAN	15 LEO	13 VIR	12 LIB	13 SAG	11 CAP	13 PIS	12 ARI	14 GEM
16 ARI	17 GEM	16 GEM	17 LEO	17 VIR	15 LIB	15 SCO	15 CAP	14 AQU	16 ARI	14 TAU	17 CAN
18 TAU	19 CAN	19 CAN	20 VIR	19 LIB	17 SCO	17 SAG	17 AQU	16 PIS	18 TAU	17 GEM	19 LEO
21 GEM	22 LEO	21 LEO	22 LIB	21 SCO	19 SAG	19 CAP	20 PIS	18 ARI	21 GEM	19 CAN	21 VIR
23 CAN	24 VIR	23 VIR	24 SCO	23 SAG	21 CAP	21 AQU	22 ARI	21 TAU	23 CAN	22 LEO	24 LIB
25 LEO	26 LIB	25 LIB	26 SAG	25 CAP	24 AQU	23 PIS	25 TAU	23 GEM	26 LEO	24 VIR	26 SCO
27 VIR	28 SCO	27 SCO	28 CAP	27 AQU	26 PIS	26 ARI	27 GEM	26 CAN	28 VIR	26 LIB	28 SAG
29 LIB		29 SAG	30 AQU	30 PIS	28 ARI	28 TAU	30 CAN	28 LEO	30 LIB	28 SCO	30 CAP
31 SCO		31 CAP				31 GEM		30 VIR		30 SAG	

1968

JAN	FEB	MAR	APR	MAY	JUN	JUL	AUG	SEP	OCT	NOV	DEC
1 AQU	2 ARI	3 TAU	2 GEM	1 CAN	2 VIR	2 LIB	3 SAG	1 CAP	2 PIS	1 ARI	1 TAU
3 PIS	4 TAU	5 GEM	4 CAN	4 LEO	5 LIB	4 SCO	5 CAP	3 AQU	5 ARI	3 TAU	3 GEM
6 ARI	7 GEM	8 CAN	7 LEO	6 VIR	7 SCO	6 SAG	7 AQU	5 PIS	7 TAU	6 GEM	6 CAN
8 TAU	9 CAN	10 LEO	9 VIR	8 LIB	9 SAG	8 CAP	9 PIS	7 ARI	10 GEM	8 CAN	8 LEO
11 GEM	12 LEO	12 VIR	11 LIB	10 SCO	11 CAP	10 AQU	11 ARI	10 TAU	12 CAN	11 LEO	11 VIR
13 CAN	14 VIR	14 LIB	13 SCO	12 SAG	13 AQU	12 PIS	13 TAU	12 GEM	15 LEO	13 VIR	13 LIB
15 LEO	16 LIB	17 SCO	15 SAG	14 CAP	15 PIS	15 ARI	16 GEM	15 CAN	17 VIR	16 LIB	15 SCO
18 VIR	18 SCO	19 SAG	17 CAP	16 AQU	17 ARI	17 TAU	18 CAN	17 LEO	19 LIB	18 SCO	17 SAG
20 LIB	20 SAG	21 CAP	19 AQU	19 PIS	20 TAU	20 GEM	21 LEO	20 VIR	21 SCO	20 SAG	19 CAP
22 SCO	22 CAP	23 AQU	21 PIS	21 ARI	22 GEM	22 CAN	23 VIR	22 LIB	23 SAG	22 CAP	21 AQU
24 SAG	25 AQU	25 PIS	24 ARI	24 TAU	25 CAN	25 LEO	25 LIB	24 SCO	25 CAP	24 AQU	23 PIS
26 CAP	27 PIS	28 ARI	26 TAU	26 GEM	27 LEO	27 VIR	28 SCO	26 SAG	27 AQU	26 PIS	26 ARI
28 AQU	29 ARI	30 TAU	29 GEM	29 CAN	30 VIR	29 LIB	30 SAG	28 CAP	30 PIS	28 ARI	28 TAU
31 PIS				31 LEO		31 SCO		30 AQU			30 GEM

1969

JAN	FEB	MAR	APR	MAY	JUN	JUL	AUG	SEP	OCT	NOV	DEC
2 CAN	1 LEO	2 VIR	1 LIB	1 SCO	1 CAP	1 AQU	1 ARI	2 GEM	2 CAN	1 LEO	1 VIR
4 LEO	3 VIR	5 LIB	3 SCO	3 SAG	3 AQU	3 PIS	3 TAU	5 CAN	4 LEO	3 VIR	3 LIB
7 VIR	6 LIB	7 SCO	5 SAG	5 CAP	5 PIS	5 ARI	6 GEM	7 LEO	7 VIR	6 LIB	5 SCO
9 LIB	8 SCO	9 SAG	8 CAP	7 AQU	7 ARI	7 TAU	8 CAN	10 VIR	9 LIB	8 SCO	8 SAG
12 SCO	10 SAG	11 CAP	10 AQU	9 PIS	10 TAU	10 GEM	11 LEO	12 LIB	12 SCO	10 SAG	10 CAP
14 SAG	12 CAP	13 AQU	12 PIS	11 ARI	12 GEM	12 CAN	13 VIR	14 SCO	14 SAG	12 CAP	12 AQU
16 CAP	14 AQU	16 PIS	14 ARI	14 TAU	15 CAN	15 LEO	16 LIB	17 SAG	16 CAP	14 AQU	14 PIS
18 AQU	16 PIS	18 ARI	16 TAU	16 GEM	17 LEO	17 VIR	18 SCO	19 CAP	18 AQU	16 PIS	16 ARI
20 PIS	18 ARI	20 TAU	19 GEM	19 CAN	20 VIR	20 LIB	20 SAG	21 AQU	20 PIS	19 ARI	18 TAU
22 ARI	21 TAU	22 GEM	21 CAN	21 LEO	22 LIB	22 SCO	22 CAP	23 PIS	22 ARI	21 TAU	20 GEM
24 TAU	23 GEM	25 CAN	24 LEO	24 VIR	25 SCO	24 SAG	24 AQU	25 ARI	25 TAU	23 GEM	23 CAN
27 GEM	26 CAN	27 LEO	26 VIR	26 LIB	27 SAG	26 CAP	26 PIS	27 TAU	27 GEM	26 CAN	25 LEO
29 CAN	28 LEO	30 VIR	29 LIB	28 SCO	29 CAP	28 AQU	29 ARI	29 GEM	29 CAN	28 LEO	28 VIR
				30 SAG		30 PIS	31 TAU				30 LIB

1970

JAN	FEB	MAR	APR	MAY	JUN	JUL	AUG	SEP	OCT	NOV	DEC
2 SCO	2 CAP	2 CAP	2 PIS	2 ARI	2 GEM	2 CAN	1 LEO	2 LIB	2 SCO	3 CAP	2 AQU
4 SAG	4 AQU	4 AQU	4 ARI	4 TAU	5 CAN	4 LEO	3 VIR	5 SCO	4 SAG	5 AQU	4 PIS
6 CAP	6 PIS	6 PIS	6 TAU	6 GEM	7 LEO	7 VIR	6 LIB	7 SAG	6 CAP	7 PIS	6 ARI
8 AQU	8 ARI	8 ARI	9 GEM	8 CAN	10 VIR	10 LIB	8 SCO	9 CAP	9 AQU	9 ARI	8 TAU
10 PIS	11 TAU	10 TAU	11 CAN	11 LEO	12 LIB	12 SCO	11 SAG	11 AQU	11 PIS	11 TAU	11 GEM
12 ARI	13 GEM	12 GEM	14 LEO	13 VIR	15 SCO	14 SAG	13 CAP	13 PIS	13 ARI	13 GEM	13 CAN
14 TAU	15 CAN	15 CAN	16 VIR	16 LIB	17 SAG	16 CAP	15 AQU	15 ARI	15 TAU	16 CAN	15 LEO
17 GEM	18 LEO	17 LEO	19 LIB	18 SCO	19 CAP	18 AQU	17 PIS	17 TAU	17 GEM	18 LEO	18 VIR
19 CAN	20 VIR	20 VIR	21 SCO	20 SAG	21 AQU	20 PIS	19 ARI	19 GEM	19 CAN	20 VIR	20 LIB
22 LEO	23 LIB	22 LIB	23 SAG	23 CAP	23 PIS	22 ARI	21 TAU	22 CAN	22 LEO	23 LIB	23 SCO
24 VIR	25 SCO	25 SCO	25 CAP	25 AQU	25 ARI	25 TAU	23 GEM	24 LEO	24 VIR	25 SCO	25 SAG
27 LIB	28 SAG	27 SAG	27 AQU	27 PIS	27 TAU	27 GEM	25 CAN	27 VIR	27 LIB	28 SAG	27 CAP
29 SCO		29 CAP	30 PIS	29 ARI	30 GEM	29 CAN	28 LEO	29 LIB	29 SCO	30 CAP	29 AQU
31 SAG		31 AQU		31 TAU			31 VIR		31 SAG		31 PIS

THE EVERYTHING ASTROLOGY BOOK

1971

JAN	FEB	MAR	APR	MAY	JUN	JUL	AUG	SEP	OCT	NOV	DEC
3 ARI	1 TAU	2 GEM	1 CAN	1 LEO	2 LIB	2 SCO	1 SAG	2 AQU	1 PIS	2 TAU	1 GEM
5 TAU	3 GEM	5 CAN	3 LEO	3 VIR	5 SCO	4 SAG	3 CAP	4 PIS	3 ARI	4 GEM	3 CAN
7 GEM	5 CAN	7 LEO	6 VIR	6 LIB	7 SAG	7 CAP	5 AQU	6 ARI	5 TAU	6 CAN	5 LEO
9 CAN	8 LEO	10 VIR	8 LIB	8 SCO	9 CAP	9 AQU	7 PIS	8 TAU	7 GEM	8 LEO	8 VIR
12 LEO	10 VIR	12 LIB	11 SCO	11 SAG	11 AQU	11 PIS	9 ARI	10 GEM	9 CAN	10 VIR	10 LIB
14 VIR	13 LIB	15 SCO	13 SAG	13 CAP	14 PIS	13 ARI	11 TAU	12 CAN	12 LEO	13 LIB	13 SCO
17 LIB	15 SCO	17 SAG	16 CAP	15 AQU	16 ARI	15 TAU	13 GEM	14 LEO	14 VIR	15 SCO	15 SAG
19 SCO	18 SAG	19 CAP	18 AQU	17 PIS	18 TAU	17 GEM	16 CAN	17 VIR	16 LIB	18 SAG	17 CAP
22 SAG	20 CAP	22 AQU	20 PIS	20 ARI	20 GEM	19 CAN	18 LEO	19 LIB	19 SCO	20 CAP	20 AQU
24 CAP	22 AQU	24 PIS	22 ARI	22 TAU	22 CAN	22 LEO	20 VIR	22 SCO	22 SAG	23 AQU	22 PIS
26 AQU	24 PIS	26 ARI	24 TAU	24 GEM	24 LEO	24 VIR	23 LIB	24 SAG	24 CAP	25 PIS	24 ARI
28 PIS	26 ARI	28 TAU	26 GEM	26 CAN	27 VIR	27 LIB	26 SCO	27 CAP	26 AQU	27 ARI	26 TAU
30 ARI	28 TAU	30 GEM	28 CAN	28 LEO	29 LIB	29 SCO	28 SAG	29 AQU	28 PIS	29 TAU	28 GEM
				30 VIR			30 CAP		31 ARI		30 CAN

1972

JAN	FEB	MAR	APR	MAY	JUN	JUL	AUG	SEP	OCT	NOV	DEC
2 LEO	3 LIB	1 LIB	2 SAG	2 CAP	1 AQU	3 ARI	1 TAU	1 CAN	1 LEO	2 LIB	1 SCO
4 VIR	5 SCO	4 SCO	5 CAP	5 AQU	3 PIS	5 TAU	3 GEM	4 LEO	3 VIR	4 SCO	4 SAG
6 LIB	8 SAG	6 SAG	7 AQU	7 PIS	5 ARI	7 GEM	5 CAN	6 VIR	5 LIB	7 SAG	7 CAP
9 SCO	10 CAP	9 CAP	9 PIS	9 ARI	7 TAU	9 CAN	7 LEO	8 LIB	8 SCO	9 CAP	9 AQU
11 SAG	12 AQU	11 AQU	12 ARI	11 TAU	9 GEM	11 LEO	10 VIR	11 SCO	10 SAG	12 AQU	11 PIS
14 CAP	15 PIS	13 PIS	14 TAU	13 GEM	11 CAN	13 VIR	12 LIB	13 SAG	13 CAP	14 PIS	14 ARI
16 AQU	17 ARI	15 ARI	16 GEM	15 CAN	14 LEO	15 LIB	14 SCO	16 CAPI	15 AQU	16 ARI	16 TAU
18 PIS	19 TAU	17 TAU	18 CAN	17 LEO	16 VIR	18 SCO	17 SAG	18 AQU	18 PIS	18 TAU	18 GEM
20 ARI	21 GEM	19 GEM	20 LEO	19 VIR	18 LIB	20 SAG	19 CAP	20 PIS	20 ARI	20 GEM	20 CAN
23 TAU	23 CAN	21 CAN	22 VIR	22 LIB	21 SCO	23 CAP	22 AQU	22 ARI	22 TAU	22 CAN	22 LEO
25 GEM	25 LEO	24 LEO	25 LIB	24 SCO	23 SAG	25 AQU	24 PIS	24 TAU	24 GEM	24 LEO	24 VIR
27 CAN	28 VIR	26 VIR	27 SCO	27 SAG	26 CAP	28 PIS	26 ARI	27 GEM	26 CAN	27 VIR	26 LIB
29 LEO		28 LIB	30 SAG	29 CAP	28 AQU	30 ARI	28 TAU	29 CAN	28 LEO	29 LIB	29 SCO
31 VIR		31 SCO			30 PIS		30 GEM		30 VIR		31 SAG

1973

JAN	FEB	MAR	APR	MAY	JUN	JUL	AUG	SEP	OCT	NOV	DEC
3 CAP	2 AQU	1 AQU	2 ARI	1 TAU	2 CAN	1 LEO	2 LIB	1 SCO	3 CAP	2 AQU	1 PIS
5 AQU	4 PIS	3 PIS	4 TAU	3 GEM	4 LEO	3 VIR	4 SCO	3 SAG	5 AQU	4 PIS	4 ARI
8 PIS	6 ARI	5 ARI	6 GEM	5 CAN	6 VIR	5 LIB	7 SAG	5 CAP	8 PIS	6 ARI	6 TAU
10 ARI	8 TAU	8 TAU	8 CAN	7 LEO	8 LIB	8 SCO	9 CAP	8 AQU	10 ARI	9 TAU	8 GEM
12 TAU	10 GEM	10 GEM	10 LEO	10 VIR	11 SCO	10 SAG	12 AQU	10 PIS	12 TAU	11 GEM	10 CAN
14 GEM	13 CAN	12 CAN	12 VIR	12 LIB	13 SAG	13 CAP	14 PIS	13 ARI	14 GEM	13 CAN	12 LEO
16 CAN	15 LEO	14 LEO	15 LIB	14 SCO	16 CAP	15 AQU	16 ARI	15 TAU	16 CAN	15 LEO	14 VIR
18 LEO	17 VIR	16 VIR	17 SCO	17 SAG	18 AQU	18 PIS	19 TAU	17 GEM	19 LEO	17 VIR	16 LIB
20 VIR	19 LIB	18 LIB	20 SAG	19 CAP	21 PIS	20 ARI	21 GEM	19 CAN	21 VIR	19 LIB	19 SCO
23 LIB	21 SCO	21 SCO	22 CAP	22 AQU	23 ARI	22 TAU	23 CAN	21 LEO	23 LIB	22 SCO	21 SAG
25 SCO	24 SAG	23 SAG	25 AQU	24 PIS	25 TAU	25 GEM	25 LEO	23 VIR	25 SCO	24 SAG	24 CAP
28 SAG	26 CAP	26 CAP	27 PIS	27 ARI	27 GEM	27 CAN	27 VIR	26 LIB	28 SAG	26 CAP	26 AQU
30 CAP		28 AQU	29 ARI	29 TAU	29 CAN	29 LEO	29 LIB	28 SCO	30 CAP	29 AQU	29 PIS
		31 PIS		31 GEM		31 VIR		30 SAG			31 ARI

1974

JAN	FEB	MAR	APR	MAY	JUN	JUL	AUG	SEP	OCT	NOV	DEC
2 TAU	1 GEM	2 CAN	1 LEO	2 LIB	1 SCO	3 CAP	2 AQU	3 ARI	2 TAU	1 GEM	1 CAN
5 GEM	3 CAN	4 LEO	3 VIR	4 SCO	3 SAG	5 AQU	4 PIS	5 TAU	5 GEM	3 CAN	3 LEO
7 CAN	5 LEO	7 VIR	5 LIB	7 SAG	6 CAP	8 PIS	7 ARI	8 GEM	7 CAN	5 LEO	5 VIR
9 LEO	7 VIR	9 LIB	7 SCO	9 CAP	8 AQU	10 ARI	9 TAU	10 CAN	9 LEO	8 VIR	7 LIB
11 VIR	9 LIB	11 SCO	9 SAG	12 AQU	11 PIS	13 TAU	11 GEM	12 LEO	11 VIR	10 LIB	9 SCO
13 LIB	11 SCO	13 SAG	12 CAP	14 PIS	13 ARI	15 GEM	13 CAN	14 VIR	13 LIB	12 SCO	11 SAG
15 SCO	14 SAG	16 CAP	14 AQU	17 ARI	15 TAU	17 CAN	15 LEO	16 LIB	15 SCO	14 SAG	14 CAP
17 SAG	16 CAP	18 AQU	17 PIS	19 TAU	18 GEM	19 LEO	17 VIR	18 SCO	18 SAG	16 CAP	16 AQU
20 CAP	19 AQU	21 PIS	19 ARI	21 GEM	20 CAN	21 VIR	19 LIB	20 SAG	20 CAP	19 AQU	19 PIS
22 AQU	21 PIS	23 ARI	22 TAU	23 CAN	22 LEO	23 LIB	22 SCO	23 CAP	22 AQU	21 PIS	21 ARI
25 PIS	24 ARI	25 TAU	24 GEM	25 LEO	24 VIR	25 SCO	24 SAG	25 AQU	25 PIS	24 ARI	24 TAU
27 ARI	26 TAU	27 GEM	26 CAN	27 VIR	26 LIB	28 SAG	26 CAP	28 PIS	27 ARI	26 TAU	26 GEM
30 TAU	28 GEM	30 CAN	28 LEO	30 LIB	28 SCO	30 CAP	29 AQU	30 ARI	30 TAU	28 GEM	28 CAN
		30 VIR			30 SAG		31 PIS				30 LEO

1975

JAN	FEB	MAR	APR	MAY	JUN	JUL	AUG	SEP	OCT	NOV	DEC
1 VIR	2 SCO	1 SCO	2 CAP	2 AQU	3 ARI	3 TAU	1 GEM	2 LEO	2 VIR	2 SCO	2 SAG
3 LIB	4 SAG	3 SAG	4 AQU	4 PIS	5 TAU	5 GEM	4 CAN	4 VIR	4 LIB	4 SAG	4 CAP
5 SCO	6 CAP	5 CAP	7 PIS	7 ARI	8 GEM	7 CAN	6 LEO	6 LIB	6 SCO	6 CAP	6 AQU
8 SAG	9 AQU	8 AQU	9 ARI	9 TAU	10 CAN	9 LEO	8 VIR	8 SCO	8 SAG	9 AQU	8 PIS
10 CAP	11 PIS	10 PIS	12 TAU	11 GEM	12 LEO	11 VIR	10 LIB	10 SAG	10 CAP	11 PIS	11 ARI
12 AQU	14 ARI	13 ARI	14 GEM	14 CAN	14 VIR	14 LIB	12 SCO	13 CAP	12 AQU	14 ARI	13 TAU
15 PIS	16 TAU	15 TAU	16 CAN	16 LEO	16 LIB	16 SCO	14 SAG	15 AQU	15 PIS	16 TAU	16 GEM
17 ARI	19 GEM	18 GEM	19 LEO	18 VIR	18 SCO	18 SAG	16 CAP	18 PIS	17 ARI	19 GEM	18 CAN
20 TAU	21 CAN	20 CAN	21 VIR	20 LIB	21 SAG	20 CAP	19 AQU	20 ARI	20 TAU	21 CAN	20 LEO
22 GEM	23 LEO	22 LEO	23 LIB	22 SCO	23 CAP	23 AQU	21 PIS	23 TAU	22 GEM	23 LEO	23 VIR
24 CAN	25 VIR	24 VIR	25 SCO	24 SAG	25 AQU	25 PIS	24 ARI	25 GEM	25 CAN	25 VIR	25 LIB
26 LEO	27 LIB	26 LIB	27 SAG	27 CAP	28 PIS	28 ARI	26 TAU	27 CAN	27 LEO	27 LIB	27 SCO
28 VIR		28 SCO	29 CAP	29 AQU	30 ARI	30 TAU	29 GEM	30 LEO	29 VIR	30 SCO	29 SAG
30 LIB		30 SAG		31 PIS			31 CAN		31 LIB		31 CAP

1976

JAN	FEB	MAR	APR	MAY	JUN	JUL	AUG	SEP	OCT	NOV	DEC
2 AQU	1 PIS	2 ARI	1 TAU	3 CAN	1 LEO	1 VIR	1 SCO	2 CAP	1 AQU	2 ARI	2 TAU
5 PIS	4 ARI	4 TAU	3 GEM	5 LEO	4 VIR	3 LIB	4 SAG	4 AQU	4 PIS	5 TAU	5 GEM
7 ARI	6 TAU	7 GEM	6 CAN	7 VIR	6 LIB	5 SCO	6 CAP	7 PIS	6 ARI	8 GEM	7 CAN
10 TAU	9 GEM	9 CAN	8 LEO	10 LIB	8 SCO	7 SAG	8 AQU	9 ARI	9 TAU	10 CAN	10 LEO
12 GEM	11 CAN	12 LEO	10 VIR	12 SCO	10 SAG	9 CAP	10 PIS	11 TAU	11 GEM	12 LEO	12 VIR
15 CAN	13 LEO	14 VIR	12 LIB	14 SAG	12 CAP	12 AQU	13 ARI	14 GEM	14 CAN	15 VIR	14 LIB
17 LEO	15 VIR	16 LIB	14 SCO	16 CAP	14 AQU	14 PIS	15 TAU	17 CAN	16 LEO	17 LIB	16 SCO
19 VIR	17 LIB	18 SCO	16 SAG	18 AQU	17 PIS	16 ARI	18 GEM	19 LEO	18 VIR	19 SCO	18 SAG
21 LIB	19 SCO	20 SAG	18 CAP	20 PIS	19 ARI	19 TAU	20 CAN	21 VIR	21 LIB	21 SAG	20 CAP
23 SCO	21 SAG	22 CAP	20 AQU	23 ARI	22 TAU	21 GEM	22 LEO	23 LIB	23 SCO	23 CAP	22 AQU
25 SAG	24 CAP	24 AQU	23 PIS	25 TAU	24 GEM	24 CAN	25 VIR	25 SCO	24 SAG	25 AQU	25 PIS
27 CAP	26 AQU	27 PIS	25 ARI	28 GEM	26 CAN	26 LEO	27 LIB	27 SAG	27 CAP	27 PIS	27 ARI
30 AQU	28 PIS	29 ARI	28 TAU	30 CAN	29 LEO	28 VIR	29 SCO	29 CAP	29 AQU	30 ARI	30 TAU
			30 GEM			30 LIB	31 SAG		31 PIS		

1977

JAN	FEB	MAR	APR	MAY	JUN	JUL	AUG	SEP	OCT	NOV	DEC
1 GEM	2 LEO	2 LEO	2 LIB	2 SCO	2 CAP	2 AQU	3 ARI	1 TAU	1 GEM	3 LEO	2 VIR
4 CAN	5 VIR	4 VIR	5 SCO	4 SAG	4 AQU	4 PIS	5 TAU	4 GEM	4 CAN	5 VIR	5 LIB
6 LEO	7 LIB	6 LIB	7 SAG	6 CAP	7 PIS	6 ARI	7 GEM	6 CAN	6 LEO	7 LIB	7 SCO
8 VIR	9 SCO	8 SCO	9 CAP	8 AQU	9 ARI	9 TAU	10 CAN	9 LEO	9 VIR	9 SCO	9 SAG
10 LIB	11 SAG	10 SAG	11 AQU	10 PIS	11 TAU	11 GEM	12 LEO	11 VIR	11 LIB	11 SAG	11 CAP
13 SCO	13 CAP	12 CAP	13 PIS	13 ARI	14 GEM	14 CAN	15 VIR	13 LIB	13 SCO	13 CAP	13 AQU
15 SAG	15 AQU	15 AQU	15 ARI	15 TAU	16 CAN	16 LEO	17 LIB	16 SCO	15 SAG	15 AQU	15 PIS
17 CAP	17 PIS	17 PIS	18 TAU	18 GEM	19 LEO	19 VIR	19 SCO	18 SAG	17 CAP	18 PIS	17 ARI
19 AQU	20 ARI	19 ARI	20 GEM	20 CAN	21 VIR	21 LIB	21 SAG	20 CAP	19 AQU	20 ARI	19 TAU
21 PIS	22 TAU	22 TAU	23 CAN	23 LEO	24 LIB	23 SCO	24 CAP	22 AQU	21 PIS	22 TAU	22 GEM
23 ARI	25 GEM	24 GEM	25 LEO	25 VIR	26 SCO	25 SAG	26 AQU	24 PIS	24 ARI	25 GEM	25 CAN
26 TAU	27 CAN	27 CAN	28 VIR	27 LIB	28 SAG	27 CAP	28 PIS	26 ARI	26 TAU	27 CAN	27 LEO
28 GEM		29 LEO	30 LIB	29 SCO	30 CAP	29 AQU	30 ARI	29 TAU	28 GEM	30 LEO	30 VIR
31 CAN		31 VIR		31 SAG		31 PIS			31 CAN		

1978

JAN	FEB	MAR	APR	MAY	JUN	JUL	AUG	SEP	OCT	NOV	DEC
1 LIB	2 SAG	1 SAG	1 AQU	1 PIS	1 TAU	1 GEM	2 LEO	1 VIR	1 LIB	2 SAG	1 CAP
3 SCO	4 CAP	3 CAP	3 PIS	3 ARI	4 GEM	4 CAN	5 VIR	4 LIB	3 SCO	4 CAP	3 AQU
5 SAG	6 AQU	5 AQU	6 ARI	5 TAU	6 CAN	6 LEO	7 LIB	6 SCO	5 SAG	6 AQU	5 PIS
7 CAP	8 PIS	7 PIS	8 TAU	8 GEM	9 LEO	9 VIR	10 SCO	8 SAG	8 CAP	8 PIS	7 ARI
9 AQU	10 ARI	9 ARI	10 GEM	10 CAN	11 VIR	11 LIB	12 SAG	10 CAP	10 AQU	10 ARI	10 TAU
11 PIS	12 TAU	12 TAU	13 CAN	13 LEO	14 LIB	13 SCO	14 CAP	12 AQU	12 PIS	12 TAU	12 GEM
13 ARI	15 GEM	14 GEM	15 LEO	15 VIR	16 SCO	16 SAG	16 AQU	14 PIS	14 ARI	15 GEM	14 CAN
16 TAU	17 CAN	16 CAN	18 VIR	17 LIB	18 SAG	18 CAP	18 PIS	17 ARI	16 TAU	17 CAN	17 LEO
18 GEM	20 LEO	19 LEO	20 LIB	20 SCO	20 CAP	20 AQU	20 ARI	19 TAU	18 GEM	20 LEO	19 VIR
21 CAN	22 VIR	21 VIR	22 SCO	22 SAG	22 AQU	22 PIS	22 TAU	21 GEM	21 CAN	22 VIR	22 LIB
23 LEO	24 LIB	24 LIB	24 SAG	24 CAP	24 PIS	24 ARI	25 GEM	23 CAN	23 LEO	25 LIB	24 SCO
26 VIR	27 SCO	26 SCO	26 CAP	26 AQU	26 ARI	26 TAU	27 CAN	26 LEO	26 VIR	27 SCO	27 SAG
28 LIB		28 SAG	29 AQU	28 PIS	29 TAU	28 GEM	30 LEO	28 VIR	28 LIB	29 SAG	29 CAP
30 SCO		30 CAP		30 ARI		31 CAN			31 SCO		31 AQU

1979

JAN	FEB	MAR	APR	MAY	JUN	JUL	AUG	SEP	OCT	NOV	DEC
2 PIS	2 TAU	2 TAU	3 CAN	2 LEO	1 VIR	1 LIB	2 SAG	1 CAP	2 PIS	1 ARI	2 GEM
4 ARI	5 GEM	4 GEM	5 LEO	5 VIR	4 LIB	4 SCO	4 CAP	3 AQU	4 ARI	3 TAU	4 CAN
6 TAU	7 CAN	6 CAN	8 VIR	7 LIB	6 SCO	6 SAG	6 AQU	5 PIS	6 TAU	5 GEM	7 LEO
8 GEM	9 LEO	9 LEO	10 LIB	10 SCO	8 SAG	8 CAP	8 PIS	7 ARI	8 GEM	7 CAN	9 VIR
11 CAN	12 VIR	11 VIR	12 SCO	12 SAG	11 CAP	10 AQU	10 ARI	9 TAU	11 CAN	9 LEO	12 LIB
13 LEO	15 LIB	14 LIB	15 SAG	14 CAP	13 AQU	12 PIS	13 TAU	11 GEM	13 LEO	12 VIR	14 SCO
16 VIR	17 SCO	16 SCO	17 CAP	16 AQU	15 PIS	14 ARI	15 GEM	13 CAN	16 VIR	14 LIB	17 SAG
18 LIB	19 SAG	19 SAG	19 AQU	18 PIS	17 ARI	16 TAU	17 CAN	16 LEO	18 LIB	17 SCO	19 CAP
21 SCO	21 CAP	21 CAP	21 PIS	21 ARI	19 TAU	18 GEM	20 LEO	18 VIR	21 SCO	19 SAG	21 AQU
23 SAG	24 AQU	23 AQU	23 ARI	23 TAU	21 GEM	21 CAN	22 VIR	21 LIB	23 SAG	22 CAP	23 PIS
25 CAP	25 PIS	25 PIS	25 TAU	25 GEM	24 CAN	23 LEO	25 LIB	23 SCO	25 CAP	24 AQU	25 ARI
27 AQU	27 ARI	27 ARI	28 GEM	27 CAN	26 LEO	26 VIR	27 SCO	26 SAG	28 AQU	26 PIS	27 TAU
29 PIS		29 TAU	30 CAN	30 LEO	29 VIR	28 LIB	30 SAG	28 CAP	30 PIS	28 ARI	30 GEM
31 ARI		31 GEM				31 SCO		30 AQU		30 TAU	

1980

JAN	FEB	MAR	APR	MAY	JUN	JUL	AUG	SEP	OCT	NOV	DEC
1 CAN	2 VIR	3 LIB	2 SCO	1 SAG	2 AQU	2 PIS	2 TAU	3 CAN	2 LEO	1 VIR	1 LIB
3 LEO	4 LIB	5 SCO	4 SAG	4 CAP	4 PIS	4 ARI	4 GEM	5 LEO	5 VIR	3 LIB	3 SCO
6 VIR	7 SCO	8 SAG	6 CAP	6 AQU	6 ARI	6 TAU	6 CAN	7 VIR	7 LIB	6 SCO	6 SAG
8 LIB	9 SAG	10 CAP	9 AQU	8 PIS	9 TAU	8 GEM	9 LEO	10 LIB	10 SCO	8 SAG	8 CAP
11 SCO	12 CAP	12 AQU	11 PIS	10 ARI	11 GEM	10 CAN	11 VIR	12 SCO	12 SAG	11 CAP	10 AQU
13 SAG	14 AQU	14 PIS	13 ARI	12 TAU	13 CAN	12 LEO	14 LIB	15 SAG	15 CAP	13 AQU	13 PIS
15 CAP	16 PIS	16 ARI	15 TAU	14 GEM	15 LEO	15 VIR	16 SCO	17 CAP	17 AQU	15 PIS	15 ARI
17 AQU	18 ARI	18 TAU	17 GEM	16 CAN	17 VIR	17 LIB	19 SAG	20 AQU	19 PIS	18 ARI	17 TAU
19 PIS	20 TAU	20 GEM	19 CAN	19 LEO	20 LIB	20 SCO	21 CAP	22 PIS	21 ARI	20 TAU	19 GEM
21 ARI	22 GEM	23 CAN	21 LEO	21 VIR	22 SCO	22 SAG	23 AQU	24 ARI	23 TAU	22 GEM	21 CAN
24 TAU	24 CAN	25 LEO	24 VIR	24 LIB	25 SAG	25 CAP	25 PIS	26 TAU	25 GEM	24 CAN	23 LEO
26 GEM	27 LEO	27 VIR	26 LIB	26 SCO	27 CAP	27 AQU	27 ARI	28 GEM	27 CAN	26 LEO	25 VIR
28 CAN	29 VIR	30 LIB	29 SCO	29 SAG	29 AQU	29 PIS	29 TAU	30 CAN	29 LEO	28 VIR	28 LIB
30 LEO				31 CAP		31 ARI	31 GEM				30 SCO

1981

	JAN	FEB	MAR	APR	MAY	JUN	JUL	AUG	SEP	OCT	NOV	DEC
	2 SAG	1 CAP	2 AQU	1 PIS	1 ARI	1 GEM	2 LEO	1 VIR	2 SCO	2 SAG	1 CAP	1 AQU
	4 CAP	3 AQU	5 PIS	3 ARI	3 TAU	3 CAN	5 VIR	3 LIB	5 SAG	5 CAP	3 AQU	3 PIS
	7 AQU	5 PIS	7 ARI	5 TAU	5 GEM	5 LEO	7 LIB	6 SCO	7 CAP	7 AQU	6 PIS	5 ARI
	9 PIS	7 ARI	9 TAU	7 GEM	7 CAN	7 VIR	10 SCO	8 SAG	10 AQU	9 PIS	8 ARI	7 TAU
	11 ARI	9 TAU	11 GEM	9 CAN	9 LEO	10 LIB	12 SAG	11 CAP	12 PIS	11 ARI	10 TAU	9 GEM
	13 TAU	12 GEM	13 CAN	11 LEO	11 VIR	12 SCO	15 CAP	13 AQU	14 ARI	13 TAU	12 GEM	11 CAN
	15 GEM	14 CAN	15 LEO	14 VIR	13 LIB	15 SAG	17 AQU	16 PIS	16 TAU	15 GEM	14 CAN	13 LEO
	17 CAN	16 LEO	18 VIR	16 LIB	16 SCO	17 CAP	19 PIS	18 ARI	18 GEM	18 CAN	16 LEO	16 VIR
	20 LEO	18 VIR	20 LIB	19 SCO	18 SAG	20 AQU	21 ARI	20 TAU	20 CAN	20 LEO	18 VIR	18 LIB
	22 VIR	21 LIB	22 SCO	21 SAG	21 CAP	22 PIS	24 TAU	22 GEM	22 LEO	22 VIR	21 LIB	20 SCO
	24 LIB	23 SCO	25 SAG	24 CAP	23 AQU	24 ARI	26 GEM	24 CAN	25 VIR	24 LIB	23 SCO	23 SAG
	27 SCO	26 SAG	27 CAP	26 AQU	26 PIS	26 TAU	28 CAN	26 LEO	27 LIB	27 SCO	26 SAG	25 CAP
	29 SAG	28 CAP	30 AQU	28 PIS	28 ARI	28 GEM	30 LEO	28 VIR	29 SCO	29 SAG	28 CAP	28 AQU
					30 TAU	30 CAN		31 LIB				30 PIS

1982

	JAN	FEB	MAR	APR	MAY	JUN	JUL	AUG	SEP	OCT	NOV	DEC
	2 ARI	2 GEM	1 GEM	2 LEO	1 VIR	2 SCO	2 SAG	1 CAP	2 PIS	2 ARI	2 GEM	2 CAN
	4 TAU	4 CAN	3 CAN	4 VIR	4 LIB	5 SAG	4 CAP	3 AQU	4 ARI	4 TAU	4 CAN	4 LEO
	6 GEM	6 LEO	6 LEO	6 LIB	6 SCO	7 CAP	7 AQU	6 PIS	7 TAU	6 GEM	6 LEO	6 VIR
	8 CAN	8 VIR	8 VIR	9 SCO	8 SAG	10 AQU	9 PIS	8 ARI	9 GEM	8 CAN	9 VIR	8 LIB
	10 LEO	11 LIB	10 LIB	11 SAG	11 CAP	12 PIS	12 ARI	10 TAU	11 CAN	10 LEO	11 LIB	10 SCO
	12 VIR	13 SCO	12 SCO	14 CAP	13 AQU	15 ARI	14 TAU	13 GEM	13 LEO	12 VIR	13 SCO	13 SAG
	14 LIB	15 SAG	15 SAG	16 AQU	16 PIS	17 TAU	16 GEM	15 CAN	15 VIR	15 LIB	15 SAG	15 CAP
	17 SCO	18 CAP	17 CAP	19 PIS	18 ARI	19 GEM	18 CAN	17 LEO	17 LIB	17 SCO	18 CAP	18 AQU
	19 SAG	20 AQU	20 AQU	21 ARI	20 TAU	21 CAN	20 LEO	19 VIR	19 SCO	19 SAG	21 AQU	20 PIS
	22 CAP	23 PIS	22 PIS	23 TAU	22 GEM	23 LEO	22 VIR	21 LIB	22 SAG	22 CAP	23 PIS	23 ARI
	24 AQU	25 ARI	24 ARI	25 GEM	24 CAN	25 VIR	24 LIB	23 SCO	24 CAP	24 AQU	25 ARI	25 TAU
	26 PIS	27 TAU	27 TAU	27 CAN	26 LEO	27 LIB	27 SCO	25 SAG	27 AQU	27 PIS	28 TAU	27 GEM
	29 ARI		29 GEM	29 LEO	29 VIR	29 SCO	29 SAG	28 CAP	29 PIS	29 ARI	30 GEM	29 CAN
	31 TAU		31 CAN		31 LIB			31 AQU		31 TAU		31 LEO

1983

JAN	FEB	MAR	APR	MAY	JUN	JUL	AUG	SEP	OCT	NOV	DEC
2 VIR	1 LIB	2 SCO	1 SAG	1 CAP	2 PIS	2 ARI	1 TAU	1 CAN	1 LEO	1 LIB	1 SCO
4 LIB	3 SCO	5 SAG	3 CAP	3 AQU	5 ARI	4 TAU	3 GEM	3 LEO	3 VIR	3 SCO	3 SAG
7 SCO	5 SAG	7 CAP	6 AQU	6 PIS	7 TAU	7 GEM	5 CAN	5 VIR	5 LIB	6 SAG	5 CAP
9 SAG	8 CAP	10 AQU	8 PIS	8 ARI	9 GEM	9 CAN	7 LEO	7 LIB	7 SCO	8 CAP	8 AQU
12 CAP	10 AQU	12 PIS	11 ARI	11 TAU	11 CAN	11 LEO	9 VIR	10 SCO	9 SAG	10 AQU	10 PIS
14 AQU	13 PIS	15 ARI	13 TAU	13 GEM	13 LEO	13 VIR	11 LIB	12 SAG	11 CAP	13 PIS	13 ARI
17 PIS	15 ARI	17 TAU	15 GEM	15 CAN	15 VIR	15 LIB	13 SCO	14 CAP	14 AQU	15 ARI	15 TAU
19 ARI	18 TAU	19 GEM	18 CAN	17 LEO	17 LIB	17 SCO	15 SAG	17 AQU	16 PIS	18 TAU	17 GEM
21 TAU	20 GEM	21 CAN	20 LEO	19 VIR	20 SCO	19 SAG	18 CAP	19 PIS	19 ARI	20 GEM	20 CAN
24 GEM	22 CAN	23 LEO	22 VIR	21 LIB	22 SAG	22 CAP	20 AQU	22 ARI	21 TAU	22 CAN	22 LEO
26 CAN	24 LEO	26 VIR	24 LIB	23 SCO	24 CAP	24 AQU	23 PIS	24 TAU	24 GEM	24 LEO	24 VIR
28 LEO	26 VIR	28 LIB	26 SCO	26 SAG	27 AQU	27 PIS	25 ARI	26 GEM	26 CAN	26 VIR	26 LIB
30 VIR	28 LIB	30 SCO	28 SAG	28 CAP	29 PIS	29 ARI	28 TAU	29 CAN	28 LEO	29 LIB	28 SCO
				31 AQU			30 GEM		30 VIR		30 SAG

1984

JAN	FEB	MAR	APR	MAY	JUN	JUL	AUG	SEP	OCT	NOV	DEC
2 CAP	3 PIS	1 PIS	2 TAU	2 GEM	1 CAN	2 VIR	3 SCO	1 SAG	1 CAP	2 PIS	1 ARI
4 AQU	5 ARI	4 ARI	5 GEM	4 CAN	3 LEO	4 LIB	5 SAG	3 CAP	3 AQU	4 ARI	4 TAU
6 PIS	8 TAU	6 TAU	7 CAN	6 LEO	5 VIR	6 SCO	7 CAP	6 AQU	5 PIS	7 TAU	6 GEM
9 ARI	10 GEM	8 GEM	9 LEO	9 VIR	7 LIB	9 SAG	9 AQU	8 PIS	8 ARI	9 GEM	9 CAN
11 TAU	12 CAN	11 CAN	11 VIR	11 LIB	9 SCO	11 CAP	12 PIS	11 ARI	10 TAU	12 CAN	11 LEO
14 GEM	15 LEO	13 LEO	13 LIB	13 SCO	11 SAG	13 AQU	14 ARI	13 TAU	13 GEM	14 LEO	13 VIR
16 CAN	16 VIR	15 VIR	15 SCO	15 SAG	13 CAP	16 PIS	17 TAU	16 GEM	15 CAN	16 VIR	15 LIB
18 LEO	18 LIB	17 LIB	17 SAG	17 CAP	16 AQU	18 ARI	19 GEM	18 CAN	18 LEO	18 LIB	17 SCO
20 VIR	20 SCO	19 SCO	20 CAP	19 AQU	18 PIS	21 TAU	22 CAN	20 LEO	20 VIR	20 SCO	20 SAG
22 LIB	23 SAG	21 SAG	22 AQU	22 PIS	21 ARI	23 GEM	24 LEO	22 VIR	22 LIB	22 SAG	22 CAP
24 SCO	25 CAP	23 CAP	25 PIS	24 ARI	23 TAU	25 CAN	26 VIR	24 LIB	24 SCO	24 CAP	24 AQU
26 SAG	28 AQU	26 AQU	27 ARI	27 TAU	26 GEM	27 LEO	28 LIB	26 SCO	26 SAG	27 AQU	26 PIS
29 CAP		28 PIS	30 TAU	29 GEM	28 CAN	29 VIR	30 SCO	28 SAG	28 CAP	29 PIS	29 ARI
31 AQU		31 ARI			30 LEO	31 LIB			30 AQU		31 TAU

1985

JAN	FEB	MAR	APR	MAY	JUN	JUL	AUG	SEP	OCT	NOV	DEC
3 GEM	2 CAN	1 CAN	2 VIR	1 LIB	2 SAG	1 CAP	2 PIS	1 ARI	3 GEM	2 CAN	1 LEO
5 CAN	4 LEO	3 LEO	4 LIB	3 SCO	4 CAP	3 AQU	4 ARI	3 TAU	5 CAN	4 LEO	4 VIR
7 LEO	6 VIR	5 VIR	6 SCO	5 SAG	6 AQU	5 PIS	7 TAU	6 GEM	8 LEO	6 VIR	6 LIB
9 VIR	8 LIB	7 LIB	8 SAG	7 CAP	8 PIS	8 ARI	9 GEM	8 CAN	10 VIR	9 LIB	8 SCO
12 LIB	10 SCO	9 SCO	10 CAP	9 AQU	11 ARI	10 TAU	12 CAN	10 LEO	12 LIB	11 SCO	10 SAG
14 SCO	12 SAG	11 SAG	12 AQU	12 PIS	13 TAU	13 GEM	14 LEO	13 VIR	14 SCO	13 SAG	12 CAP
16 SAG	14 CAP	14 CAP	14 PIS	14 ARI	16 GEM	15 CAN	16 VIR	15 LIB	16 SAG	15 CAP	14 AQU
18 CAP	17 AQU	16 AQU	17 ARI	17 TAU	18 CAN	18 LEO	18 LIB	17 SCO	18 CAP	17 AQU	16 PIS
20 AQU	19 PIS	18 PIS	20 TAU	19 GEM	20 LEO	20 VIR	20 SCO	19 SAG	20 AQU	19 PIS	19 ARI
23 PIS	21 ARI	21 ARI	22 GEM	22 CAN	23 VIR	22 LIB	22 SAG	21 CAP	23 PIS	21 ARI	21 TAU
25 ARI	24 TAU	23 TAU	25 CAN	24 LEO	25 LIB	24 SCO	25 CAP	23 AQU	25 ARI	24 TAU	24 GEM
28 TAU	27 GEM	26 GEM	27 LEO	26 VIR	27 SCO	26 SAG	27 AQU	25 PIS	28 TAU	26 GEM	26 CAN
30 GEM		28 CAN	29 VIR	29 LIB	29 SAG	28 CAP	29 PIS	28 ARI	30 GEM	29 CAN	29 LEO
		31 LEO		31 SCO		31 AQU		30 TAU			31 VIR

1986

JAN	FEB	MAR	APR	MAY	JUN	JUL	AUG	SEP	OCT	NOV	DEC
2 LIB	1 SCO	2 SAG	2 AQU	2 PIS	3 TAU	3 GEM	2 CAN	3 VIR	2 LIB	1 SCO	2 CAP
4 SCO	3 SAG	4 CAP	5 PIS	4 ARI	5 GEM	5 CAN	4 LEO	5 LIB	4 SCO	3 SAG	4 AQU
6 SAG	5 CAP	6 AQU	7 ARI	7 TAU	8 CAN	8 LEO	6 VIR	7 SCO	7 SAG	5 CAP	6 PIS
8 CAP	7 AQU	8 PIS	9 TAU	9 GEM	11 LEO	10 VIR	9 LIB	9 SAG	9 CAP	7 AQU	9 ARI
11 AQU	9 PIS	11 ARI	12 GEM	12 CAN	13 VIR	12 LIB	11 SCO	11 CAP	11 AQU	9 PIS	11 TAU
13 PIS	11 ARI	13 TAU	14 CAN	14 LEO	15 LIB	15 SCO	13 SAG	14 AQU	13 PIS	11 ARI	14 GEM
15 ARI	14 TAU	16 GEM	17 LEO	17 VIR	17 SCO	17 SAG	15 CAP	16 PIS	15 ARI	14 TAU	16 CAN
17 TAU	16 GEM	18 CAN	19 VIR	19 LIB	19 SAG	19 CAP	17 AQU	18 ARI	18 TAU	16 GEM	19 LEO
20 GEM	19 CAN	21 LEO	21 LIB	21 SCO	21 CAP	21 AQU	19 PIS	20 TAU	20 GEM	19 CAN	21 VIR
22 CAN	21 LEO	23 VIR	24 SCO	23 SAG	23 AQU	23 PIS	22 ARI	23 GEM	23 CAN	21 LEO	24 LIB
25 LEO	23 VIR	25 LIB	26 SAG	25 CAP	26 PIS	25 ARI	24 TAU	25 CAN	25 LEO	24 VIR	26 SCO
27 VIR	26 LIB	27 SCO	28 CAP	27 AQU	28 ARI	28 TAU	26 GEM	28 LEO	27 VIR	26 LIB	28 SAG
29 LIB	28 SCO	29 SAG	30 AQU	29 PIS	30 TAU	30 GEM	29 CAN	30 VIR	30 LIB	28 SCO	30 CAP
		31 CAP		31 ARI			31 LEO			30 SAG	

1987

JAN	FEB	MAR	APR	MAY	JUN	JUL	AUG	SEP	OCT	NOV	DEC
1 AQU	1 ARI	1 ARI	2 GEM	2 CAN	3 VIR	3 LIB	1 SCO	2 CAP	1 AQU	2 ARI	1 TAU
3 PIS	4 TAU	3 TAU	4 CAN	4 LEO	5 LIB	5 SCO	4 SAG	4 AQU	3 PIS	4 TAU	4 GEM
5 ARI	6 GEM	5 GEM	7 LEO	7 VIR	8 SCO	7 SAG	6 CAP	6 PIS	6 ARI	6 GEM	6 CAN
7 TAU	9 CAN	8 CAN	9 VIR	9 LIB	10 SAG	9 CAP	8 AQU	8 ARI	8 TAU	9 CAN	8 LEO
10 GEM	11 LEO	10 LEO	12 LIB	11 SCO	12 CAP	11 AQU	10 PIS	10 TAU	10 GEM	11 LEO	11 VIR
12 CAN	14 VIR	13 VIR	14 SCO	13 SAG	14 AQU	13 PIS	12 ARI	13 GEM	12 CAN	14 VIR	14 LIB
15 LEO	16 LIB	15 LIB	16 SAG	15 CAP	16 PIS	15 ARI	14 TAU	15 CAN	15 LEO	16 LIB	16 SCO
17 VIR	18 SCO	18 SCO	18 CAP	17 AQU	18 ARI	18 TAU	16 GEM	17 LEO	17 VIR	18 SCO	18 SAG
20 LIB	21 SAG	20 SAG	20 AQU	20 PIS	20 TAU	20 GEM	19 CAN	20 VIR	20 LIB	21 SAG	20 CAP
22 SCO	23 CAP	22 CAP	22 PIS	22 ARI	23 GEM	22 CAN	21 LEO	22 LIB	22 SCO	23 CAP	22 AQU
24 SAG	25 AQU	24 AQU	25 ARI	24 TAU	25 CAN	25 LEO	24 VIR	25 SCO	24 SAG	25 AQU	24 PIS
26 CAP	27 PIS	26 PIS	27 TAU	26 GEM	28 LEO	27 VIR	26 LIB	27 SAG	26 CAP	27 PIS	26 ARI
28 AQU		28 ARI	29 GEM	29 CAN	30 VIR	30 LIB	29 SCO	29 CAP	29 AQU	29 ARI	29 TAU
30 PIS		30 TAU		31 LEO			31 SAG		31 PIS		31 GEM

1988

JAN	FEB	MAR	APR	MAY	JUN	JUL	AUG	SEP	OCT	NOV	DEC
2 CAN	1 LEO	2 VIR	1 LIB	3 SAG	1 CAP	1 AQU	1 ARI	2 GEM	1 CAN	2 VIR	2 LIB
5 LEO	4 VIR	4 LIB	3 SCO	5 CAP	3 AQU	3 PIS	3 TAU	4 CAN	4 LEO	5 LIB	5 SCO
7 VIR	6 LIB	7 SCO	5 SAG	7 AQU	5 PIS	5 ARI	5 GEM	6 LEO	6 VIR	7 SCO	7 SAG
10 LIB	9 SCO	9 SAG	8 CAP	9 PIS	8 ARI	7 TAU	8 CAN	9 VIR	9 LIB	10 SAG	9 CAP
12 SCO	11 SAG	11 CAP	10 AQU	11 ARI	10 TAU	9 GEM	10 LEO	11 LIB	11 SCO	12 CAP	12 AQU
15 SAG	13 CAP	14 AQU	12 PIS	13 TAU	12 GEM	11 CAN	13 VIR	14 SCO	14 SAG	14 AQU	14 PIS
17 CAP	15 AQU	16 PIS	14 ARI	16 GEM	14 CAN	14 LEO	15 LIB	16 SAG	16 CAP	17 PIS	16 ARI
19 AQU	17 PIS	18 ARI	16 TAU	18 CAN	17 LEO	16 VIR	18 SCO	19 CAP	18 AQU	19 ARI	18 TAU
21 PIS	19 ARI	20 TAU	18 GEM	20 LEO	19 VIR	19 LIB	20 SAG	21 AQU	20 PIS	21 TAU	20 GEM
23 ARI	21 TAU	22 GEM	20 CAN	23 VIR	22 LIB	21 SCO	22 CAP	23 PIS	22 ARI	23 GEM	22 CAN
25 TAU	23 GEM	24 CAN	23 LEO	25 LIB	24 SCO	24 SAG	24 AQU	25 ARI	24 TAU	25 CAN	25 LEO
27 GEM	26 CAN	27 LEO	25 VIR	28 SCO	26 SAG	26 CAP	26 PIS	27 TAU	26 GEM	27 LEO	27 VIR
30 CAN	28 LEO	29 VIR	28 LIB	30 SAG	29 CAP	28 AQU	28 ARI	29 GEM	29 CAN	30 VIR	30 LIB
		30 SCO				30 PIS	30 TAU		31 LEO		

1989

JAN	FEB	MAR	APR	MAY	JUN	JUL	AUG	SEP	OCT	NOV	DEC
1 SCO	2 CAP	2 CAP	2 PIS	2 ARI	2 GEM	2 CAN	3 VIR	1 LIB	1 SCO	2 CAP	2 AQU
4 SAG	4 AQU	4 AQU	4 ARI	4 TAU	4 CAN	4 LEO	5 LIB	4 SCO	4 SAG	5 AQU	4 PIS
6 CAP	6 PIS	6 PIS	6 TAU	6 GEM	7 LEO	6 VIR	8 SCO	6 SAG	6 CAP	7 PIS	7 ARI
8 AQU	8 ARI	8 ARI	8 GEM	8 CAN	9 VIR	9 LIB	10 SAG	9 CAP	9 AQU	9 ARI	9 TAU
10 PIS	11 TAU	10 TAU	10 CAN	10 LEO	11 LIB	11 SCO	12 CAP	11 AQU	11 PIS	11 TAU	11 GEM
12 ARI	13 GEM	12 GEM	13 LEO	13 VIR	14 SCO	14 SAG	15 AQU	13 PIS	13 ARI	13 GEM	13 CAN
14 TAU	15 CAN	14 CAN	15 VIR	15 LIB	16 SAG	16 CAP	17 PIS	15 ARI	15 TAU	15 CAN	15 LEO
16 GEM	17 LEO	17 LEO	18 LIB	18 SCO	19 CAP	18 AQU	19 ARI	17 TAU	17 GEM	17 LEO	17 VIR
19 CAN	20 VIR	19 VIR	20 SCO	20 SAG	21 AQU	20 PIS	21 TAU	19 GEM	19 CAN	20 VIR	19 LIB
21 LEO	22 LIB	22 LIB	23 SAG	22 CAP	23 PIS	23 ARI	23 GEM	21 CAN	21 LEO	22 LIB	22 SCO
23 VIR	25 SCO	24 SCO	25 CAP	25 AQU	25 ARI	25 TAU	25 CAN	24 LEO	23 VIR	25 SCO	24 SAG
26 LIB	27 SAG	27 SAG	28 AQU	27 PIS	27 TAU	27 GEM	28 LEO	26 VIR	26 LIB	27 SAG	27 CAP
29 SCO		29 CAP	30 PIS	29 ARI	30 GEM	29 CAN	30 VIR	29 LIB	28 SCO	30 CAP	29 AQU
31 SAG		31 AQU		31 TAU		31 LEO			31 SAG		

1990

JAN	FEB	MAR	APR	MAY	JUN	JUL	AUG	SEP	OCT	NOV	DEC
1 PIS	1 TAU	2 GEM	1 CAN	3 VIR	1 LIB	1 SCO	2 CAP	1 AQU	1 PIS	2 TAU	1 GEM
3 ARI	3 GEM	5 CAN	3 LEO	5 LIB	4 SCO	4 SAG	5 AQU	3 PIS	3 ARI	4 GEM	3 CAN
5 TAU	5 CAN	7 LEO	5 VIR	8 SCO	6 SAG	6 CAP	7 PIS	6 ARI	5 TAU	6 CAN	5 LEO
7 GEM	8 LEO	9 VIR	8 LIB	10 SAG	9 CAP	9 AQU	9 ARI	8 TAU	7 GEM	8 LEO	7 VIR
9 CAN	10 VIR	12 LIB	10 SCO	13 CAP	11 AQU	11 PIS	11 TAU	10 GEM	9 CAN	10 VIR	9 LIB
11 LEO	12 LIB	14 SCO	13 SAG	15 AQU	14 PIS	13 ARI	14 GEM	12 CAN	11 LEO	12 LIB	12 SCO
13 VIR	15 SCO	16 SAG	15 CAP	17 PIS	16 ARI	15 TAU	16 CAN	14 LEO	14 VIR	15 SCO	14 SAG
16 LIB	17 SAG	19 CAP	18 AQU	20 ARI	18 TAU	17 GEM	18 LEO	16 VIR	16 LIB	17 SAG	17 CAP
18 SCO	20 CAP	21 AQU	20 PIS	22 TAU	20 GEM	19 CAN	20 VIR	19 LIB	18 SCO	20 CAP	19 AQU
21 SAG	22 AQU	24 PIS	22 ARI	24 GEM	22 CAN	21 LEO	22 LIB	21 SCO	21 SAG	22 AQU	22 PIS
23 CAP	24 PIS	26 ARI	24 TAU	26 CAN	24 LEO	24 VIR	25 SCO	24 SAG	23 CAP	25 PIS	24 ARI
26 AQU	26 ARI	28 TAU	26 GEM	28 LEO	26 VIR	26 LIB	27 SAG	26 CAP	26 AQU	27 ARI	26 TAU
28 PIS	28 TAU	30 GEM	28 CAN	30 VIR	29 LIB	28 SCO	30 CAP	29 AQU	28 PIS	29 TAU	28 GEM
30 ARI			30 LEO			31 SAG			30 ARI		30 CAN

1991

JAN	FEB	MAR	APR	MAY	JUN	JUL	AUG	SEP	OCT	NOV	DEC
1 LEO	2 LIB	2 LIB	3 SAG	2 CAP	1 AQU	1 PIS	2 TAU	3 CAN	2 LEO	2 LIB	2 SCO
3 VIR	4 SCO	4 SCO	5 CAP	5 AQU	4 PIS	3 ARI	4 GEM	5 LEO	4 VIR	5 SCO	4 SAG
6 LIB	7 SAG	6 SAG	8 AQU	7 PIS	6 ARI	6 TAU	6 CAN	7 VIR	6 LIB	7 SAG	7 CAP
8 SCO	9 CAP	9 CAP	10 PIS	10 ARI	8 TAU	8 GEM	8 LEO	9 LIB	8 SCO	10 CAP	9 AQU
11 SAG	12 AQU	11 AQU	12 ARI	12 TAU	10 GEM	10 CAN	10 VIR	11 SCO	11 SAG	12 AQU	12 PIS
13 CAP	14 PIS	14 PIS	15 TAU	14 GEM	12 CAN	12 LEO	12 LIB	13 SAG	13 CAP	15 PIS	14 ARI
16 AQU	17 ARI	16 ARI	17 GEM	16 CAN	14 LEO	14 VIR	15 SCO	16 CAP	16 AQU	17 ARI	17 TAU
18 PIS	19 TAU	18 TAU	19 CAN	18 LEO	16 VIR	16 LIB	17 SAG	18 AQU	18 PIS	19 TAU	19 GEM
20 ARI	21 GEM	20 GEM	21 LEO	20 VIR	19 LIB	18 SCO	20 CAP	21 PIS	21 ARI	21 GEM	21 CAN
23 TAU	23 CAN	22 CAN	23 VIR	22 LIB	21 SCO	21 SAG	22 AQU	23 ARI	23 TAU	23 CAN	23 LEO
25 GEM	25 LEO	25 LEO	25 LIB	25 SCO	23 SAG	23 CAP	25 PIS	25 TAU	25 GEM	25 LEO	25 VIR
27 CAN	27 VIR	27 VIR	28 SCO	27 SAG	26 CAP	26 AQU	27 ARI	28 GEM	27 CAN	28 VIR	27 LIB
29 LEO		29 LIB	30 SAG	30 CAP	29 AQU	28 PIS	29 TAU	30 CAN	29 LEO	30 LIB	29 SCO
31 VIR		31 SCO				31 ARI	31 GEM		31 VIR		

1992

JAN	FEB	MAR	APR	MAY	JUN	JUL	AUG	SEP	OCT	NOV	DEC
1 SAG	2 AQU	3 PIS	1 ARI	1 TAU	2 CAN	1 LEO	2 LIB	2 SAG	2 CAP	1 AQU	1 PIS
3 CAP	4 PIS	5 ARI	4 TAU	3 GEM	4 LEO	3 VIR	4 SCO	5 CAP	4 AQU	3 PIS	3 ARI
6 AQU	7 ARI	8 TAU	6 GEM	5 CAN	6 VIR	5 LIB	6 SAG	7 AQU	7 PIS	6 ARI	6 TAU
8 PIS	9 TAU	10 GEM	8 CAN	8 LEO	8 LIB	7 SCO	8 CAP	10 PIS	10 ARI	8 TAU	8 GEM
11 ARI	12 GEM	12 CAN	10 LEO	10 VIR	10 SCO	10 SAG	11 AQU	12 ARI	12 TAU	11 GEM	10 CAN
13 TAU	14 CAN	14 LEO	12 VIR	12 LIB	13 SAG	12 CAP	13 PIS	15 TAU	14 GEM	13 CAN	12 LEO
15 GEM	16 LEO	16 VIR	15 LIB	14 SCO	15 CAP	15 AQU	16 ARI	17 GEM	17 CAN	15 LEO	14 VIR
17 CAN	18 VIR	18 LIB	17 SCO	16 SAG	17 AQU	17 PIS	18 TAU	19 CAN	19 LEO	17 VIR	16 LIB
19 LEO	20 LIB	20 SCO	19 SAG	19 CAP	20 PIS	20 ARI	21 GEM	21 LEO	21 VIR	19 LIB	19 SCO
21 VIR	22 SCO	23 SAG	21 CAP	21 AQU	22 ARI	22 TAU	23 CAN	24 VIR	23 LIB	21 SCO	21 SAG
23 LIB	24 SAG	25 CAP	24 AQU	24 PIS	25 TAU	24 GEM	25 LEO	25 LIB	25 SCO	24 SAG	23 CAP
25 SCO	27 CAP	27 AQU	26 PIS	26 ARI	27 GEM	27 CAN	27 VIR	28 SCO	27 SAG	26 CAP	26 AQU
28 SAG	29 AQU	30 PIS	29 ARI	28 TAU	29 CAN	29 LEO	29 LIB	30 SAG	29 CAP	28 AQU	28 PIS
30 CAP				31 GEM		31 VIR	31 SCO				31 ARI

1993

JAN	FEB	MAR	APR	MAY	JUN	JUL	AUG	SEP	OCT	NOV	DEC
2 TAU	1 GEM	2 CAN	1 LEO	2 LIB	1 SCO	2 CAP	1 AQU	2 ARI	2 TAU	1 GEM	3 LEO
4 GEM	3 CAN	5 LEO	3 VIR	4 SCO	3 SAG	5 AQU	3 PIS	5 TAU	4 GEM	3 CAN	5 VIR
7 CAN	5 LEO	7 VIR	5 LIB	6 SAG	5 CAP	7 PIS	6 ARI	7 GEM	7 CAN	5 LEO	7 LIB
9 LEO	7 VIR	8 LIB	7 SCO	9 CAP	7 AQU	10 ARI	8 TAU	10 CAN	9 LEO	8 VIR	9 SCO
11 VIR	9 LIB	10 SCO	9 SAG	11 AQU	10 PIS	12 TAU	11 GEM	12 LEO	11 VIR	10 LIB	11 SAG
13 LIB	11 SCO	13 SAG	11 CAP	13 PIS	12 ARI	15 GEM	13 CAN	14 VIR	13 LIB	12 SCO	13 CAP
15 SCO	13 SAG	15 CAP	14 AQU	16 ARI	15 TAU	17 CAN	15 LEO	16 LIB	15 SCO	14 SAG	15 AQU
17 SAG	16 CAP	17 AQU	16 PIS	18 TAU	17 GEM	19 LEO	17 VIR	18 SCO	17 SAG	16 CAP	18 PIS
19 CAP	18 AQU	20 PIS	19 ARI	21 GEM	19 CAN	21 VIR	19 LIB	20 SAG	19 CAP	18 AQU	20 ARI
22 AQU	21 PIS	22 ARI	21 TAU	23 CAN	22 LEO	23 LIB	21 SCO	22 CAP	22 AQU	20 PIS	23 TAU
24 PIS	23 ARI	25 TAU	24 GEM	25 LEO	24 VIR	25 SCO	24 SAG	24 AQU	24 PIS	23 ARI	25 GEM
27 ARI	26 TAU	27 GEM	26 CAN	28 VIR	26 LIB	27 SAG	26 CAP	27 PIS	27 ARI	26 TAU	28 CAN
29 TAU	28 GEM	30 CAN	28 LEO	30 LIB	28 SCO	30 CAP	28 AQU	29 ARI	29 TAU	28 GEM	30 LEO
			30 VIR		30 SAG		31 PIS			30 CAN	

1994

JAN	FEB	MAR	APR	MAY	JUN	JUL	AUG	SEP	OCT	NOV	DEC
1 VIR	2 SCO	1 SCO	1 CAP	1 AQU	2 ARI	2 TAU	1 GEM	2 LEO	2 VIR	2 SCO	2 SAG
3 LIB	4 SAG	3 SAG	4 AQU	3 PIS	5 TAU	4 GEM	3 CAN	4 VIR	4 LIB	4 SAG	4 CAP
5 SCO	6 CAP	5 CAP	6 PIS	6 ARI	7 GEM	7 CAN	6 LEO	6 LIB	6 SCO	6 CAP	6 AQU
8 SAG	8 AQU	7 AQU	9 ARI	8 TAU	10 CAN	9 LEO	8 VIR	8 SCO	8 SAG	8 AQU	8 PIS
10 CAP	11 PIS	10 PIS	11 TAU	11 GEM	12 LEO	11 VIR	10 LIB	10 SAG	10 CAP	11 PIS	10 ARI
12 AQU	13 ARI	12 ARI	14 GEM	13 CAN	14 VIR	14 LIB	12 SCO	13 CAP	12 AQU	13 ARI	13 TAU
14 PIS	16 TAU	15 TAU	16 CAN	16 LEO	16 LIB	16 SCO	14 SAG	15 AQU	14 PIS	15 TAU	15 GEM
17 ARI	18 GEM	17 GEM	18 LEO	18 VIR	19 SCO	18 SAG	16 CAP	17 PIS	17 ARI	18 GEM	18 CAN
19 TAU	20 CAN	20 CAN	21 VIR	20 LIB	21 SAG	20 CAP	18 AQU	19 ARI	19 TAU	20 CAN	20 LEO
22 GEM	23 LEO	22 LEO	23 LIB	22 SCO	23 CAP	22 AQU	21 PIS	22 TAU	22 GEM	23 LEO	23 VIR
24 CAN	25 VIR	24 VIR	25 SCO	24 SAG	25 AQU	24 PIS	23 ARI	24 GEM	24 CAN	25 VIR	25 LIB
26 LEO	27 LIB	26 LIB	27 SAG	26 CAP	27 PIS	27 ARI	26 TAU	27 CAN	27 LEO	28 LIB	27 SCO
28 VIR		28 SCO	29 CAP	28 AQU	29 ARI	29 TAU	28 GEM	29 LEO	29 VIR	30 SCO	29 SAG
31 LIB		30 SAG		31 PIS			31 CAN		31 LIB		31 CAP

1995

JAN	FEB	MAR	APR	MAY	JUN	JUL	AUG	SEP	OCT	NOV	DEC
2 AQU	1 PIS	2 ARI	1 TAU	1 GEM	2 LEO	2 VIR	3 SCO	1 SAG	2 AQU	1 PIS	3 TAU
4 PIS	3 ARI	5 TAU	3 GEM	3 CAN	5 VIR	4 LIB	5 SAG	3 CAP	5 PIS	3 ARI	5 GEM
6 ARI	5 TAU	7 GEM	6 CAN	6 LEO	7 LIB	6 SCO	7 CAP	5 AQU	7 ARI	5 TAU	8 CAN
9 TAU	8 GEM	10 CAN	9 LEO	8 VIR	9 SCO	8 SAG	9 AQU	7 PIS	9 TAU	8 GEM	10 LEO
11 GEM	10 CAN	12 LEO	11 VIR	10 LIB	11 SAG	10 CAP	11 PIS	9 ARI	12 GEM	10 CAN	13 VIR
14 CAN	13 LEO	14 VIR	13 LIB	13 SCO	13 CAP	12 AQU	13 ARI	12 TAU	14 CAN	13 LEO	15 LIB
16 LEO	15 VIR	17 LIB	15 SCO	15 SAG	15 AQU	14 PIS	15 TAU	14 GEM	17 LEO	15 VIR	17 SCO
19 VIR	17 LIB	19 SCO	17 SAG	17 CAP	17 PIS	17 ARI	18 GEM	17 CAN	19 VIR	18 LIB	19 SAG
21 LIB	19 SCO	21 SAG	19 CAP	19 AQU	19 ARI	19 TAU	20 CAN	19 LEO	21 LIB	20 SCO	21 CAP
23 SCO	22 SAG	23 CAP	21 AQU	21 PIS	22 TAU	22 GEM	23 LEO	22 VIR	23 SCO	22 SAG	23 AQU
25 SAG	24 CAP	25 AQU	24 PIS	23 ARI	24 GEM	24 CAN	25 VIR	24 LIB	26 SAG	24 CAP	25 PIS
27 CAP	26 AQU	27 PIS	26 ARI	26 TAU	27 CAN	27 LEO	28 LIB	26 SCO	28 CAP	26 AQU	28 ARI
30 AQU	28 PIS	30 ARI	28 TAU	28 GEM	29 LEO	29 VIR	30 SCO	28 SAG	30 AQU	28 PIS	30 TAU
				31 CAN		31 LIB		30 CAP		30 ARI	

1996

JAN	FEB	MAR	APR	MAY	JUN	JUL	AUG	SEP	OCT	NOV	DEC
1 GEM	3 LEO	1 LEO	2 LIB	2 SCO	2 CAP	2 AQU	2 ARI	1 TAU	3 CAN	2 LEO	2 VIR
4 CAN	5 VIR	3 VIR	4 SCO	4 SAG	4 AQU	4 PIS	4 TAU	3 GEM	5 LEO	4 VIR	4 LIB
6 LEO	8 LIB	6 LIB	7 SAG	6 CAP	6 PIS	6 ARI	7 GEM	6 CAN	8 VIR	7 LIB	6 SCO
9 VIR	10 SCO	8 SCO	9 CAP	8 AQU	9 ARI	8 TAU	9 CAN	8 LEO	10 LIB	9 SCO	9 SAG
11 LIB	12 SAG	10 SAG	11 AQU	10 PIS	11 TAU	11 GEM	12 LEO	11 VIR	13 SCO	11 SAG	11 CAP
14 SCO	14 CAP	13 CAP	13 PIS	12 ARI	13 GEM	13 CAN	14 VIR	13 LIB	15 SAG	13 CAP	13 AQU
16 SAG	16 AQU	15 AQU	15 ARI	15 TAU	16 CAN	16 LEO	17 LIB	15 SCO	17 CAP	16 AQU	15 PIS
18 CAP	18 PIS	17 PIS	17 TAU	17 GEM	18 LEO	18 VIR	19 SCO	18 SAG	19 AQU	18 PIS	17 ARI
20 AQU	20 ARI	19 ARI	20 GEM	19 CAN	21 VIR	21 LIB	21 SAG	20 CAP	21 PIS	20 ARI	19 TAU
22 PIS	23 TAU	21 TAU	22 CAN	22 LEO	23 LIB	23 SCO	24 CAP	22 AQU	23 ARI	22 TAU	22 GEM
24 ARI	25 GEM	23 GEM	25 LEO	24 VIR	26 SCO	25 SAG	26 AQU	24 PIS	26 TAU	24 GEM	24 CAN
26 TAU	27 CAN	26 CAN	27 VIR	27 LIB	28 SAG	27 CAP	28 PIS	26 ARI	28 GEM	27 CAN	26 LEO
29 GEM		28 LEO	30 LIB	29 SCO	30 CAP	29 AQU	30 ARI	28 TAU	30 CAN	29 LEO	29 VIR
31 CAN		31 VIR		31 SAG		31 PIS		30 GEM			31 LIB

1997

JAN	FEB	MAR	APR	MAY	JUN	JUL	AUG	SEP	OCT	NOV	DEC
3 SCO	1 SAG	1 SAG	1 AQU	1 PIS	1 TAU	1 GEM	2 LEO	3 LIB	3 SCO	1 SAG	1 CAP
5 SAG	4 CAP	3 CAP	4 PIS	3 ARI	3 GEM	3 CAN	4 VIR	6 SCO	5 SAG	4 CAP	3 AQU
7 CAP	6 AQU	5 AQU	6 ARI	5 TAU	6 CAN	5 LEO	7 LIB	8 SAG	8 CAP	6 AQU	5 PIS
9 AQU	8 PIS	7 PIS	8 TAU	7 GEM	8 LEO	8 VIR	9 SCO	10 CAP	10 AQU	8 PIS	8 ARI
11 PIS	10 ARI	9 ARI	10 GEM	9 CAN	11 VIR	10 LIB	12 SAG	12 AQU	12 PIS	10 ARI	10 TAU
13 ARI	12 TAU	11 TAU	12 CAN	12 LEO	13 LIB	13 SCO	14 CAP	14 PIS	14 ARI	12 TAU	12 GEM
15 TAU	14 GEM	13 GEM	14 LEO	14 VIR	16 SCO	15 SAG	16 AQU	16 ARI	16 TAU	14 GEM	14 CAN
18 GEM	16 CAN	16 CAN	17 VIR	17 LIB	18 SAG	18 CAP	18 PIS	18 TAU	18 GEM	17 CAN	16 LEO
20 CAN	19 LEO	18 LEO	19 LIB	19 SCO	20 CAP	20 AQU	20 ARI	21 GEM	20 CAN	19 LEO	19 VIR
23 LEO	21 VIR	21 VIR	22 SCO	22 SAG	22 AQU	22 PIS	22 TAU	23 CAN	23 LEO	21 VIR	21 LIB
25 VIR	24 LIB	23 LIB	24 SAG	24 CAP	24 PIS	24 ARI	24 GEM	25 LEO	25 VIR	24 LIB	24 SCO
28 LIB	26 SCO	26 SCO	27 CAP	26 AQU	26 ARI	26 TAU	27 CAN	28 VIR	28 LIB	26 SCO	26 SAG
30 SCO		28 SAG	29 AQU	28 PIS	29 TAU	28 GEM	29 LEO	30 LIB	30 SCO	29 SAG	28 CAP
		30 CAP		30 ARI		30 CAN	31 VIR				31 AQU

1998

JAN	FEB	MAR	APR	MAY	JUN	JUL	AUG	SEP	OCT	NOV	DEC
2 PIS	2 TAU	2 TAU	2 CAN	2 LEO	3 LIB	3 SCO	2 SAG	3 AQU	2 PIS	1 ARI	2 GEM
4 ARI	4 GEM	4 GEM	4 LEO	4 VIR	5 SCO	5 SAG	4 CAP	5 PIS	4 ARI	3 TAU	4 CAN
6 TAU	7 CAN	6 CAN	7 VIR	7 LIB	8 SAG	8 CAP	6 AQU	7 ARI	6 TAU	5 GEM	6 LEO
8 GEM	9 LEO	8 LEO	9 LIB	9 SCO	10 CAP	10 AQU	8 PIS	9 TAU	8 GEM	7 CAN	9 VIR
10 CAN	11 VIR	11 VIR	12 SCO	12 SAG	13 AQU	12 PIS	11 ARI	11 GEM	10 CAN	9 LEO	11 LIB
13 LEO	14 LIB	13 LIB	14 SAG	14 CAP	15 PIS	14 ARI	13 TAU	13 CAN	13 LEO	11 VIR	14 SCO
15 VIR	16 SCO	16 SCO	17 CAP	16 AQU	17 ARI	16 TAU	15 GEM	15 LEO	15 VIR	14 LIB	16 SAG
18 LIB	19 SAG	18 SAG	19 AQU	19 PIS	19 TAU	18 GEM	17 CAN	18 VIR	17 LIB	16 SCO	18 CAP
20 SCO	21 CAP	21 CAP	21 PIS	21 ARI	21 GEM	21 CAN	19 LEO	20 LIB	20 SCO	19 SAG	21 AQU
23 SAG	23 AQU	23 AQU	23 ARI	23 TAU	23 CAN	23 LEO	21 VIR	23 SCO	23 SAG	21 CAP	23 PIS
25 CAP	25 PIS	25 PIS	25 TAU	25 GEM	25 LEO	25 VIR	24 LIB	25 SAG	25 CAP	24 AQU	25 ARI
27 AQU	27 ARI	27 ARI	27 GEM	27 CAN	28 VIR	28 LIB	26 SCO	28 CAP	27 AQU	26 PIS	28 TAU
29 PIS		29 TAU	29 CAN	29 LEO	30 LIB	30 SCO	29 SAG	30 AQU	30 PIS	28 ARI	30 GEM
31 ARI		31 GEM		31 VIR			31 CAP			30 TAU	

1999

JAN	FEB	MAR	APR	MAY	JUN	JUL	AUG	SEP	OCT	NOV	DEC
1 CAN	1 VIR	1 VIR	2 SCO	2 SAG	3 AQU	2 PIS	1 ARI	2 GEM	1 CAN	1 VIR	1 LIB
3 LEO	4 LIB	3 LIB	4 SAG	4 CAP	5 PIS	5 ARI	3 TAU	4 CAN	3 LEO	4 LIB	3 SCO
5 VIR	6 SCO	6 SCO	7 CAP	7 AQU	8 ARI	7 TAU	5 GEM	6 LEO	5 VIR	6 SCO	6 SAG
7 LIB	9 SAG	8 SAG	9 AQU	9 PIS	10 TAU	9 GEM	7 CAN	8 VIR	8 LIB	9 SAG	8 CAP
10 SCO	11 CAP	11 CAP	12 PIS	11 ARI	12 GEM	11 CAN	9 LEO	10 LIB	10 SCO	11 CAP	11 AQU
12 SAG	14 AQU	13 AQU	14 ARI	13 TAU	14 CAN	13 LEO	12 VIR	13 SCO	12 SAG	14 AQU	13 PIS
15 CAP	16 PIS	15 PIS	16 TAU	15 GEM	16 LEO	15 VIR	14 LIB	15 SAG	15 CAP	16 PIS	16 ARI
17 AQU	18 ARI	17 ARI	18 GEM	17 CAN	18 VIR	17 LIB	16 SCO	18 CAP	17 AQU	18 ARI	18 TAU
19 PIS	20 TAU	19 TAU	20 CAN	19 LEO	20 LIB	20 SCO	19 SAG	20 AQU	20 PIS	21 TAU	20 GEM
22 ARI	22 GEM	21 GEM	22 LEO	21 VIR	23 SCO	22 SAG	21 CAP	22 PIS	22 ARI	23 GEM	22 CAN
24 TAU	24 CAN	23 CAN	24 VIR	24 LIB	25 SAG	25 CAP	24 AQU	25 ARI	24 TAU	25 CAN	24 LEO
26 GEM	26 LEO	26 LEO	27 LIB	26 SCO	28 CAP	27 AQU	26 PIS	27 TAU	26 GEM	27 LEO	26 VIR
28 CAN		28 VIR	29 SCO	29 SAG	30 AQU	30 PIS	28 ARI	29 GEM	28 CAN	29 VIR	28 LIB
30 LEO		30 LIB		31 CAP			30 TAU		30 LEO		31 SCO

2000

JAN	FEB	MAR	APR	MAY	JUN	JUL	AUG	SEP	OCT	NOV	DEC
2 SAG	1 CAP	2 AQU	1 PIS	2 TAU	1 GEM	2 LEO	1 VIR	2 SCO	1 SAG	3 AQU	2 PIS
5 CAP	4 AQU	4 PIS	3 ARI	5 GEM	3 CAN	4 VIR	3 LIB	4 SAG	4 CAP	5 PIS	5 ARI
7 AQU	6 PIS	7 ARI	5 TAU	7 CAN	5 LEO	7 LIB	5 SCO	6 CAP	6 AQU	8 ARI	7 TAU
10 PIS	8 ARI	9 TAU	7 GEM	9 LEO	7 VIR	9 SCO	8 SAG	9 AQU	9 PIS	10 TAU	9 GEM
12 ARI	11 TAU	11 GEM	9 CAN	11 VIR	9 LIB	11 SAG	10 CAP	11 PIS	11 ARI	12 GEM	11 CAN
14 TAU	13 GEM	13 CAN	11 LEO	13 LIB	12 SCO	14 CAP	13 AQU	14 ARI	13 TAU	14 CAN	13 LEO
16 GEM	15 CAN	15 LEO	14 VIR	15 SCO	14 SAG	16 AQU	15 PIS	16 TAU	16 GEM	16 LEO	15 VIR
18 CAN	17 LEO	17 VIR	16 LIB	18 SAG	17 CAP	19 PIS	18 ARI	18 GEM	18 CAN	18 VIR	18 LIB
20 LEO	19 VIR	19 LIB	18 SCO	20 CAP	19 AQU	21 ARI	20 TAU	20 CAN	20 LEO	20 LIB	20 SCO
23 VIR	21 LIB	22 SCO	20 SAG	23 AQU	22 PIS	24 TAU	22 GEM	23 LEO	22 VIR	23 SCO	22 SAG
25 LIB	23 SCO	24 SAG	23 CAP	25 PIS	24 ARI	26 GEM	24 CAN	25 VIR	24 LIB	25 SAG	25 CAP
27 SCO	26 SAG	27 CAP	26 AQU	28 ARI	26 TAU	28 CAN	26 LEO	27 LIB	26 SCO	27 CAP	27 AQU
29 SAG	28 CAP	29 AQU	28 PIS	30 TAU	28 GEM	30 LEO	28 VIR	29 SCO	29 SAG	30 AQU	30 PIS
			30 ARI		30 CAN		30 LIB	30 LIB	31 CAP		

2001

JAN	FEB	MAR	APR	MAY	JUN	JUL	AUG	SEP	OCT	NOV	DEC
1 ARI	2 GEM	1 GEM	2 LEO	1 VIR	2 SCO	1 SAG	3 AQU	1 PIS	1 ARI	2 GEM	2 CAN
4 TAU	4 CAN	4 CAN	4 VIR	3 LIB	4 SAG	4 CAP	5 PIS	4 ARI	4 TAU	4 CAN	4 LEO
6 GEM	6 LEO	6 LEO	6 LIB	6 SCO	7 CAP	6 AQU	8 ARI	6 TAU	6 GEM	7 LEO	6 VIR
8 CAN	8 VIR	8 VIR	8 SCO	8 SAG	9 AQU	9 PIS	10 TAU	9 GEM	8 CAN	9 VIR	8 LIB
10 LEO	10 LIB	10 LIB	10 SAG	10 CAP	11 PIS	11 ARI	12 GEM	11 CAN	10 LEO	11 LIB	10 SCO
12 VIR	12 SCO	12 SCO	13 CAP	13 AQU	14 ARI	14 TAU	15 CAN	13 LEO	12 VIR	13 SCO	12 SAG
14 LIB	15 SAG	14 SAG	15 AQU	15 PIS	16 TAU	16 GEM	17 LEO	15 VIR	15 LIB	15 SAG	15 CAP
16 SCO	17 CAP	16 CAP	18 PIS	18 ARI	19 GEM	18 CAN	19 VIR	17 LIB	17 SCO	17 CAP	17 AQU
18 SAG	20 AQU	19 AQU	20 ARI	20 TAU	21 CAN	20 LEO	21 LIB	19 SCO	19 SAG	20 AQU	20 PIS
21 CAP	22 PIS	22 PIS	23 TAU	22 GEM	23 LEO	22 VIR	23 SCO	21 SAG	21 CAP	22 PIS	22 ARI
23 AQU	25 ARI	24 ARI	25 GEM	24 CAN	25 VIR	24 LIB	25 SAG	24 CAP	23 AQU	25 ARI	25 TAU
26 PIS	27 TAU	26 TAU	27 CAN	27 LEO	27 LIB	26 SCO	27 CAP	26 AQU	26 PIS	27 TAU	27 GEM
28 ARI		29 GEM	29 LEO	29 VIR	29 SCO	29 SAG	30 AQU	29 PIS	28 ARI	30 GEM	29 CAN
31 TAU		31 CAN		31 LIB		31 CAP			31 TAU		31 LEO

2002

JAN	FEB	MAR	APR	MAY	JUN	JUL	AUG	SEP	OCT	NOV	DEC
2 VIR	1 LIB	2 SCO	1 SAG	2 AQU	1 PIS	1 ARI	2 GEM	1 CAN	1 LEO	1 LIB	1 SCO
4 LIB	3 SCO	4 SAG	3 CAP	5 PIS	4 ARI	4 TAU	5 CAN	3 LEO	3 VIR	3 SCO	3 SAG
6 SCO	5 SAG	6 CAP	5 AQU	7 ARI	6 TAU	6 GEM	7 LEO	5 VIR	5 LIB	5 SAG	5 CAP
9 SAG	7 CAP	9 AQU	8 PIS	10 TAU	9 GEM	8 CAN	9 VIR	7 LIB	7 SCO	7 CAP	7 AQU
11 CAP	10 AQU	11 PIS	10 ARI	12 GEM	11 CAN	11 LEO	11 LIB	9 SCO	9 SAG	10 AQU	9 PIS
13 AQU	12 PIS	14 ARI	13 TAU	15 CAN	13 LEO	13 VIR	13 SCO	12 SAG	11 CAP	12 PIS	12 ARI
16 PIS	15 ARI	16 TAU	15 GEM	17 LEO	15 VIR	15 LIB	15 SAG	14 CAP	13 AQU	15 ARI	14 TAU
18 ARI	17 TAU	19 GEM	18 CAN	19 VIR	18 LIB	17 SCO	18 CAP	16 AQU	16 PIS	17 TAU	17 GEM
21 TAU	20 GEM	21 CAN	20 LEO	21 LIB	20 SCO	19 SAG	20 AQU	19 PIS	18 ARI	20 GEM	19 CAN
23 GEM	22 CAN	24 LEO	22 VIR	23 SCO	22 SAG	21 CAP	22 PIS	21 ARI	21 TAU	22 CAN	22 LEO
26 CAN	24 LEO	26 VIR	24 LIB	25 SAG	24 CAP	24 AQU	25 ARI	24 TAU	23 GEM	24 LEO	24 VIR
28 LEO	26 VIR	28 LIB	26 SCO	28 CAP	26 AQU	26 PIS	27 TAU	26 GEM	26 CAN	27 VIR	26 LIB
30 VIR	28 LIB	30 SCO	28 SAG	30 AQU	29 PIS	28 ARI	30 GEM	29 CAN	28 LEO	29 LIB	28 SCO
			30 CAP			31 TAU			30 VIR		30 SAG

2003

JAN	FEB	MAR	APR	MAY	JUN	JUL	AUG	SEP	OCT	NOV	DEC
1 CAP	2 PIS	1 PIS	3 TAU	2 GEM	1 CAN	1 LEO	2 LIB	2 SAG	1 CAP	2 PIS	2 ARI
3 AQU	5 ARI	4 ARI	5 GEM	5 CAN	4 LEO	3 VIR	4 SCO	4 CAP	4 AQU	5 ARI	4 TAU
6 PIS	7 TAU	6 TAU	8 CAN	7 LEO	6 VIR	5 LIB	6 SAG	6 AQU	6 PIS	7 TAU	7 GEM
8 ARI	10 GEM	9 GEM	10 LEO	10 VIR	8 LIB	7 SCO	8 CAP	9 PIS	8 ARI	10 GEM	9 CAN
11 TAU	12 CAN	11 CAN	12 VIR	12 LIB	10 SCO	10 SAG	10 AQU	11 ARI	11 TAU	12 CAN	12 LEO
13 GEM	14 LEO	14 LEO	14 LIB	14 SCO	12 SAG	12 CAP	12 PIS	13 TAU	13 GEM	15 LEO	14 VIR
16 CAN	16 VIR	16 VIR	16 SCO	16 SAG	14 CAP	14 AQU	15 ARI	16 GEM	16 CAN	17 VIR	16 LIB
18 LEO	18 LIB	18 LIB	18 SAG	18 CAP	16 AQU	16 PIS	17 TAU	18 CAN	18 LEO	19 LIB	19 SCO
20 VIR	21 SCO	20 SCO	20 CAP	20 AQU	19 PIS	18 ARI	20 GEM	21 LEO	21 VIR	21 SCO	21 SAG
22 LIB	23 SAG	22 SAG	23 AQU	22 PIS	21 ARI	21 TAU	22 CAN	23 VIR	23 LIB	23 SAG	23 CAP
24 SCO	25 CAP	24 CAP	25 PIS	25 ARI	23 TAU	23 GEM	24 LEO	25 LIB	25 SCO	25 CAP	25 AQU
26 SAG	27 AQU	26 AQU	27 ARI	27 TAU	26 GEM	26 CAN	27 VIR	27 SCO	27 SAG	27 AQU	27 PIS
29 CAP		29 PIS	30 TAU	30 GEM	28 CAN	28 LEO	29 LIB	29 SAG	29 CAP	29 PIS	29 ARI
31 AQU		31 ARI				30 VIR	31 SCO		31 AQU		

2004

JAN	FEB	MAR	APR	MAY	JUN	JUL	AUG	SEP	OCT	NOV	DEC
1 TAU	2 CAN	3 LEO	1 VIR	1 LIB	2 SAG	1 CAP	1 PIS	2 TAU	2 GEM	1 CAN	1 LEO
3 GEM	4 LEO	5 VIR	4 LIB	3 SCO	4 CAP	3 AQU	4 ARI	5 GEM	5 CAN	3 LEO	3 VIR
6 CAN	7 VIR	7 LIB	6 SCO	5 SAG	6 AQU	5 PIS	6 TAU	7 CAN	7 LEO	6 VIR	6 LIB
8 LEO	9 LIB	9 SCO	8 SAG	7 CAP	8 PIS	7 ARI	8 GEM	10 LEO	10 VIR	8 LIB	8 SCO
10 VIR	11 SCO	11 SAG	10 CAP	9 AQU	10 ARI	10 TAU	11 CAN	12 VIR	12 LIB	10 SCO	10 SAG
13 LIB	13 SAG	14 CAP	12 AQU	11 PIS	12 TAU	12 GEM	13 LEO	14 LIB	14 SCO	13 SAG	12 CAP
15 SCO	15 CAP	16 AQU	14 PIS	14 ARI	15 GEM	15 CAN	16 VIR	17 SCO	16 SAG	15 CAP	14 AQU
17 SAG	17 AQU	18 PIS	16 ARI	16 TAU	17 CAN	17 LEO	18 LIB	19 SAG	18 CAP	17 AQU	16 PIS
19 CAP	20 PIS	20 ARI	19 TAU	19 GEM	20 LEO	20 VIR	20 SCO	21 CAP	20 AQU	19 PIS	18 ARI
21 AQU	22 ARI	23 TAU	21 GEM	21 CAN	22 VIR	22 LIB	23 SAG	23 AQU	23 PIS	21 ARI	21 TAU
23 PIS	24 TAU	25 GEM	24 CAN	24 LEO	25 LIB	24 SCO	25 CAP	25 PIS	25 ARI	23 TAU	23 GEM
25 ARI	27 GEM	28 CAN	26 LEO	26 VIR	27 SCO	26 SAG	27 AQU	27 ARI	27 TAU	26 GEM	25 CAN
28 TAU	29 CAN	30 LEO	29 VIR	28 LIB	29 SAG	28 CAP	29 PIS	30 TAU	29 GEM	28 CAN	28 LEO
30 GEM				31 SCO		30 AQU	31 ARI				31 VIR

2005

JAN	FEB	MAR	APR	MAY	JUN	JUL	AUG	SEP	OCT	NOV	DEC
2 LIB	1 SCO	2 SAG	3 AQU	2 PIS	3 TAU	2 GEM	1 CAN	2 VIR	2 LIB	1 SCO	2 CAP
4 SCO	3 SAG	4 CAP	5 PIS	4 ARI	5 GEM	5 CAN	3 LEO	5 LIB	4 SCO	3 SAG	4 AQU
6 SAG	5 CAP	6 AQU	7 ARI	6 TAU	7 CAN	7 LEO	6 VIR	7 SCO	7 SAG	5 CAP	7 PIS
8 CAP	7 AQU	8 PIS	9 TAU	9 GEM	10 LEO	10 VIR	8 LIB	9 SAG	9 CAP	7 AQU	9 ARI
10 AQU	9 PIS	10 ARI	11 GEM	11 CAN	12 VIR	12 LIB	11 SCO	12 CAP	11 AQU	9 PIS	11 TAU
12 PIS	11 ARI	13 TAU	14 CAN	14 LEO	15 LIB	15 SCO	13 SAG	14 AQU	13 PIS	11 ARI	13 GEM
15 ARI	13 TAU	15 GEM	16 LEO	16 VIR	17 SCO	17 SAG	15 CAP	16 PIS	15 ARI	14 TAU	15 CAN
17 TAU	16 GEM	17 CAN	19 VIR	18 LIB	19 SAG	19 CAP	17 AQU	18 ARI	17 TAU	16 GEM	18 LEO
19 GEM	18 CAN	20 LEO	21 LIB	21 SCO	21 CAP	21 AQU	19 PIS	20 TAU	19 GEM	18 CAN	20 VIR
22 CAN	21 LEO	22 VIR	23 SCO	23 SAG	23 AQU	23 PIS	21 ARI	22 GEM	22 CAN	21 LEO	23 LIB
24 LEO	23 VIR	25 LIB	26 SAG	25 CAP	25 PIS	25 ARI	23 TAU	24 CAN	24 LEO	23 VIR	25 SCO
27 VIR	25 LIB	27 SCO	28 CAP	27 AQU	28 ARI	27 TAU	26 GEM	27 LEO	27 VIR	26 LIB	28 SAG
29 LIB	28 SCO	29 SAG	30 AQU	29 PIS	30 TAU	29 GEM	28 CAN	29 VIR	29 LIB	28 SCO	30 CAP
		31 CAP		31 ARI			31 LEO			30 SAG	

2006

JAN	FEB	MAR	APR	MAY	JUN	JUL	AUG	SEP	OCT	NOV	DEC
1 AQU	1 ARI	1 ARI	1 GEM	1 CAN	2 VIR	2 LIB	1 SCO	2 CAP	1 AQU	2 ARI	1 TAU
3 PIS	3 TAU	3 TAU	4 CAN	3 LEO	5 LIB	5 SCO	3 SAG	4 AQU	4 PIS	4 TAU	3 GEM
5 ARI	6 GEM	5 GEM	6 LEO	6 VIR	7 SCO	7 SAG	6 CAP	6 PIS	6 ARI	6 GEM	6 CAN
7 TAU	8 CAN	7 CAN	8 VIR	8 LIB	10 SAG	9 CAP	8 AQU	8 ARI	8 TAU	8 CAN	8 LEO
9 GEM	10 LEO	10 LEO	11 LIB	11 SCO	12 CAP	11 AQU	10 PIS	10 TAU	10 GEM	10 LEO	10 VIR
12 CAN	13 VIR	12 VIR	14 SCO	13 SAG	14 AQU	13 PIS	12 ARI	12 GEM	12 CAN	13 VIR	13 LIB
14 LEO	16 LIB	15 LIB	16 SAG	15 CAP	16 PIS	15 ARI	14 TAU	14 CAN	14 LEO	15 LIB	15 SCO
17 VIR	18 SCO	17 SCO	18 CAP	18 AQU	18 ARI	17 TAU	16 GEM	17 LEO	17 VIR	18 SCO	18 SAG
19 LIB	20 SAG	20 SAG	20 AQU	20 PIS	20 TAU	20 GEM	18 CAN	19 VIR	19 LIB	20 SAG	20 CAP
22 SCO	23 CAP	22 CAP	22 PIS	22 ARI	22 GEM	22 CAN	21 LEO	22 LIB	22 SCO	23 CAP	22 AQU
24 SAG	25 AQU	24 AQU	25 ARI	24 TAU	25 CAN	24 LEO	23 VIR	24 SCO	24 SAG	25 AQU	24 PIS
26 CAP	27 PIS	26 PIS	27 TAU	26 GEM	27 LEO	27 VIR	26 LIB	27 SAG	26 CAP	27 PIS	27 ARI
28 AQU		28 ARI	29 GEM	28 CAN	29 VIR	29 LIB	28 SCO	29 CAP	29 AQU	29 ARI	29 TAU
30 PIS		30 TAU		31 LEO			31 SAG		31 PIS		31 GEM

2007

JAN	FEB	MAR	APR	MAY	JUN	JUL	AUG	SEP	OCT	NOV	DEC
2 CAN	1 LEO	2 VIR	1 LIB	1 SCO	2 CAP	2 AQU	2 ARI	1 TAU	2 CAN	3 VIR	3 LIB
4 LEO	3 VIR	5 LIB	3 SCO	3 SAG	4 AQU	4 PIS	4 TAU	3 GEM	4 LEO	5 LIB	5 SCO
7 VIR	5 LIB	7 SCO	6 SAG	6 CAP	7 PIS	6 ARI	6 GEM	5 CAN	7 VIR	8 SCO	8 SAG
9 LIB	8 SCO	10 SAG	8 CAP	8 AQU	9 ARI	8 TAU	9 CAN	7 LEO	9 LIB	10 SAG	10 CAP
12 SCO	10 SAG	12 CAP	11 AQU	10 PIS	11 TAU	10 GEM	11 LEO	9 VIR	12 SCO	13 CAP	13 AQU
14 SAG	13 CAP	14 AQU	13 PIS	12 ARI	13 GEM	12 CAN	13 VIR	12 LIB	14 SAG	15 AQU	15 PIS
16 CAP	15 AQU	17 PIS	15 ARI	14 TAU	15 CAN	14 LEO	15 LIB	14 SCO	17 CAP	18 PIS	17 ARI
19 AQU	17 PIS	19 ARI	17 TAU	16 GEM	17 LEO	17 VIR	18 SCO	17 SAG	19 AQU	20 ARI	19 TAU
21 PIS	19 ARI	21 TAU	19 GEM	18 CAN	19 VIR	19 LIB	20 SAG	19 CAP	21 PIS	22 TAU	21 GEM
23 ARI	21 TAU	23 GEM	21 CAN	21 LEO	22 LIB	22 SCO	23 CAP	22 AQU	23 ARI	24 GEM	23 CAN
25 TAU	23 GEM	25 CAN	23 LEO	23 VIR	24 SCO	24 SAG	25 AQU	24 PIS	25 TAU	26 CAN	25 LEO
27 GEM	25 CAN	27 LEO	26 VIR	25 LIB	27 SAG	27 CAP	27 PIS	26 ARI	27 GEM	28 LEO	27 VIR
29 CAN	28 LEO	29 VIR	28 LIB	28 SCO	29 CAP	29 AQU	29 ARI	28 TAU	29 CAN	30 VIR	30 LIB
				31 SAG		31 PIS		30 GEM	31 LEO		

E Index

midpoints, vs. aspects,
118–119
Moon, 5, 54–55, 57–58
conjunctions with, 132,
135–137
nodes of, 12–13
oppositions, 187–189
sextiles and trines,
172–175
in the signs, 66–67
Moon charts, 283–312
Moon squares, 155–157
mutual reception, 56

N

nadir. *See* imum coeli (IC)
natal charts. *See* birth charts
Neptune, 5, 63
conjunctions with, 134,
136, 138, 141, 143–144,
146–147, 149–150
oppositions, 198
sextiles and trines,
183–184
in the signs, 80–81
Neptune charts, 277
Neptune squares, 166–167
ninth house, 92, 97–98
nodes, lunar, 12–13
North Node, 5, 12–13
conjunctions with, 134,
136, 139, 141, 143, 145,
146, 148–150

O

oppositions, 5, 115, 123–124, 185
Jupiter, 194–196
Mars, 193–194
Mercury, 189–191
Moon, 187–189
Neptune, 198
Pluto, 199
Saturn, 196–197
Sun, 186–187
Uranus, 197–198
Venus, 191–193
orbs, 116–119
outer planets, 54–55

P

past-life astrology, 11–13
physical traits
of Aquarius, 49
of Aries, 18
of Cancer, 27
of Capricorn, 46
of Gemini, 24
of Leo, 30
of Libra, 38
of Pisces, 52
of Sagittarius, 43
of Scorpio, 40
of Taurus, 21
of Virgo, 33
Pisces, 5
characteristics of,
49–52
children, 113–114

in the houses, 94
love compatibility with,
229–232
men, 51
women, 50–51
Pisces Moon, 67
planetary energy, 53–54
planetary motion, 55
planets, 5
See also specific planets
basics, 54–55
horizon placement of, 86
inner and outer, 54–55
orbs and, 118
in the signs, 65–83
strengths and weaknesses
of, 56
Pluto, 5, 63–64
conjunctions with, 134, 136,
138, 141, 143, 145–151
oppositions, 199
sextiles and trines, 184
in the signs, 81–83
Pluto charts, 276
Pluto squares, 167
predictions, 2
Ptolemy, xi, 120

R

religions, astrology and, xi
retrograde motion, 55
rising sign. *See* ascendant sign
(AS)

The EVERYTHING Series!

BUSINESS & PERSONAL FINANCE

Everything® Budgeting Book
Everything® Business Planning Book
Everything® Coaching and Mentoring Book
Everything® Fundraising Book
Everything® Get Out of Debt Book
Everything® Grant Writing Book
Everything® Home-Based Business Book, 2nd Ed.
Everything® Homebuying Book, 2nd Ed.
Everything® Homeselling Book, 2nd Ed.
Everything® Investing Book, 2nd Ed.
Everything® Landlording Book
Everything® Leadership Book
Everything® Managing People Book
Everything® Negotiating Book
Everything® Online Business Book
Everything® Personal Finance Book
Everything® Personal Finance in Your 20s and 30s Book
Everything® Project Management Book
Everything® Real Estate Investing Book
Everything® Robert's Rules Book, $7.95
Everything® Selling Book
Everything® Start Your Own Business Book
Everything® Wills & Estate Planning Book

COMPUTERS

Everything® Online Auctions Book
Everything® Blogging Book

COOKING

Everything® Barbecue Cookbook
Everything® Bartender's Book, $9.95
Everything® Chinese Cookbook
Everything® Cocktail Parties and Drinks Book
Everything® College Cookbook
Everything® Cookbook
Everything® Cooking for Two Cookbook
Everything® Diabetes Cookbook
Everything® Easy Gourmet Cookbook
Everything® Fondue Cookbook
Everything® Gluten-Free Cookbook
Everything® Glycemic Index Cookbook
Everything® Grilling Cookbook

Everything® Healthy Meals in Minutes Cookbook
Everything® Holiday Cookbook
Everything® Indian Cookbook
Everything® Italian Cookbook
Everything® Low-Carb Cookbook
Everything® Low-Fat High-Flavor Cookbook
Everything® Low-Salt Cookbook
Everything® Meals for a Month Cookbook
Everything® Mediterranean Cookbook
Everything® Mexican Cookbook
Everything® One-Pot Cookbook
Everything® Pasta Cookbook
Everything® Quick Meals Cookbook
Everything® Slow Cooker Cookbook
Everything® Slow Cooking for a Crowd Cookbook
Everything® Soup Cookbook
Everything® Tex-Mex Cookbook
Everything® Thai Cookbook
Everything® Vegetarian Cookbook
Everything® Wild Game Cookbook
Everything® Wine Book, 2nd Ed.

CRAFT SERIES

Everything® Crafts—Baby Scrapbooking
Everything® Crafts—Bead Your Own Jewelry
Everything® Crafts—Create Your Own Greeting Cards
Everything® Crafts—Easy Projects
Everything® Crafts—Polymer Clay for Beginners
Everything® Crafts—Rubber Stamping Made Easy
Everything® Crafts—Wedding Decorations and Keepsakes

HEALTH

Everything® Alzheimer's Book
Everything® Diabetes Book
Everything® Health Guide to Adult Bipolar Disorder
Everything® Health Guide to Controlling Anxiety
Everything® Health Guide to Fibromyalgia
Everything® Hypnosis Book

Everything® Low Cholesterol Book
Everything® Massage Book
Everything® Menopause Book
Everything® Nutrition Book
Everything® Reflexology Book
Everything® Stress Management Book

HISTORY

Everything® American Government Book
Everything® American History Book
Everything® Civil War Book
Everything® Irish History & Heritage Book
Everything® Middle East Book

GAMES

Everything® 15-Minute Sudoku Book, $9.95
Everything® 30-Minute Sudoku Book, $9.95
Everything® Blackjack Strategy Book
Everything® Brain Strain Book, $9.95
Everything® Bridge Book
Everything® Card Games Book
Everything® Card Tricks Book, $9.95
Everything® Casino Gambling Book, 2nd Ed.
Everything® Chess Basics Book
Everything® Craps Strategy Book
Everything® Crossword and Puzzle Book
Everything® Crossword Challenge Book
Everything® Cryptograms Book, $9.95
Everything® Easy Crosswords Book
Everything® Easy Kakuro Book, $9.95
Everything® Games Book, 2nd Ed.
Everything® Giant Sudoku Book, $9.95
Everything® Kakuro Challenge Book, $9.95
Everything® Large-Print Crosswords Book
Everything® Lateral Thinking Puzzles Book, $9.95
Everything® Pencil Puzzles Book, $9.95
Everything® Poker Strategy Book
Everything® Pool & Billiards Book
Everything® Test Your IQ Book, $9.95
Everything® Texas Hold 'Em Book, $9.95
Everything® Travel Crosswords Book, $9.95
Everything® Word Games Challenge Book
Everything® Word Search Book

Bolded titles are new additions to the series.
All Everything® books are priced at $12.95 or $14.95, unless otherwise stated. Prices subject to change without notice.

HOBBIES

Everything® Candlemaking Book
Everything® Cartooning Book
Everything® Drawing Book
Everything® Family Tree Book, 2nd Ed.
Everything® Knitting Book
Everything® Knots Book
Everything® Photography Book
Everything® Quilting Book
Everything® Scrapbooking Book
Everything® Sewing Book
Everything® Woodworking Book

HOME IMPROVEMENT

Everything® Feng Shui Book
Everything® Feng Shui Decluttering Book, $9.95
Everything® Fix-It Book
Everything® Home Decorating Book
Everything® Homebuilding Book
Everything® Lawn Care Book
Everything® Organize Your Home Book

KIDS' BOOKS

All titles are $7.95

Everything® Kids' Animal Puzzle &
   Activity Book
Everything® Kids' Baseball Book, 4th Ed.
Everything® Kids' Bible Trivia Book
Everything® Kids' Bugs Book
Everything® Kids' Christmas Puzzle
   & Activity Book
Everything® Kids' Cookbook
Everything® Kids' Crazy Puzzles Book
Everything® Kids' Dinosaurs Book
**Everything® Kids' Gross Hidden Pictures
Book**
Everything® Kids' Gross Jokes Book
Everything® Kids' Gross Mazes Book
Everything® Kids' Gross Puzzle and
   Activity Book
Everything® Kids' Halloween Puzzle
   & Activity Book
Everything® Kids' Hidden Pictures Book
Everything® Kids' Horses Book
Everything® Kids' Joke Book
Everything® Kids' Knock Knock Book
Everything® Kids' Math Puzzles Book
Everything® Kids' Mazes Book
Everything® Kids' Money Book
Everything® Kids' Nature Book

Everything® Kids' Pirates Puzzle and
   Activity Book
Everything® Kids' Puzzle Book
Everything® Kids' Riddles & Brain Teasers Book
Everything® Kids' Science Experiments Book
Everything® Kids' Sharks Book
Everything® Kids' Soccer Book
Everything® Kids' Travel Activity Book

KIDS' STORY BOOKS

Everything® Fairy Tales Book

LANGUAGE

Everything® Conversational Japanese Book
   (with CD), $19.95
Everything® French Grammar Book
Everything® French Phrase Book, $9.95
Everything® French Verb Book, $9.95
**Everything® German Practice Book with
CD, $19.95**
Everything® Inglés Book
Everything® Learning French Book
Everything® Learning German Book
Everything® Learning Italian Book
Everything® Learning Latin Book
Everything® Learning Spanish Book
Everything® Sign Language Book
Everything® Spanish Grammar Book
Everything® Spanish Phrase Book, $9.95
Everything® Spanish Practice Book
   (with CD), $19.95
Everything® Spanish Verb Book, $9.95

MUSIC

Everything® Drums Book (with CD), $19.95
Everything® Guitar Book
**Everything® Guitar Chords Book with CD,
$19.95**
Everything® Home Recording Book
Everything® Playing Piano and Keyboards
   Book
Everything® Reading Music Book (with CD),
   $19.95
Everything® Rock & Blues Guitar Book
   (with CD), $19.95
Everything® Songwriting Book

NEW AGE

Everything® Astrology Book, 2nd Ed.
Everything® Dreams Book, 2nd Ed.
Everything® Love Signs Book, $9.95

Everything® Numerology Book
Everything® Paganism Book
Everything® Palmistry Book
Everything® Psychic Book
Everything® Reiki Book
Everything® Tarot Book
Everything® Wicca and Witchcraft Book

PARENTING

Everything® Baby Names Book, 2nd Ed.
Everything® Baby Shower Book
Everything® Baby's First Food Book
Everything® Baby's First Year Book
Everything® Birthing Book
Everything® Breastfeeding Book
Everything® Father-to-Be Book
Everything® Father's First Year Book
Everything® Get Ready for Baby Book
Everything® Get Your Baby to Sleep Book,
   $9.95
Everything® Getting Pregnant Book
Everything® Homeschooling Book
Everything® Mother's First Year Book
Everything® Parent's Guide to Children
   and Divorce
Everything® Parent's Guide to Children
   with ADD/ADHD
Everything® Parent's Guide to Children
   with Asperger's Syndrome
Everything® Parent's Guide to Children
   with Autism
Everything® Parent's Guide to Children with
   Bipolar Disorder
Everything® Parent's Guide to Children
   with Dyslexia
Everything® Parent's Guide to Positive
   Discipline
Everything® Parent's Guide to Raising a
   Successful Child
**Everything® Parent's Guide to Raising
Boys**
**Everything® Parent's Guide to Raising
Siblings**
Everything® Parent's Guide to Tantrums
Everything® Parent's Guide to the Overweight
   Child
Everything® Parent's Guide to the Strong-
   Willed Child
Everything® Parenting a Teenager Book
Everything® Potty Training Book, $9.95
Everything® Pregnancy Book, 2nd Ed.

Bolded titles are new additions to the series.
All Everything® books are priced at $12.95 or $14.95, unless otherwise stated. Prices subject to change without notice.

Everything® Pregnancy Fitness Book
Everything® Pregnancy Nutrition Book
Everything® Pregnancy Organizer, $15.00
Everything® Toddler Book
Everything® Toddler Activities Book
Everything® Tween Book
Everything® Twins, Triplets, and More Book

PETS

Everything® Boxer Book
Everything® Cat Book, 2nd Ed.
Everything® Chihuahua Book
Everything® Dachshund Book
Everything® Dog Book
Everything® Dog Health Book
Everything® Dog Training and Tricks Book
Everything® German Shepherd Book
Everything® Golden Retriever Book
Everything® Horse Book
Everything® Horse Care Book
Everything® Horseback Riding Book
Everything® Labrador Retriever Book
Everything® Poodle Book
Everything® Pug Book
Everything® Puppy Book
Everything® Rottweiler Book
Everything® Small Dogs Book
Everything® Tropical Fish Book
Everything® Yorkshire Terrier Book

REFERENCE

Everything® Car Care Book
Everything® Classical Mythology Book
Everything® Computer Book
Everything® Divorce Book
Everything® Einstein Book
Everything® Etiquette Book, 2nd Ed.
Everything® Inventions and Patents Book
Everything® Mafia Book
Everything® Mary Magdalene Book
 Everything® Philosophy Book
Everything® Psychology Book
Everything® Shakespeare Book

RELIGION

Everything® Angels Book
Everything® Bible Book
Everything® Buddhism Book
Everything® Catholicism Book

Everything® Christianity Book
Everything® Freemasons Book
Everything® History of the Bible Book
Everything® Jewish History & Heritage Book
Everything® Judaism Book
Everything® Kabbalah Book
Everything® Koran Book
Everything® Prayer Book
Everything® Saints Book
Everything® Torah Book
Everything® Understanding Islam Book
Everything® World's Religions Book
Everything® Zen Book

SCHOOL & CAREERS

Everything® Alternative Careers Book
Everything® College Major Test Book
Everything® College Survival Book, 2nd Ed.
Everything® Cover Letter Book, 2nd Ed.
Everything® Get-a-Job Book
Everything® Guide to Being a Paralegal
**Everything® Guide to Being a Real Estate
    Agent**
Everything® Guide to Starting and Running
    a Restaurant
Everything® Job Interview Book
Everything® New Nurse Book
Everything® New Teacher Book
Everything® Paying for College Book
Everything® Practice Interview Book
Everything® Resume Book, 2nd Ed.
Everything® Study Book
Everything® Teacher's Organizer, $16.95

SELF-HELP

Everything® Dating Book, 2nd Ed.
Everything® Great Sex Book
Everything® Kama Sutra Book
Everything® Self-Esteem Book

SPORTS & FITNESS

Everything® Fishing Book
Everything® Golf Instruction Book
Everything® Pilates Book
Everything® Running Book
Everything® Total Fitness Book
Everything® Weight Training Book
Everything® Yoga Book

TRAVEL

Everything® Family Guide to Hawaii
Everything® Family Guide to Las Vegas,
    2nd Ed.
Everything® Family Guide to New York City,
    2nd Ed.
Everything® Family Guide to RV Travel &
    Campgrounds
Everything® Family Guide to the Walt Disney
    World Resort®, Universal Studios®,
    and Greater Orlando, 4th Ed.
Everything® Family Guide to Cruise Vacations
Everything® Family Guide to the Caribbean
Everything® Family Guide to Washington
    D.C., 2nd Ed.
Everything® Guide to New England
Everything® Travel Guide to the Disneyland
    Resort®, California Adventure®,
    Universal Studios®, and the
    Anaheim Area

WEDDINGS

Everything® Bachelorette Party Book, $9.95
Everything® Bridesmaid Book, $9.95
Everything® Elopement Book, $9.95
Everything® Father of the Bride Book, $9.95
Everything® Groom Book, $9.95
Everything® Mother of the Bride Book, $9.95
Everything® Outdoor Wedding Book
Everything® Wedding Book, 3rd Ed.
Everything® Wedding Checklist, $9.95
Everything® Wedding Etiquette Book, $9.95
Everything® Wedding Organizer, $15.00
Everything® Wedding Shower Book, $9.95
Everything® Wedding Vows Book, $9.95
Everything® Weddings on a Budget Book, $9.95

WRITING

Everything® Creative Writing Book
Everything® Get Published Book, 2nd Ed.
Everything® Grammar and Style Book
Everything® Guide to Writing a Book Proposal
Everything® Guide to Writing a Novel
Everything® Guide to Writing Children's Books
Everything® Guide to Writing Research Papers
Everything® Screenwriting Book
Everything® Writing Poetry Book
Everything® Writing Well Book